DOES
COLLEGE
MAKE
A DIFFERENCE?

**Recent Titles in
Contributions to the Study of Education**

Managing Institutions of Higher Education into the 21st Century:
Issues and Implications
Ronald R. Sims and Serbrenia J. Sims, editors

Identity and Ideology: Sociocultural Theories of Schooling
Stanley William Rothstein

Moral Education and the Liberal Arts
Michael H. Mitias, editor

Physicians in the Academic Marketplace
Dolores L. Burke

Student Outcomes Assessment: A Historical Review and Guide to
Program Development
Serbrenia J. Sims

The Vision of the Public Junior College, 1900-1940: Professional Goals
and Popular Aspirations
John H. Frye

Adult Education for Community Development
Edwin Hamilton

Archetypal Forms in Teaching
William A. Reinsmith

Labor Relations in Education: An International Perspective
Bruce S. Cooper, editor

The Emerging Worldwide Electronic University
Parker Rossman

A New History of Educational Philosophy
James S. Kaminsky

DOES
COLLEGE
MAKE
A DIFFERENCE?

Long–Term Changes
in Activities and Attitudes

**William E. Knox,
Paul Lindsay,
and Mary N. Kolb**

Foreword by Ernest T. Pascarella

Contributions to the Study of Education, Number 59

GREENWOOD PRESS
Westport, Connecticut • London

Library of Congress Cataloging-in-Publication Data

Knox, William E.
  Does college make a difference? : long-term changes in activities
and attitudes / William E. Knox, Paul Lindsay, and Mary N. Kolb ;
foreword by Ernest T. Pascarella.
      p.   cm.—(Contributions to the study of education, ISSN
0196-707X ; no. 59)
  Includes bibliographical references (p.) and index.
  ISBN 0-313-28528-4 (alk. paper)
  1. College graduates—United States—Attitudes—Longitudinal
studies. 2. High school graduates—United States—Attitudes—
Longitudinal studies. 3. College graduates—Employment—United
States—Longitudinal studies. 4. High school graduates—Employment—
United States—Longitudinal studies. 5. Attitude change—
Longitudinal studies. 6. Education, Higher—United States—
Longitudinal studies. 7. Education, Higher—Economic aspects—
United States—Longitudinal studies.   I. Lindsay, Paul.
II. Kolb, Mary N.   III. Title.   IV. Series.
LB2824.K58   1993
378'.01'0973—dc20   93-9318

British Library Cataloguing in Publication Data is available.

Library of Congress Catalog Card Number: 93-9318
ISBN: 0-313-28528-4
ISSN: 0196-707X

First published in 1993

Greenwood Press, 88 Post Road West, Westport, CT 06881
An imprint of Greenwood Publishing Group, Inc.

Printed in the United States of America

The paper used in this book complies with the
Permanent Paper Standard issued by the National
Information Standards Organization (Z39.48-1984).

10 9 8 7 6 5 4 3 2 1

Copyright Acknowledgment

The authors and publisher are grateful for permission to reprint a revised version of
chapter 6, which originally appeared as:

"Higher Education, College Characteristics and Student Experiences: Long Term Effects
on Educational Satisfactions and Perceptions" by William E. Knox, Paul Lindsay, and
Mary N. Kolb, *Journal of Higher Education*, Vol. 63, No. 3 (May/June 1992) is reprinted by
permission. © 1992 by the Ohio State University Press. All rights reserved.

To Diana, Caroline, and Kurt

CONTENTS

TABLES

FOREWORD

America has always had a special relationship with its colleges and universities. They have frequently been considered the crown jewels in our educational system and, until recently, we have supported them with an almost unprecedented public and private generosity. Perhaps much of this generous underwriting of higher education stems from a deeply held cultural belief about what our postsecondary institutions accomplish, and indeed we frequently expect them to accomplish great things. These include, but are certainly not limited to, the facilitation of students' ability to think critically, analytically and reflectively; the development of their value structures and moral sensibilities; the fostering of their personal development and self-identity; and the solidification of their career identity, vocational competence, and attitudes toward work. In addition, a college degree is probably still perceived as the single most important nonascribed or noninherited determinant of middle- and upper-middle-class occupational and economic status in our society.

Yet, it is probably the case that cultural and societal beliefs about what college accomplishes are rarely founded on carefully collected and skillfully analyzed evidence. Consequently, we often form assumptions about the impact of college attendance, the impact of certain experiences and achievements during college, and the impact of attending certain kinds of colleges, for which there may be little or no empirical support. It is to this issue, the documentation of the impacts of college, that the work of Bill Knox, Paul Lindsay, and Mary Kolb speaks powerfully and eloquently. The book they have written, *Does College Make a Difference?*, is destined to be considered a major contribution to the growing body of research on how college affects students.

There are several reasons why Knox, Lindsay, and Kolb's work is so important. However, I believe these various reasons can be reduced to two major characteristics of their research: 1) the significance of the data they employ; and 2) the conceptual and methodological rigor of their analyses. By selecting as their data base the *National Longitudinal Study of the High School Class of 1972* (NLS-72), the authors have at their disposal what is perhaps the single most significant and potentially rich source of longitudinal information about college impact collected in the past decade. (The only possible exception is Alexander Astin's Cooperative Institutional Research Program Data, but this data base typically does not survey individuals not entering college, nor does it routinely trace individuals as long as the 14-year longitudinal follow-up that is now a part of the NLS-72 data.) The NLS-72 data permit them to look at such wide-ranging outcomes of postsecondary education as civic and political activity, self-esteem, various dimensions of personal values and goals, educational attainment, occupational achievement, and earnings. Moreover, the design of the NLS-72 data file permits the authors to address what are probably the five most salient questions about college impact:

1. What are the net or unique effects of attaining different levels of postsecondary education?
2. What are the impacts of different aggregate college characteristics (e.g., academic selectivity, control, and enrollment)?
3. How do different individual experiences (e.g., academic major and academic success) shape the impact of college?
4. Are the effects of college different for different kinds of students (e.g., men versus women)?
5. What are the long-term or enduring impacts of college?

While the quality of the data they explore is a central determinant of the importance of their work, it is the conceptual and methodological rigor that Knox, Lindsay, and Kolb apply in a comprehensive set of analyses of that data that makes their work exceptional. The simple and inescapable fact is that the degree of certitude with which we can make reasonable conclusions about the true impact of college is largely a function of methodological and analytical rigor. This is a particularly strong feature of the authors' investigative style. By carefully taking into account the different background characteristics of students who attain different levels of postsecondary education, who attend different kinds of colleges, and who have different individual experiences and involvements during college, Knox, Lindsay, and Kolb take a major step in separating the specious effects of differential student recruitment from the actual socialization or status-allocating impacts of college. Supplementing this care and rigor in the analysis of their data is a refreshing candor and openness in pointing out the limitations of both their methods and their conclusions.

Does College Make a Difference? will be of great value to almost anyone with a scholarly interest in the impact of college on students. Sociologists, psychologists, higher education faculty, and other behavioral scientists will enjoy its strong theoretical grounding in the work of John Meyer and Robert Bellah, as well as its adroit and comprehensive analysis of a major national data base. Moreover, a significant segment of academic and student affairs administrators will also find it of value, particularly as it maps the various impacts of college on individual values, goals, and self-image. Its lucid and nontechnical writing will be especially appealing to the latter groups.

The publication of *Does College Make a Difference?* is undoubtedly a major event for those interested in the influence of postsecondary education. It will in all likelihood take its place among works such as Astin's *Four Critical Years*, Feldman and Newcomb's *The Impact of College on Students* and Hyman and Wright's *Education's Lasting Influence on Values* as books that have significantly advanced our understanding of how college impacts the lives of students.

Ernest T. Pascarella
Chicago, Illinois

PREFACE

The strains of Elgar's familiar *Pomp and Circumstance March #1* announce to the gathered parents, grandparents, brothers, and sisters that the ceremony has begun. Everyone is excited. The graduating college seniors slowly approach the front of the auditorium. The emotional pitch of the audience is high and hundreds of cameras are ready. "Land of Hope and Glory" engulfs graduates and their well-wishers in welcome.

Throughout the ceremony there are words, sometimes solemn, sometimes joyous, sometimes jesting, but always centering on the occasion's significance. Not only the featured speaker, but the giver of each prayer, award, or introduction takes the obligatory notice of the meaning of the occasion. Most of these words celebrate the growth in mind, spirit, and character of the graduates during their years in the institution, expressing the ideals, hopes, and dreams of the teachers, administrators, students, and families. Pervading the event are feelings of relief, a sense of pride and accomplishment, hopeful anticipation, as well as fatigue, anxiety, and sadness that the graduates may be parting from their friends.

In a society with few unambiguous rites to denote passage from one phase to another, surely this is an occasion of high ritual significance. It represents the assumption of a new identity and a status—college graduate—that is recognized throughout the nation and world. Both the graduate and society as a whole have a big stake in this identity and a big investment in dollars and time in attaining it.

Americans exhibit an almost unquestioning faith in the power of education, especially higher education. We complain about it. We agonize over it. We worry about it. "Education presidents," "education governors," and corporate leaders worry over how our schools affect our abilities to stay economically competitive. The United States spends a much higher proportion of its education budget on higher education than other industrialized societies. The United States has a much higher proportion of young persons in higher education than other Western countries.

Middle-class parents brood over how their children are doing in school and how this will affect their chances for college, work, and income. These aspirations are, of course, relative. For the upper middle class, the expected and normal course is to go to Harvard or Yale or other elite schools. For a broader group, the major flagship state university holds high enough prestige and social status associations. When we ask our students why they are in college, the answer is, overwhelmingly, "to get a degree to get a job." Unlike graduation-day speakers, they seldom mention cultivating the intellect, becoming active citizens, enriching the mind and spirit, or developing character.

What do colleges really do, in the long term, for the individuals who are processed through them? This is the primary question for this book. Most Americans expect two kinds of lasting outcomes from higher education. First, they want degrees to get jobs, opportunities to enter professional careers, a better chance in the job market, higher incomes—utilitarian outcomes. Second, they want the kinds of individual changes the graduation speakers talk about—intellectual growth and change, skills and attitudes and values reflecting the "educated" person, commitment to helping others and improving the community. How are students with various levels and types of education sorted into the job market, leading to different levels of income and occupational status? How do they come to express motivations for success in work, fulfillment in leisure, and service to others? To what extent do students really get these kinds of benefits?

In this book we take a close, careful look at a national sample of high school seniors, some of whom went on to college and some of whom did not. How are they different, fourteen years after high school? The focus is what colleges actually do for students, how they affect in the long run students' attitudes and values, social and political participation, conceptions of self, and responses to college. Our data preclude examining questions about knowledge and skills. Instead, we explore incomes, occupational status, activities and attitudes about work and leisure and the community, and conceptions of self and schooling.

To relieve some anxiety, we can say at the outset that the conventional wisdom is confirmed here—college graduation does enhance income and occupational status. Getting a degree will probably help you get a better job! Investments in education are rewarded with extrinsic benefits. We will explore some of the underlying reasons that this part of common sense is confirmed. What is considerably more problematic, and what we focus on particularly, are the outcomes the graduation speakers address. Are college alumni, compared with high school graduates, more likely to value the intrinsic rewards of work, such as the opportunity to do creative and interesting work? Do college students develop leisure attitudes and skills that lead to more fulfilling personal lives? Are graduates more engaged in community service and civic concerns? Do they graduate with a stronger sense of self, of being competent, worthwhile people who control their own lives? Most students are quite utilitarian about their education; that is, they evince a strong interest in instrumental career success. However, the vast investment by students, parents, and the taxpaying public suggests that Americans are looking for something beyond individual economic benefits. Graduation exercises reflect this hope. What are the facts? What is the reality?

Many alumni in our study, looking back on their own experience, remember college as a time of growth and change. The more higher education they have, the more they are satisfied with their education and the more likely they are to report meeting interesting people, learning new ideas, and having done well. Americans' unquestioning faith in the power of education seems to be reinforced by the college experience. There is some evidence, then, for both the pragmatic, common-sense view and the idealistic view of the lasting effects of college. The first emphasizes extrinsic benefits to individuals from higher education; the second, intrinsic benefits. These views correspond to two approaches sociologists have emphasized in analyzing effects of schools and colleges: *allocation* of persons to positions in society, especially occupational positions; and *socialization* of individuals—the development of values, attitudes, skills and roles appropriate for adults.

As professors, two of the authors spend a large part of our time teaching college students. We enjoy doing this and, like most professors in the recent Carnegie survey (Carnegie Foundation 1989), we want students to grow and change intellectually and believe that they do sometimes. We have seen students light up with enthusiasm about ideas, experience the satisfaction of seeing connections between their college courses and their own experience, grow from shy freshmen to self-confident seniors and then to mature adults. As college students, we enjoyed many experiences in and out of class. College benefited us. As par-

ents, we have vicariously enjoyed our own children's experiences
in colleges, which, again, have been positive contributions to
them and their life-long interests and fulfillment. We shudder
when we see many states cutting back on university libraries,
faculties, and facilities because of economic depression and
fiscal problems. Higher education has become more than a
preparation for life; it is a central concern of the lives we have
chosen. Out of this affection for students and for colleges our
research emerged.

It is all the more sobering, then, to have to report that this
more objective look at a national sample of high school seniors
and their experience with higher education leads us to believe
that some of our own ideals and some popular American beliefs
about the impact of college are simply illusions. Higher education is powerful, but not in the ways some of us would like to
believe. Higher education primarily confers status rather than
new values, life goals, or motivation for constructive social
engagement. Parents and students who take a utilitarian approach to college are closer to the truth about higher education
than pundits and philosophers and professors and graduation
speakers with high ideals and expectations. Our analysis reveals
that the common sense of these parents and students is closer
to the sociological reality than the fragile ideals of those most
vocal about the benefits of college.

The central question is: What is higher education supposed
to do for young adults and what does it actually do? The
outcomes are changes in attitudes and activities related to
central American values: success, individual fulfillment and
concern for the community.   These central themes and the
methods and data for this study are the subject of chapter 1.

Chapter 2 deals with the effects of higher education upon
success goals and rewards, such as annual earnings, occupational status, and participation in professional associations and
other job-related groups; and on occupational goals such as job
security, success, opportunities for one's own advancement and
for one's children, job autonomy, and interesting work.

Expressive individualism, reflected in both social participation and life goals, is the theme of chapter 3. The themes of this
chapter are how young adults changed after high school and how
higher education affects participation in cultural groups, sports,
and other leisure activities, and how higher education affects
values regarding family and marriage, friendships, leisure, good
education and the importance of working with friendly people on
the job.

The topic of chapter 4 is civic commitment. Changes in voting and other political involvement, and community activities, volunteer work and non-worship church activities, commitment to community leadership and social justice are central, as is the question of how these are affected by attending college.

In chapter 5 we weigh the effects of educational attainment and college characteristics and experiences on two crucial aspects of self-concept: self-direction and self-esteem.

Satisfaction with schooling and perceptions of educational experience are the subject of chapter 6. Included are analyses of academic and social aspects of high school and college experiences—teaching, learning, friendships, sports and recreational facilities, counseling and placement opportunities, and prestige of the institution. We also consider how individuals view their educations: how challenging the courses were, how much was learned, and whether interesting ideas and people were encountered.

Finally, in the concluding chapter, we present the implications of the findings for postsecondary education curriculum policy, the unresolved challenges and questions, the issues involved in learning from one cohort, and suggestions for those who advise prospective students.

ACKNOWLEDGMENTS

The support of many people and organizations was vital to the successful completion of this book. It is incredible how many people must cooperate and how many decisions must dovetail to carry out large-scale quantitative research.

Glen H. Elder, Jr. was a kindly and interested Dutch uncle who read and critiqued early drafts of our research proposal and who helped us greatly to improve it. The Spencer Foundation, under the presidency of H. Thomas James, generously supported the two first-named authors half-time for the academic year 1987–1988 and furnished computer support, other services, and supplies. The University of North Carolina at Greensboro (UNCG) also provided each of them with a half salary for that year. This made it possible for them to devote a full academic year to the research. In addition, Spencer Foundation funds supported Mary N. Kolb, the third author, half-time during that year, and that led to our later collaboration. The Institute for Research in Social Science was generous in granting us visiting scholar standing and in providing us with office space, electronic communications, and telephone service for the 1987–1988 academic year. Glen Elder was kind enough to draw the attention of all three authors to their similar research interests. Dr. James, now retired from the Spencer Foundation, and the other foundation board members were far-sighted enough to respond to our early pleas to underwrite essential data-gathering efforts. To save costs the Department of Education had ordered cuts of most subjective and social and political participation items from the 1986 wave of the *National Longitudinal Study of the High School Class of 1972* (NLS-72). Dropping these items, which had all appeared in earlier waves, would have precluded the use of the survey to study many aspects of how these people entered young adulthood. Such slashes would have made this project impossible. We had become aware of the possibility of this draconian retrenchment from C. Dennis Carroll and Andrew Kolstad of the Office of Longitudinal Studies of the Center for Education Statistics, U. S. Department of Education. Carroll and Kolstad had maintained effective liaison with the many public data-users in the field. Knox and Lindsay, among many others, urged saving these "soft" data. Dennis Carroll, chief of longitudinal studies at the center, indicated the center's willingness to include the items scheduled for deletion provided we obtained outside funding.

We prevailed upon the Spencer Foundation to help fund the items slated for elimination. Tom James made strenuous efforts at the highest levels in the U.S. Department of Education to have the items funded federally instead of privately, trenchantly quoting a Spencer Foundation board member, "When the poor pay the rich, the devil laughs!" Since the foundation had already pledged to support piggyback data-gathering on NLS-72, it lived up to its word when negotiations for federal funding were unavailing. Not only did the present study benefit from Spencer's generosity, so also did the study of young adulthood, for the data are now in the public domain.

Marion M. Faldet, vice-president of the Spencer Foundation, deserves a special word of praise. She is the ideal administrator for a foundation, always grasping the scholar's situation and needs, ever thoughtful and tactful.

We have a peculiar debt to Everett Wilson, who stuck his nose in our office in the summer of 1987 and asked, "What are you people up to?" We said that we were investigating the long-term effects of education. He said in a ruefully knowing and jocular way, "Lots of Luck!" We realized that this was the voice of experience, giving support in what many had come to regard as a lost cause, but we also accepted it as something of a challenge. We are especially indebted to an offhand, but enthusiastic remark of Gary Gaddy of the University of North Carolina at Chapel Hill's Institute for Research in Social Science (IRSS). After we made a presentation at the IRSS as part of its Colloquium Series—a presentation that contained a wealth of empirical findings, Gary said, "You have a book here." Angel Beza, then Acting Director of IRSS, was present and concurred. This moment was a turning-point in our commitment to this project and provided the catalyst we needed.

Catherine Zimmer of the Sociology Department at North Carolina State University has been nothing less than a marvel, for she gave us frequent and unstinting advice on statistical techniques and questions of research design. She read through many drafts of much of our material, especially the appendixes, and her critiques, rooted in her good sociological judgment and statistical wisdom, were indispensable. She has all the qualities of a great teacher, for she never made us feel like fools even when we asked some obvious questions. Richard Jaeger of UNCG's School of Education provided us with essential statistical expertise, particularly on design effects. David Mitchell of UNCG's Sociology Department was especially helpful on problems of measurement and factor analysis. M. Elaine Burgess of UNCG's Sociology Department kindly called our attention to the many issues and pitfalls in the measurement of occupational standing, and Rachel Rosenfeld of the Sociology Department of the University of North Carolina at Chapel Hill was most helpful in bringing us up to date in the literature on assessing that topic. Barry Hirsch, now of the Economics Department of Florida Sate University, aided us in thinking about how to measure income.

The work of The National Opinion Research Center (NORC) as contractor responsible for gathering, processing, and disseminating the data was up to its usual high standard, and Penny Sebring of NORC was most helpful as liaison.

The personnel of the Academic Computing Center at the University of North Carolina at Greensboro were most gracious and patient in helping us carry out many technical tasks in managing, transporting, and merging large data-sets. Gary M. Grandon, director of the computing center, provided us with abundant support, facilitating UNCG's generous contribution when we exceeded our original budget for computer time and services by a great amount. His vision and ability to expedite matters led to UNCG's substantial expansion of its computer capabilities just in time for our heavy computational and data storage needs. The center's staff was constantly informative and kind. Marlene R. Pratto, the assistant director for user services, and Host and Network Support staff members Terri Kirchen and Judy Martin, all helped cheerfully, effectively, and frequently in problems of complex computations and in data-set management and transportation.

The personnel of The Institute for Research in Social Science (IRSS) of the University of North Carolina at Chapel Hill were also consistently gracious and helped us over many of the hurdles that confronted us through the year we worked there. This was a most stimulating climate for doing research and for professional renewal. In particular, Angell Beza, then the acting director, ever knowledgeable and personable, was decisive in providing us with office space, telecommunications, and telephone service for the academic year 1987-1988. He also encouraged us to do this book. Kenneth Hardy, a fine methodologist and sociologist at IRSS, often availed us of his invaluable analytical and statistical advice. Richard Lennox, then statistician with IRSS, also helped us with many decisions concerning factor analysis, the reliability of measures, research design, and the interpretation of results. IRSS's many fine programming consultants were always willing to assist us with the knottiest of problems. Finally, Mike Crane, supervisor of the machine room and a virtuoso who could get anything electronic to work, deserves special thanks for helping out with our complex communications needs.

Small grants from the Research Council of UNCG helped facilitate the early phases of our work. Joanne V. Creighton, former dean of UNCG's College of Arts and Sciences, gave sympathetic support and helped us arrange for reduced course loads in the academic year 1989-1990 to complete the writing of this book.

Carol Sanders of UNCG's Office of Budgeting and Accounting was most helpful in ironing out technical budgetary problems, as was Debbie Otis of the same office in accounting and handling budgetary details. They are both administrators who expedite getting essential little things done.

Terry Dziedziek, Sue Sippel, and Lisa Swanson proved most diligent in library research and attention to the minutiae of preparing the bibliography. Joan Roach was a model of cooperation, patience, and expertise in the arduous and complex task of typing statistical tables. Selena Mobbs was wonderfully perfectionistic as she prepared the tables and helped us clean both text and tables for inconsistencies and other flaws. Gail and Jack Owens of The Chapel Hill Press proofread the manuscript and provided camera-ready copy with consummate skill, patience, and good humor. We owe a debt of gratitude to several anonymous readers who helped us strengthen the argument of the book. Paul Betz, now with the Oxford University Press, helped us with a variety of matters from writing style and organization to the wisdom and lore of scholarly publishing. He gave us early encouragement to do the book and met with us several times over the years; his active, gentle role in helping us shape the book was welcome indeed. We are indebted to several anonymous readers who helped us strengthen the details of the argument. George Butler, acquisitions editor at Greenwood Publishing Group, is last but far from least in our gratitude. He responded immediately and with keen interest upon our submission of the manuscript and has unerringly guided us and brought a sense of perspective and wisdom to our endeavors.

The merits of this book owe much to those we have cited above. It is a pleasure to give them heartfelt thanks. We also are grateful to many persons who cooperated in gathering, processing, storing, and disseminating the data but who must go unsung since they are not known to us. This book's deficiencies are, of course, the responsibility of the authors.

To the authors, this enterprise has been, above all, serious and joyous—a wonderful exercise in collegiality and authenticity in communication. Each author made singular essential contributions to the whole.

Finally, our families—spouses and children alike—did more than stand patiently by through the years of research and writing. They gave us loving support. They adapted their schedules to ours and helped restore a sense of perspective to our lives. They also read much of our material, raised large questions, and critiqued our work creatively.

DOES
COLLEGE
MAKE
A DIFFERENCE?

Introduction: College—What For?

Everybody's gettin' so goddam educated in this country there'll be nobody to take away the garbage. . . . You stand on the street today and spit, you're gonna hit a college man.

Arthur Miller, *All My Sons*

In L. Frank Baum's *The Wonderful Wizard of Oz*, the wizard endows the scarecrow with brains, a mixture of pins and needles and bran held in place in the scarecrow's head by straw. Thirty-nine years after the book's publication in 1900, the popular motion picture appeared. The screenplay departs markedly from the book in that the wizard responds to the scarecrow's request for brains by giving him a college degree.

"Why, anybody can have a brain," the wizard says. "That's a very mediocre commodity. . . . Back where I come from, we have universities, seats of great learning—where men go to become great thinkers, and when they come out, they think deep thoughts—and with no more brains than you have—but! they have one thing you haven't got! A diploma. . . . Therefore, by virtue of the authority vested in me by the Universitatus Committeeatum e pluribus unum, I hereby confer upon you the honorary degree of Th.D. . . . Doctor of Thinkology."

"Oh, joy, rapture!" smiles the scarecrow with disbelief. "I've got a brain! How can I ever thank you enough?" (Baum 1984; Langley, Ryerson, and Woolf 1989). The scarecrow, exuding a new self-confidence, is elated with his transformation and new status.

In those first few decades of the twentieth century, a college diploma became an omnipotent symbol of status, a powerfully defining entreé to the middle-class American dream. At the turn of the century, when *The Wizard of Oz* was published, twenty-nine thousand bachelor's and advanced degrees were conferred, four out of five upon men. In 1939, the year the film was released, 217,000 degrees were awarded, an increase of over seven times. In 1987, 1.4 million degrees were earned, half of them by women (National Center for Education Statistics [NCES] 1989). The proportion of American adults with four or more years of college has risen steadily from 11 percent in 1970 to 20 percent in 1988 (NCES 1989). Today, one of twenty persons in the United States is enrolled in some form of higher education, over twice the proportion of most other industrial nations (Rasell and Mishel 1989).

Joe Keller, in Arthur Miller's play *All My Sons*, set in the 1940s, was successful in business without a college degree. He suffered acutely from his lack of sophisticated verbal facility: "I ain't got the vocabulary" (Miller 1947, 45), but he saw clearly how society was changing. With only slight modification, Joe's comment is truer now than ever: "You stand on the street today and spit, you're gonna hit a college man or woman."

What do young adults get for their investment of time, money, and effort? And what does society get? Are students receiving the benefits promised and fulfilling their dreams? What is college supposed to do? And what is it actually doing?

College is supposed to do many things. Students typically seek through education jobs that are stable, well paying and satisfying.[1] Parents of all social classes want their children to have higher education credentials for their economic and career advantages. For many working-class families, this may mean a one- or two-year certificate at a local community college, or a four-year degree at a nearby state university. The more affluent middle class simply expects college attendance from earliest childhood, and a child who drops out, even temporarily, causes the parents grief. In any case, middle-class adults and their children usually agree that education after high school is a necessary step on the way to an acceptable job. Working-class people who do not go on to college often blame themselves for a presumed lack of effort or intelligence, a phenomenon sociologists include among the "hidden injuries of class" (Sennett and Cobb 1972; Rubin 1976).

College has other aims as well. For most students, especially among the more affluent, enjoyment of collegiate social life is a high priority. They look forward to fraternities, sororities, college sports, and extracurricular activities as an interval of dalliance prior to assuming adult responsibilities. At the university one often meets a future spouse and builds life-long friendships and business associations. Visits to college campuses and knowledge of the student body are major considerations in deciding among colleges.

At the same time, political, business, and educational leaders emphasize specialized training of scientists, technicians, and business persons for a more competitive state or national economy. Corporate employers want graduates with a combination of liberal arts and practical skills—analytical and communication skills, familiarity with the language of business and the nature of work in corporate settings, skills for coping with corporate environments, and attitudes favorable to business (Useem, 1989). Large research universities, so essential to the economic and technical requirements of an advanced industrial society, provide specialized graduate and undergraduate training, traditional liberal arts education, and training in a large variety of vocational skills. Public monies also support four-year and two-year institutions to train people for thousands of occupations—teaching, nursing, business, textile design, computer programming, and many more.

There is considerable evidence that higher education provides a significant economic return to the nation. Leslie and Brinkman (1988) devote much attention to showing that there continues to be a significant social, as opposed to individual, return to the investment in education. Solmon (1985) discusses not only differences in individual earnings but also cognitive and behavioral changes consequent upon education at all levels cross-nationally. He suggests, however, that in all these respects quality education, including higher education, is not as advantageous to developed societies as it once may have been, but that developing countries may get a significant boost by investing in high-quality education for lesser numbers of students than by trying to offer a diluted product to the many.

The professors stress different aims; the primary goal is cultivating the intellect of students. For five thousand faculty members recently surveyed by the Carnegie Foundation for Advancement of Teaching, the most important purpose of undergraduate education is encouraging creative thinking (Carnegie Foundation 1989). Basic understanding of mathematics and science, knowledge of history and social sciences, and appreciation of literature and the arts also ranked high.

For many educational administrators and leading members of the higher education establishment, college ought also to contribute, on the other hand, to the personal and social development of students: understanding and relating to other people, clarifying values and philosophy of life, commitment to ideas and life-long learning, and skills for the enjoyment of leisure. Others see altruistic social and political values and engagement as the most important outcome of higher education. As Boyer expresses it, "The aim of the undergraduate experience is not only to prepare the young for productive careers, but also to enable them to live lives of dignity and purpose; not only to generate new knowledge, but to channel that knowledge to humane ends; not merely to study government, but to help shape a citizenry that can promote the public good" (1987, 297).

Is higher education fulfilling all these high expectations? What, in fact, does education after high school have to do with young adults—their work and leisure, their attitudes and values, their community and political commitments, their self-development, and their opinions of higher educational institutions?

AMERICAN VALUES AND HIGHER EDUCATION

What we want from education grows out of the basic core values of Americans and American culture. One of the most provocative recent statements of mainstream American goals is *Habits of the Heart* (Bellah et al. 1985). The authors group American values into three types: utilitarian, expressive, and civic. Most of all, we prize work, success, achievement through competition, and material rewards—what the authors term utilitarian individualism. Benjamin Franklin exemplifies this commitment, as in his advice to Europeans considering immigration to America: "If they are poor, they begin first as Servants or Journeymen: and if they are sober, industrious, and frugal, they soon become Masters, establish themselves in Business, marry, raise Families, and become respectable Citizens" (Cited in Bellah et al. 1985, 33). Franklin assumes that hard work will lead to higher social standing. This faith in meritocracy—success through competition and striving—is still powerful in contemporary America. Franklin's simple stratification system seems quaint in comparison with today's complex social system, in which over twenty thousand occupations confer varying degrees of income, prestige, and power. Access to the middle and higher rungs of this occupational ladder typically requires documented completion of the requirements of the educational system—with its high school diplomas, one- and two-year postsecondary certificates and degrees, and bachelor's, master's and doctoral degrees. Bellah and his coauthors use the entrepreneur and the well-educated bureaucratic manager, both usually male, as modern roles symbolizing the importance of utilitarian individualism.

At the same time, Americans value personal happiness, freedom, friendship, marriage, family, and leisure—expressive individualism. Walt Whitman proclaims this emphatically: "I celebrate myself. . . . I loaf and invite my soul" (cited in Bellah et al. 1985, 34). By the late twentieth century, many Americans have come to believe that work is not all there is to life. In countless ways, people take time to socialize with close friends and family—in homes and outdoor leisure locales such as parks and wilderness areas, at sports events, and in night clubs, bowling alleys, and bars. Social circles of people with similar tastes and ethnic communities share music, sports, and popular arts, and express their commonality with distinctive language, clothes, and consumer goods. Schools and communities express their solidarity through intense loyalty to their athletic teams.[2] In *Habits of the Heart* the therapist is the contemporary symbol of expressive individualism. Accepting the economic and social system as it is, the therapist helps the individual adjust and find happiness. The aim is to liberate people from stifling norms and relationships, for work and love and a sense of individual well-being—the pursuit of happiness.

Americans have historically esteemed equality, justice, democracy, and even community—civic commitment. These values dominated the Biblical and Republican traditions of the colonial period. Thomas Jefferson exemplifies the American tradition of civic commitment. His faith in education as the foundation of democracy reinforced his belief that "all men are created equal." "I know of no safe depository of the ultimate powers of the society but the people themselves," said Jefferson, "and if we think them not enlightened enough to exercise their control with a wholesome discretion, the remedy is not to take it from them, but to inform their discretion by education" (Padover 1939, 89-90). The themes of equality, justice, democracy, and community have reappeared in many social movements and educational reforms in the years since Jefferson. But Bellah and his associates believe that utilitarian and expressive individualism overwhelm today's dominant middle-class white culture. Even when social movements, politics, or community service actively engage people, the only way they have to articulate their commitment is the language of expressive individualism with a vocabulary of personal idiosyncratic preference. In Bellah and his coauthors' view, we lack a vocabulary of civic concern.

These conflicting values have played a critical role in the development of American higher education. The tension between views of education as a narrow preparation for work and as a broadening and liberalizing influence are as ancient as ancient Greece. Both perspectives agree that education ought to prepare students for life. But those advocating utilitarian education are intent on occupational life, whereas proponents of liberal education emphasize the range of knowledge that will also aid in leisure, human relationships, and citizenship.

The humanities dominated the earliest higher education in this country in its preparation of an elite of ministers and lawyers. The liberal arts and humanities curricula have yielded ground to more practical studies throughout the history of American education. The rise of rationalism and empiricism represented the increasing ascendancy of an emergent bourgeoisie. First, in the late eighteenth century, mathematics and the natural sciences joined the curriculum. Then the escalation in research and multiplication of specialty areas in the second half of the nineteenth century divided universities into schools, departments, and specialties. The Morrill Act of 1862 established land grant institutions and added a flood of formerly apprenticeship programs to the curricula. It reflected agricultural and middle-class interests. Finally, after World War II the student clientele mushroomed to include a huge variety of social and age groups. This further undermined elite efforts toward a common humanities curriculum (Commission on the Humanities, 1980).

Most students enter college for instrumental reasons: they expect the further schooling to pay off in better jobs. This instrumental orientation is reflected in their enrollment patterns. The number of recent high school graduates who enroll in college, and the particular types of programs they enroll in, corresponds to the market for college graduates (Freeman 1976). For example, academic and scientific enrollments have increased recently, as have business-oriented and traditional professional specialties. Generally, the trend since about 1970 has been toward studies related to work: decreases in the number of degrees awarded in letters and foreign languages, social sciences, and philosophy and religion were exceeded by growth in computer science, protective service, and communications graduates (Snyder 1987, Table 154). Katchadourian and Boli's (1985) study of Stanford graduates, however, finds that students compartmentalized their careerist and intellectualist values, and most students embraced both perspectives.

Individualism, both utilitarian and expressive, and civic commitment encompass some of the most frequently mentioned aims of higher education. The pursuits of success, of happiness, and of the common good frame our questions fittingly. How does college foster or hinder these basic, albeit often conflicting, values and activities? The next three chapters deal in succession with utilitarian, expressive, and civic issues.

Two further questions remain, both of which are elaborations on the theme of expressive individualism. One is the development of individual identity or personality—in other words, the self. How does postsecondary schooling affect self-esteem and sense of self-direction? Accordingly, the fifth chapter is entitled "In Pursuit of Self." Finally, as Astin (1985) suggests, if we want to know how higher education affects people, why not ask the clients? How satisfied are former students with their academic and social experiences in high school and college? Chapter 6, "The Pursuit of Educational Experiences," concerns these issues.

HIGHER EDUCATION'S EFFECTS:
SORTING AND SOCIALIZING

What effects do colleges have on students' self-esteem, sense of self-direction, values, and social and political participation? Do such effects endure beyond the years of schooling into adulthood? How do colleges make an impact on their students? Sociologists have emphasized two kinds of effects of schools and colleges: socialization of individuals and allocation of these persons to positions in society, especially occupational positions (Kerckhoff 1976). Riesman and Jencks (1962, 78) stress both: "College is an initiation rite for separating the upper-middle from the lower-middle class, and for changing the semi-amorphous adolescent into a semi-identified adult."

The socialization approach to the study of higher education, in contrast to the allocation approach, inquires into the conditions under which various types of change take place for students. What features of the college environment, for example, lead to value changes? What types and characteristics of institutions, what arrangements of curricula and teaching methods, make a difference in student outcomes? (Anderson 1984a, 1984b; Pascarella and Terenzini 1991) Underlying these questions is the frequent assumption that we can create college environments that help develop competent, critical, and socially concerned human beings.

The development of students is, then, a subject quite apart from the certification function of education, although we shall see that the two are interrelated. Several generations of social scientists have searched for the impact of higher education on students. The search for socialization effects of colleges on their students, especially the different effects of particular colleges, has a long, rich, and checkered history. Serious methodological shortcomings and unduly optimistic expectations have tended to be the rule, not the exception. Meyer (1977, 58) acerbically refers to this search as a quest for the grail.

The most notable attempts include Newcomb's classic study of Bennington College students (1943), which showed a remarkable liberalization in the political values of students in their college years. Yet, as Newcomb was aware, this had the limitations of a case study; it was not possible to generalize from the experiences of a distinctive group of students at a unique juncture of a particular college's development in the late years of the Great Depression. Jacob (1957) surveyed many more institutions and students and was pessimistic about the socialization effects of colleges. As he mordantly observed, students of the 1950s were self-centered, traditional, conformist, and "gloriously contented." The little value change that did take place during the college years stemmed from distinctive experiences rather than differences between college environments, although Jacob does discuss the "peculiar potency" of a very few colleges.

Sanford's *The American College* (1962) acknowledged the dearth of systematic empirical knowledge about college effects but pioneered in bringing together sociological and psychological perspectives. The explicit goal was to make college environments more effective and more humane. Webster, Freedman, and Heist (1962) reported changes in students' knowledge, personality and values, but recognized that the causes were unknown. Freedman (1962) found attitudes to be rather stable after the senior year. In a follow-up of the earlier Bennington study, Newcomb et al. (1967) showed a striking persistence into young adulthood of the values developed in the college years, especially when sustained by congenial, supporting social environments. In all these studies, the possibility remains that normal life-course changes could have accounted for most of the findings, for none of the above pieces of research could compare the students to their peers who did *not* go on to college.

Many of the fifteen hundred empirical studies in Feldman and Newcomb's (1969) comprehensive survey of college impact on values, attitudes, and personality had this or other methodological shortcomings. As they sought the conditions that led to changes in different types of students, the authors discovered some common themes: students appeared to be changing in college, but self-selection into college environments and student personality characteristics confounded attempts to isolate preexisting conditions from actual changes. Apart from the effects of small, residential four-year colleges, most of these did not isolate institutional effects. Only two studies included those not attending college; some were longitudinal during the college years, but few examined effects beyond the college years.

Astin's (1977) study was a major advance, with a large national sample and a wide array of college and personality characteristics. He found changes in values, activities, and personality characteristics in the college years. Attending four-year rather than two-year colleges and small, rather than large, institutions magnified the changes. Again, there were no comparisons with those who did not go to college and the study did not go beyond the college years. Astin concluded that the greatest obstacle to knowledge of the effects of college education was lack of adequate longitudinal data, an obstacle that the present study helps to overcome.

From a perspective sharply different in substance and method, Hyman, Wright, and Reed (1975) and Hyman and Wright (1979) made two ingenious studies of the long-term effects of educational attainment on both knowledge and values, respectively. They found large and generally consistent differences in knowledge and values for those of differing levels of education, from elementary school through college. They conclude that the differences are indeed long-lasting and independent of socioeconomic background, ethnic origin, region, and gender. They could not, however, control for academic abilities, values, and knowledge prior to entering school. Neither study addressed the process by which education had such a massive impact on knowledge and values.

Finally, Pascarella and Terenzini's (1991) comprehensive synthesis, analyzing over 2,600 studies of the 1970s and 1980s, provides the best source for knowledge of recent research in the field as well as the definitive starting place for empirical research on the effects of higher education for the foreseeable future. The authors not only encompass virtually all relevant works with clarity and precision, but they point out weaknesses and omissions and key theoretical and methodological challenges for future research. Two "families" of models and theories have dominated the research they review. One is based on psychological theories of individual human growth and development. The other family of theories, which they classify as sociological college impact models, focuses on structural and organizational characteristics of colleges and their environments. College impact perspectives emphasize external sources of change in students' attitudes and behavior, not necessarily based on particular patterns of internal development. Each approach has strengths and limitations and both types contribute to understanding of the processes by which institutions affect individuals. In either case, Pascarella and Terenzini make a strong case for research that is better designed and more carefully grounded in theory.[3]

Not only do schools socialize, they also certify students and allocate them to positions in society. To Durkheim we owe the latter line of thought. Schools exist primarily for the survival and functioning of society (Durkheim 1956) rather than for the personal development of students. The aim of education is to instill in students the norms, values, knowledge, and skills needed for performance of adult roles in society. Schools evaluate the performance and capacities of their students, sorting and certifying them for positions in the social order. "Education, far from having as its unique or principal object the individual and his interests, is above all the means by which society perpetually recreates the conditions of its very existence" (1956, 123). Education's allocation function has been emphasized in such widely divergent approaches as status attainment research (e.g., Alexander and Eckland 1973; Alexander and McDill 1976; Blau and Duncan 1967; Kerckhoff 1976; Kerckhoff and Jackson 1982; Sewell and Hauser 1976, 1980; Meyer 1977) and neo-Marxist analyses (Bowles and Gintis 1976; Collins 1979).

Meyer's comprehensive theory of the effects of education as an institution (1977) distinguishes incisively how schools socialize and allocate students and how these processes are related. At the same time, Meyer places these effects within the much more inclusive and pervasive legitimation function of education. Universities produce knowledge and define certain types of knowledge and ways of thinking as legitimate (e.g., astronomy as opposed to astrology). Moreover, the educational system defines social positions corresponding to various types of specialized competence and certifies those who have achieved expertise in these areas. These systems of classification become institutionalized and enforced by rules of the state. For example, a certain amount of schooling becomes compulsory for all citizens and practicing medicine requires a medical doctorate from an accredited institution. Education systems in modern nations thus do what religious systems did in earlier societies: "Mysteries are rationalized, brought under symbolic control, and incorporated into the social system" (Meyer 1977, 67).

From Meyer's perspective, the most important things schools and colleges do for students is give them a new social identity, to confer status. And this carries with it entitlements to an improved position in the economy. After students fulfill a prescribed number of courses or credits, the school grants them certificates or degrees defining a new status, for example, high school graduate or college graduate. Failure to complete requirements also results in a new status, for example, high school dropout. As students are processed through the educational system, they learn the personal and social qualities appropriate to the positions to which the school is authorized to assign them; people learn to play the roles associated with their statuses. The status conferred by the school or college remains with the graduates for the rest of their lives, affecting their values and behavior long after the completion of schooling. As Meyer puts it, the student experiences "(a) the immediate socializing organization, (b) the fact that this organization has the allocating power to confer status on him, and (c) the broader fact that this allocation power has the highest level of legitimacy in society. The education he receives has a very special status and authority: its levels and content categories have the power to redefine him legitimately in the eyes of everyone around him and thus take on overwhelming ceremonial significance" (75).

Meyer's articles (1970, 1977) are a sociological interpretation of college effects that are impressive in their closure and comprehensiveness. Kamens (1971, 1974, 1977) elaborated these ideas specifically for higher education. The theory does not deny that there are socialization effects of higher education but argues that the allocation-placement hypothesis largely subsumes them. Both Feldman (1972) and Meyer hold that, for an institution to produce changes through socialization, it must motivate its charges to want to be socialized. This ability to motivate, in turn, inheres in the institution's power to confer credentials that provide access to future status—identities that students perceive to be advantageous. However, education's part in certifying young people to take particular roles in society goes beyond simply allocating individuals to existing places in the social structure. Meyer (1977) and Kamens (1977), in the context of their legitimation theory, highlight the impact of educational systems on defining and constructing social statuses and fields of expertise. This, then, is not the usual stimulus-response interpretation, but one that takes actors to interpret their situations and, accordingly, to choose courses of action. It also takes into account the different strengths, real or imagined, of educational institutions to promise future benefits by sorting people into categories with desirable and esteemed social standing. It is an extension of the question that nearly every child in America hears again and again: "What are you going to be when you grow up?"

Meyer (1970) theorizes that most American colleges have weak charters in that there is no clear social and political elite to which the typical college can promise access. To the extent that institutions are roughly equivalent in having relatively weak charters, we would anticipate that educational attainment itself and, especially, the receiving of credentials would account for most of the differences in individual outcomes. Graduation from most colleges confers some level of middle-class status; hence, we may expect similar and not very pronounced socialization effects of the slight variations in college characteristics in themselves. In Meyer's view there are a small number of institutions that avoid "diffuse socialization" through their strong charters. Such institutions are likely to be prestigious and visible and to provide a clear channel to enhanced status identities. To the extent that institutional characteristics and individual experiences explain such outcomes, the strength of the institution's charter may play a part. There is evidence that attendance at elite universities and colleges enhances graduates' placement in high-status positions and their income (Kingston and Lewis, 1990). The observed effects, however, might be largely accounted for by individual characteristics before the study. Also, less than 1 percent of postsecondary students attend these elite universities and colleges. The focus in our study will be on the effects of a much broader segment of two-year and four-year institutions on a nationally representative sample of students.

The shifts in values, goals, and activities attributable to higher education in the domains of commitments, self-concept, and satisfactions with and perceptions of higher education occupy us here. We have sought to distinguish the extent to which alterations would have occurred anyway in the usual course of young adult development, the degree to which changes result from particular environments or student experiences there, and the pervasiveness of a certification effect whereby the attainment of educational levels is accompanied by taking on values and activities consistent with the social status conferred.

PERVASIVE INEQUITIES: SOCIAL CLASS, RACE, GENDER AND ACADEMIC ABILITIES

A study of the consequences of higher education would not be complete without taking account of complex and pervasive inequities in American schools and society. Higher education is a diverse resource that is not uniformly available, in either quantity or quality, to all categories of people. These groups do not use education uniformly, and education does not necessarily have the same meaning for them. Gender, race, social class origins, and academic abilities affect where students go to college, what they study, and how long they stay in school. These relationships make it more difficult to isolate the effects of educational credentials, college characteristics, and student experience; therefore, we consider the influence of these background factors.

Does higher education open doors to equality of opportunity, or is it one of the causes of inequality? Ironically, as Carnoy and Levin (1985) argue, both propositions may be accurate. In the recent past there has been less discrimination toward minorities and women, for example, and more opportunity for these groups within educational institutions than in the workplace. At the same time, schools and colleges tend to reproduce the inequalities that students bring with them to school. Many studies explore these relationships (e.g., Sewell and Hauser 1976; Persell 1977; Featherman and Hauser 1978; Jencks et al. 1979; Buchmann 1989). There is evidence of change: since the 1960s, women and minorities have been attaining more education than their counterparts did in earlier years. Gender differences in the proportion of degrees awarded finally disappeared by the late 1980s, although the fields in which these were conferred tend to be polarized by sex. The race gap in educational attainment appeared to be closing through the late 1970s, but the proportion of black students going on to higher education began a decline that lasted through the mid-1980s.

Our own analyses show that while race and gender differences are important in the educational attainment process, social class origins are even more powerful in determining success. Sixty-one percent of those from the top quartile of family socioeconomic status completed four or more years of college, while only 18 percent of those from low quartile families did so (Table 1.1). The overall effect of social class is actually understated by these figures. About 16 percent of the age group of our sample did not complete high school (U.S. Department of Education 1989). These dropouts were disproportionately from low-income and minority groups.

Gender, race, and class origins helped determine where these high school graduates went to college and their experiences there (Table 1.2). Whites were more likely than blacks to go to more selective schools and to get better grades. Women were more likely to get better grades than men and to major in education, while men had a better chance of majoring in business. In subsequent chapters we examine the effects of these decisions

Table 1.1
Percent Completing Four Years or More of College
by Family Socioeconomic Status, Race, and Gender

	Total	Men	Women	White	Black
Family Socioeconomic Status					
High Quartile	61	63	59	61	61
Middle Two Quartiles	31	34	28	31	33
Low Quartile	18	18	19	18	22
N =	5409	2593	2816	4950	459

SOURCE: National Longitudinal Study of the High School of Class of 1972 (see Appendixes A and B).

about college majors on utilitarian, expressive, and civic out-comes for young adults. Again, social class had stronger effects than race and gender. College students from higher-status fami-lies were more likely to go to colleges that are private, more selective, larger, and have higher proportions of students living on campus. These higher-status students less often went to vocationally oriented schools and they more often lived on cam-pus. Opportunities to participate in the more educationally beneficial milieux, then, are greater for higher-status students. Those beginning with more advantages reap more benefits.

Unraveling the effects of class, race, and gender on educa-tional attainment is difficult because these factors are inter-twined with another powerful influence on school success—academic abilities. In this study we measure academic abilities by scores on standardized tests taken in the senior year of high school for reading, vocabulary, mathematics, and induc-tive reasoning. These tests measure what Howard Gardner (1983) calls logical-mathematical and linguistic intelligences. These are a narrow range of competencies, partly innate and partly acquired, that contribute to success in school. As Gardner points out, such tests fail to take account of other types of intelligences which may be just as valuable to society: spatial, musical, and bodily-kinesthetic abilities; interpersonal skills; and understanding oneself.[4] Academic abilities begin developing earliest for children in middle- and upper-class families in which reading and writing are common and parents speak the language that is taught in schools.

Social class differences in educational success and effects of expanding higher education in industrial societies have been

Table 1.2
Correlations of Background Factors with
College Characteristics and Student Experiences

	Background Factors			
	Whites	Women	Family Socioeconomic Status	Academic Abilities
College Characteristics				
Student Enrollment	.07	-.05	.15	.19
Selectivity	.19	-.09	.29	.39
Private Control	-.03	-.04	.14	.12
Full-time Students	-.04	-.04	.02	.07
Vocational Emphasis	-.01	.03	-.13	-.20
Highly Residential	.03	-.05	.17	.20
Student Experiences				
Business Major	.02-	.14	.06	.01
Education Major	-.01	.18	-.03-	-.06
Arts & Sciences Major	-.04	-.01	.03	.12
Ever Lived on Campus	-.02	.04	.20	.24
College Grades	.12	.20	.08	.34

N = 2702

NOTE: For data transformations and calculation procedures see Appendixes A and B.

explored critically by Pierre Bourdieu (Bourdieu and Passeron 1977; Bourdieu 1977; Swartz 1977, 1990). Contrary to the intentions and expectations of many in these societies, the expansion of educational institutions, Bourdieu shows, actually creates new and more complex forms of social inequality. Basing his work primarily on an analysis of the French educational system, Bourdieu shows how dominant elites pass on their cultural advantages to their children, who are more successful in schools than working- and middle-class children. Consequently, the social class structure reproduces itself from generation to generation. Upper-class children begin school with great advantages in the "cultural capital" valued by schools and universities—verbal facility, knowledge, and academic skills. Moreover, upper-class children bring a different set of attitudes and aspirations (habitus)—expectations prevalent in one's social group of future academic and status attainment. Systems of examinations, competition for admission to elite schools and universities, and self-selection all combine to sort out those destined for higher achievement from ordinary middle- and working-class youth. Even working-class youth with especially high academic abilities and motivation, qualities that are supposed to make people successful in meritocratic systems, find themselves at a disadvantage with their lack of broad cultural knowledge that is learned in families rather than in school. Cultural capital, then, is transformed into scholastic capital (educational credentials), which later leads to financial success and higher social status.

Bourdieu, like Meyer, Kamens, and Kingston and Lewis, cited above, also examines the effects of attending elite higher education institutions on careers, especially those requiring graduate and professional education. In societies where higher education is ever expanding and bachelor's degrees become more common, the type and prestige of the school attended for the bachelor's degree are likely to become more important status-defining characteristics of the graduate. However, as noted in our earlier discussion, the present study will focus on the effects of undergraduate education for the average student rather than the elite student.

Research in American education has confirmed empirically the advantages of children from higher educational and economic classes for school success (e.g., Jencks et al., 1979). Middle-class children begin school with more highly developed academic abilities. They expect to go to college and their parents are committed to providing the resources. In contrast, children from working-class and poor families lack the cultural capital valued by schools. One consequence is that they are placed in lower ability groups than similarly able but more advantaged students.[5] Parents who are working class or poor often do not or cannot help their children do the things that would make them successful in school. Like students of higher social classes, high ability students get the best of what postsecondary education has to offer. They are more likely to attend institutions that are highly selective, larger, private, with higher proportions of students living on campus, and they are more likely to live on campus themselves (see Table 1.2). Even if opportunities were equalized among students of different social classes, races, and genders, the policy question would remain whether those of higher academic abilities should be given more opportunities in the educational system (Jencks et al. 1979; Alexander, Cook, and McDill 1978). As Alexander Astin concludes, "The American higher education system is, in effect, a de facto tracking system whereby students are sorted into different institutions on the basis of their differing levels of academic preparation. . . . The basic problem for minorities is not institutional racism. The basic problem is that the higher education system favors the best-prepared students"(1985, 91-92, 99).

The data do not allow us directly to address outcomes for those who attended two-year colleges, whether community or technical colleges or hybrids. Brint and Karabel (1989) present a definitive study of the historical forces behind the emergence of the two-year college, its national diffusion, and the process by which it changed from an orientation to transfer to a four-year college to an essentially vocational one. They argue convincingly the failure of two-year colleges to live up to their democratic promise of higher educational access for all and epitomize this in the title, *The Diverted Dream*. While community colleges have opened higher educational opportunities to many working-class and minority students, the aggregate effect has been to accentuate rather than reduce social inequality by further refining the higher education tracking system. They are especially critical of the increasing emphasis on narrowly focused vocational education, which prepares students neither for successful four-year college pursuits nor for critical democratic participation as citizens. Howard London (1978) presents a revealing symbolic interactionist account of the ambiguities, the complexities, and the essentially blue-collar tenor of the community college. Such colleges seem poor stepping stones to success. Pascarella and Terenzini (1991) confirm these findings in other studies: students entering two-year colleges planning to attain bachelor's degrees are at a disadvantage compared to students of similar abilities entering four-year schools.

When we started the analyses for this book, we had expected that the effects of higher education would differ more clearly and profoundly for men and women than they did. With few exceptions, most notably in chapter 2 dealing with life chances, most of the gender differences that do show up are attributable to gender differences in development and the life cycle. The data in hand do not afford a way of assessing precisely the deep differences between men and women in consciousness and life perspectives. Valuable inroads on how women are affected by and use educational experiences and contexts and how they interpret them have already been made (Weis 1988; Holland and Eisenhart 1990). In their brilliant ethnographic account, Holland and Eisenhart show how young women confront educational institutions with institutionalized gender inequality. For a further incisive probing of the part educational institutions play in reproducing gender inequality largely through implicit sexist agendas, the reader should see Weis's critical anthology.

Social class, race, gender, and academic abilities, then, are sources of pervasive inequities in the process of postsecondary education. They especially determine school success and eventual educational attainment. In some respects these antecedents directly influence changes in the values, activities, and personality factors we examine. In other ways, these factors indirectly affect the outcomes we examine, through their powerful impact on educational attainment.

UNIQUENESS OF THIS STUDY

With the ever-increasing plethora of information and opinion about higher education published in the United States, why yet another study? Most of the work—nonscholarly and, indeed, even scholarly—is long on advice and short on analysis. With the hopes and fears of so many people so bound up with higher education, it is small wonder that there is so much material. Some of the material reflects an ideology of uncritical acceptance, or nearly hysterical adulation, of education. As Bowen says in his excellent review of the social science literature on higher education, "America has thus far in its history had a love affair with education" (1977, 449).

What makes this study unique is, first of all, its dual conceptual framework. We will examine the lasting socialization and allocation effects of higher education within the context of the status-conferring function of educational institutions. Moreover, we ask how higher education contributes to the character of the contemporary United States by affecting the utilitarian, expressive, and civic goals and activities of adults.

The analysis is based on a sample of 5,409 black and white women and men from the *National Longitudinal Study of the High School Class of 1972* (NLS-72). They are a nationwide and reasonably representative sample of their class from all fifty of the United States, from large and small schools in urban and rural areas and communities of diverse income levels. (For a full technical discussion of the sample see Appendix B.) Just before their high school graduation, the students answered extensive questionnaires including information about their values and life goals and their sense of self-esteem and self-direction. Two years after high school graduation, the respondents answered questions about their social and political participation—voting, church-related activities, volunteer work, social clubs, and sports. In 1986, at about thirty-two years of age, they responded again to these same questions. How did they change in their ideas about work, marriage, education, and leisure? How did their patterns of participation in the community change? Most important for this study, how did higher education affect these changes? Comparing those attaining different levels of schooling helps ascertain the difference higher education makes. Fourteen years after high school graduation, 22 percent of these young adults had no further formal education after high school. Twenty-five percent had completed less than two years of post-secondary schooling. Eighteen percent completed two or more years of college without achieving a bachelor's degree (this group includes those with two-year degrees). Twenty-five percent earned bachelor's degrees at a wide variety of institutions, and 11 percent earned advanced degrees.

What kinds of postsecondary institutions did our sample attend and what kind of student careers did they have? Those who went to college answered questions about their major field of study, whether they lived on campus, and their course grades. We obtained information about their postsecondary schools as well. The institutional data came from several sources and include size of the student body, selectivity of the college, the proportion of students who live on campus and who are full-time, the proportion of programs that are vocational, and whether the institution is public or private. Information on these characteristics for 2,702 people provides the basis for analysis of the effects of college characteristics. (See Appendix B for sources of institutional data and measurement of college characteristics.) Correlations among the characteristics of institutions in this broad sample of two-year, four-year, and graduate institutions are presented in Table 1.3. Selectivity is associated positively with private control, proportion of students living on campus, size of the student body, and proportion of students who are full-time; on the other hand, selectivity is correlated negatively with vocational emphasis. Larger institutions are more likely to be public and to have fewer full-time students. Private colleges are more likely to be residential and to have full-time students and less likely to emphasize vocational programs.

These institutional characteristics and varying individual student careers seemed most likely to influence our outcomes, which are goals, activities, and aspects of personality. Feldman and Newcomb (1969), Astin (1977), and Pascarella and Terenzini (1991) found that the impact of small residential four-year colleges owes both to their having a homogeneous faculty and student body and the opportunity they provide for interaction between students and faculty inside and outside the classroom. Since greater participation enhances socializing effects (Astin 1985), smaller colleges with higher proportions of students living on campus or who are full-time may have greater impact. Since private colleges are often, but not always, small and residential, private versus public control is a separate dimension. Liberal arts and sciences programs often predominate in small colleges.

Table 1.3
Correlation Matrix of College Characteristics for Last Postsecondary Institution Attended

	Student Enrollment	Selectivity	Full-Time Students	Private Control	Vocational Emphasis
Selectivity	.31				
Full-Time Students	-.23	.15			
Private Control	-.39	.33	.19		
Vocational Emphasis	-.02	-.49	-.21	-.29	
Highly Residential	-.02	.44	.35	.26	-.25

N = 2702

NOTE: See Appendix A for discussion of measurement of these college characteristics.

Differing curricular opportunities may have profound effects on the climate of colleges and their impact on students. Inclusion of the proportion of programs that are vocational versus academic helps explore this issue.

Finally, among attributes of colleges, the selectivity of institutions mesmerizes students, their families and the public. At the pinnacle of the prestige hierarchy of American higher education are Ivy League universities, the "public ivy's" (Moll 1985), and prestigious liberal arts colleges. These colleges and universities have the best resources and strong reputations, and demand for admission is high. Their student bodies originate from the wealthiest families. Following these high-prestige institutions is a snakelike procession of institutions lower in the prestige hierarchy, each trying to be a little more like the institutions in front of them in line (Riesman 1958). What difference does selectivity make? After taking account of initial differences between students, are graduates of more selective schools more satisfied with their education? Do they have higher earnings? Are they more involved in political and community affairs? Are their life goals different from those of graduates of community colleges or comprehensive state universities? In short, what evidence is there that college selectivity makes a difference?

In most recent research, institutional characteristics have shown some, but disappointingly little, socializing impact on students (Feldman and Newcomb 1969; Astin 1977; Bowen 1977; Pascarella and Terenzini 1991). More promising than institutional differences is the hypothesis that varying individual student careers will effect changes in goals, activities, and personality. First, individual residence on campus can immerse the student in activities with socializing impact. There is much evidence for this hypothesis (Chickering 1974; Astin 1977; Pascarella and Terenzini 1991). Second, in choosing a major field of study, each student makes a crucial decision. To graduate, the student must eventually earn sufficient course credits in this field. College major may influence changes in attitudes and behavior, especially to accentuate or reinforce initial differences (Feldman and Newcomb 1969; Astin 1977; Pascarella and Terenzini 1991). Students often change majors, and studies of college have usually been based on students' initial choices. The student's last major may be more likely to have long-term impact; thus, the student's final major is the criterion here: those majoring in business, education, and arts and sciences, versus others. While it would have been interesting to define the field of study more narrowly, the numbers of students in each group would have been too small for meaningful analysis. Finally, college grades are indicators of academic status attained in the higher education process. While grades are central to students' undergraduate experience (Becker, Greer, and Hughes 1968), with the exception of admission to another school, their impact on life after college is little known. That is why the long-term effects of undergraduate grades command attention.

This study makes a significant contribution through a unique combination of seven major methodological strengths[6]:

1. A longitudinal or panel design, that is, long-term follow-up of the same individuals;
2. Inclusion of those with no formal education after high school;
3. A fourteen-year time span;
4. National representativeness;
5. A wide range of individual attitudes and behavioral reports;
6. Data on characteristics of educational institutions after high school; and
7. Data on student experiences in educational settings after high school.

This singular set of strengths overcomes many design limitations of most earlier studies (Smart 1986; Pascarella and Terenzini 1991). We can place a high level of confidence in our success in specifying the contribution of different elements to changes in young adults: how student careers, college characteristics, and level of education affect a rich array of outcomes; changes in values, personality, and activities taking place in early adulthood; and also relative success in the world of work. The members of the high school class of 1972, their parents, and society made a large educational investment. How has all this schooling and the resulting educational credentials changed their lives and contributed to their development?

LIMITATIONS OF THIS STUDY

The NLS-72 data, although extraordinary, have limitations. We have made some deliberate decisions for good and sufficient reasons in designing this research, but these leave gaps in our understanding that need to be filled. We sought the most elemental variables for consistent attention throughout the book. In so doing, we attained a uniform degree of clarity regarding the direct effects of the level of education attainment, college characteristics, and college experiences. Future researchers may well wish to complicate their analyses to gain more complete understanding of some of these matters. We shall sketch some of the study's limitations, many of which represent opportunities for further work.

First, our models simplify in two basic respects. We ruled out many indirect causal paths as beyond the scope of our analysis. For example, socioeconomic status affects how much education one receives. Therefore, it works through educational attainment indirectly to affect whatever outcomes educational attainment itself affects. In addition, our choice of recursive models postpones analysis incorporating time-series and feedback loops. Thus, more adequate attention to the order of events in complex causal processes is in store for the future. Also, there are many events in the life course that need to be incorporated for complete explanations of outcomes; while we set these to one side for clarity, they ought not be ignored indefinitely.

Second, the definition of educational attainment in broad groupings is a useful simplification. It may, however, be limited in capturing the social and personal consequences and the meaning of credentialing and identity transformation. Scholars may wish to use more precise and particular categories in an attempt to analyze this process.

Third, some measurement constraints could not be avoided. Gathering data on so many facets of the consequences of education resulted in many single-item measures. The future researcher will want to construct composite measures from several items to gain assurance of reliability. However, one must assess any gain in reliability against the increased costs; in 1986, it cost $64,000 to add four pages to the NLS-72 questionnaire intended for 14,500 respondents.

Fourth, and closely related to the third point, there has been a sampling of items representing various domains that leaves us thirsting for more information. For example, there is only one item that bears directly on political liberalism-conservatism: the goal of working to correct social and economic inequalities. There are no items dealing with knowledge or how knowledge is used. There are no measures of whether the respondent has learned how to learn. One has to try to fill in the gaps by piecing together existing studies or designing new data collection efforts.

Fifth, we have not distinguished adequately between educational careers commonly regarded as normal versus those regarded as in some sense atypical. Thus, given our task, we could not capture the complexities of sequences of individual activities and institutional environments. Interruptions of educational careers and the reasons for such interruptions may have significant consequences for the outcomes under study. Being on-time or being off-time (either early or late) clearly can influence many changes in outcomes. Going to several different schools is a related complication. Had we limited the analysis to those who attended one school for four years without interruption, we might well have found greater effects. It is quite likely that interruptions and a variety of contexts result in effects that are weaker—and that these complexities are increasingly common. While our analysis begs such questions of interruptions in time or place, these difficulties, while not insuperable, do require special analyses. We have also not confronted variations in effects connected with the amount of time elapsed since schooling and disjointed educational careers.

Sixth, the aggregate nature of our study imposes another limitation. While varying the characteristics of higher education does not have much effect on individual change during and after college, very few students in the sample attended any given institution. Thus, the uniqueness of an institution and the distinctive differences between particular institutions are lost. However, the study that can take into account the "genius" of a setting typically can support only limited generalizations, if at all. These two types of study are both necessary, for they complement one another. With the rise of mass education, the simple four-year career at a college in less typical than it used to be. Hence, in the future it will become increasingly difficult to show clear-cut results attributable to intensive experience of particular contexts.

There is a seventh and final limitation concerning the many difficulties in analyzing one cohort in sociohistorical isolation. We treat this issue separately in chapter 7.

WHAT DO COLLEGES DO?

What, then, do young adults and the society get for their investment in higher education? By the time they are thirty-two years old, how did postsecondary education or the lack of it effect changes in the high school class of 1972? The types of changes are individualism—utilitarian and expressive—and civic commitment. To these, the themes of *Habits of the Heart* (Bellah et al. 1985), we also add self-concept and opinions of one's own educational institution and experiences there. These provide the framework for the five chapters of empirical analysis that follow.

NOTES

1. The American Council on Education and the Graduate School at the University of California, Los Angeles sponsor the Cooperative Institutional Research Program, a national survey of first-time full-time college freshmen conducted annually since 1966. These reports indicate that attending college because of concerns about jobs and money is on the increase, from only one half of freshmen reporting this reason in 1971 (American Council on Education, 1986) to nearly three-quarters in 1988 (Astin et al. 1988).

2. See Cheek and Burch (1976) for a comprehensive statement of the function of leisure in human societies and its expressions in the contemporary United States.

3. For a thorough discussion of these issues, see Pascarella and Terenzini (1991, chapter 2.

4. Gardner's argument is only one of many dealing with the controversies surrounding use of standardized tests of ability to determine placement in schools, curricula, and college admissions. For a good overview of the issues, see Wigdor and Garner (1982).

5. In these lower ability groups or tracks, the teaching methods, content, and student interactions provide fewer opportunities than those for higher groups for intellectual growth and learning skills necessary for further schooling (Rosenbaum 1976; Alexander, Cook, and McDill 1978; Persell 1977; Goodlad 1984; Oakes 1985).

6. See Appendix B for detailed discussion of the study design.

In Pursuit of Success

[College] was no religious retreat, no perception of pure learning.
It was a little apprentice-shop where one was further equipped
for making money. . . . It pretended to exist by the religious virtue
of knowledge. But the religious virtue of knowledge was become
a flunkey to the god of material success.

D. H. Lawrence, *The Rainbow*

Nearly everyone in America, indeed the world over, believes in a
powerful connection between education and occupational success. Lawrence's sardonic comment anticipates the bland truism
of U.S. Vice-President Dan Quayle, who said with unintentional
humor, "Education is truly the linchpin to opportunity in our
society" (*PBS Morning Edition* 1988). Quayle's attempt to be iconic
and to resonate with public opinion was, instead, sadly ironic in
view of his riches and the administration's failure to give more
than lip service to education. For all the contrast between their
moral judgments, Lawrence's and Quayle's belief in education's
mighty linkage to success in the world of work is identical and
generally taken for granted, especially in America.

Bellah and his associates sum up this ethos distinctively and
cogently:

In the past hundred years, individualism and its ambiguities
have been linked to middle class status. . . . In the true sense
of the term, the middle class is defined not merely by the desire
for material betterment but by a conscious, calculating effort
to move up the ladder of success. . . . Status mobility has
increasingly depended on advanced education and competence
in managerial and professional occupations that require specialized knowledge. For those oriented primarily to upward

mobility, to "success," major features of American society appear to be "the normal outcome of the operation of individual achievement." (1985, 149)

How useful are both allocation and socialization explanations[1] of long-term changes in young adults' work lives? There are several issues to be considered when we look at the connection between education and occupation. First, what are the possible mechanisms linking education and occupation? Second, since educational and occupational career paths customarily have tended to diverge sharply for men and women, how does gender influence the linkage? Third, how do higher education and degree attainment affect work goals, work values, and monetary and status rewards? Fourth, holding constant the effects of level of education attained, how do postsecondary institutions and students' educational careers after high school affect outcomes? Thus, the long-term outcomes in 1986 for the high school class of 1972 shed light on a number of questions: How much do level of higher education and degree attainment *by themselves* change individuals' work goals and values and affect the acquisition of monetary and status rewards? How much do differences between postsecondary institutions and students' careers as students *by themselves* influence such results?

LINKING EDUCATION AND OCCUPATIONAL OUTCOMES

How those with more education come to earn more and have more prestigious jobs can usually be grouped under one of two schooling functions: *socializing* (schooling as causing personal change that has payoffs) and *status conferral* (the power of education as an institution to assign students to new and legitimate status identities, e.g., dropout, college graduate).[2] Theories proposing that students learn things in school that make them better workers are consistent with socialization arguments. There are many interpretations of why this might be so, or, in other words, of how socialization might work.

Preeminent among these is human capital theory (e.g., Becker 1975), whereby employers are supposed to believe that schooling makes workers more productive through increasing their specific and general cognitive skills. Dore, however, decries the emphasis on amount of schooling at the expense of educational content (1976). He isolates a variety of mechanisms by which investment in schooling may increase work productivity and, hence, lifetime earnings.

Bowles and Gintis (1976) argue, instead, that schools are detrimental to students and essentially teach disciplined work compliance. Each level of schooling has different consequences, for there is a "correspondence principle" that links education and occupation: high school graduates learn the respect for authority and promptness appropriate to line workers, while college-educated workers learn to organize their own time and meet deadlines as befits managers. Berg (1971), however, argues that the behaviors and attitudes that employers assume to be characteristic of more educated employees—ambition and discipline, for example—may have nothing to do with job performance.

Collins (1971, 1979) also emphasizes the attitudes and behavior learned in school but believes that schools teach cultures: "What is learned in school has much more to do with conventional standards of sociability and propriety than with instrumental and cognitive skills" (Collins 1979, 19). Employers set educational requirements consonant with the culture of those doing the hiring and with the level of prestige the organization wishes to maintain. That companies headed by chief executives with liberal arts degrees are dramatically more likely to recruit liberal arts graduates (Useem and Karabel 1986) is consistent with Collins' argument.

By contrast, allocation theories hold that education does not necessarily *merely* affect individuals in ways that increase work productivity. Schools sort students by putative intelligence so that only those believed to be most intelligent achieve the highest levels of schooling. Employers can then screen for educational attainment as an inexpensive and efficient way for them to estimate learning capacity. Schooling becomes simply a signal to the employer of the relative costs of training a prospective employee (Arrow 1973; Spence 1974; Gottfredson 1985). Educational attainment, then, screens applicants into ranked "labor queues," with the most desirable positions going to those with the most education (Thurow 1975). Meyer emphasizes how schools allocate students to social roles: "Schools may teach people useful skills and values. Whether they do or not in particular cases, they certainly *allocate* people to positions of higher social status, and this affects the anticipations and socialization of the students (and non-students) as well as the experience and later socialization of the graduates (and non-graduates)" (Meyer 1977, 74). This certifying function refers to many roles but has particularly potent implications for work roles: education "defines which persons have access to valued positions in society" (Meyer 1977, 55).[3]

The socialization and allocation theories are not necessarily mutually exclusive.[4] How much the impact of higher education on job status and earnings operates primarily through the amount, rather than the type, of education attained, lends credence to screening or allocation types of hypotheses (e.g., Anderson 1985; Bills 1988a; Kolb 1990; Mueller 1988; Solmon 1975; Tinto 1977). However, the extent to which variations in key characteristics of higher education institutions or individual careers in college affect these outcomes directly supports socialization theories but can also support allocation theories to the extent that a charter is involved.[5]

In general, any changes in work goals and values attributable to either educational attainment or differing educational environments or careers support the premise that schools socialize students. If divergent institutional characteristics result in noticeably different value shifts, then—depending on the specific nature of the changes—this supports a human capital model. Allocation theories provide a more encompassing interpretation of the effects of education than socialization theories by themselves. Of course, a highly prestigious institution can, through its charter, create powerful effects for a select elite. Here, however, we are addressing the effects of the vast preponderance of institutions with uncertain and diffuse charters.[6] If the changes in student goals and values are linked to the level of education attained but independent of variations in colleges and careers, and if the work values or goals acquired are compatible with the occupational roles that correspond to the educational credential, then Meyer's allocation arguments explain the impact of higher education more adequately than a simple socialization account.

Occupational Attitudes and Behavior as Outcomes

What types of changes in work values and goals would be consistent with the white-collar and professional roles for which higher education prepares people? Individual motivations in the world of work take both expressive and instrumental forms, commonly referred to as intrinsic and extrinsic values.[7] An intrinsic value means work as an end in itself. It entails rewards integral to work, such as opportunities to exercise one's talents or to do something socially useful and important. In contrast, extrinsic values point to ends outside of the work itself. They are rewards, typically money and social status, that work can be exchanged for. But they may also be rewards in the sense of security: the avoidance of downward mobility.

Blue-collar rather than white-collar jobs have often been thought of as involving an instrumental orientation toward work, one with less variety, autonomy, and responsibility.[8] However, the persistent correlation between education or occupational position and apparently extrinsic interests suggests that "social stratification apparently matters more in determining whether men are forced to focus on the extrinsic than in determining whether they are free to focus on the intrinsic" (Kohn and Schooler 1983, 15). From this perspective, if higher education socializes young people for particular types of occupational roles, college may decrease the salience of instrumental—or extrinsic—factors, in the sense of success, while enhancing intrinsic work goals.

Most previous discussions have not adequately distinguished, however, between two possible dimensions of extrinsic work motivation. If the emphasis is on avoiding downward mobility and diminished life chances, then the motivation becomes one of seeking job security, and we shall refer to it as that. If the emphasis is on attaining career success or wealth and income, then one can think of upward mobility as an aim. Thus, what *utilitarian, instrumental,* and *extrinsic* mean ought always to be clearly specified.

Three items covering "determining the kind of work I plan to be doing" comprise a measure of job security as a goal. These are the importance of "job openings in the occupation," "good income to start or within a few years," and "job security and permanence." Note the temporizing phrase, "or within a few years," which suggests that one will accept less than good income for the time being.[9] The success goal is shown in the importance of the life goal, "being successful in my line of work." "Having lots of money" indicates financial success as a goal. An additional indicator of getting ahead in one's job as a goal is the importance of opportunity for advancement. The life goal, "being able to give my children better opportunities than I've had," provides further evidence of concern with status attainment in the sense that one's children are extensions of oneself. A score of the intrinsic work value was constructed from two measures, "freedom to make my own decisions" and "work that seems important and interesting to me." One activity that indicates occupational identity is participation in occupational groups. Such organizations are, by definition, premised on protecting and advancing the employment-related interests of particular occupations or industries. The NLS-72 respondents report whether they actively participated in or were members of a "union, farm, trade, or professional association," and this is our index of participation in occupational groups.

Occupational Status and Earnings as Outcomes

Work confers occupational status and earnings as two types of individual reward. Two distinct issues are the effects of education on obtaining a prestigious job and the impact of education on job performance once the job is acquired.[10]

Wages are commonly treated as stemming from job performance, although the processes governing pay rates may vary among occupations. The 1986 annual wages of NLS-72 respondents are an indicator of how much material rewards can be attributed to higher education.[11] A revised Duncan Socioeconomic Index (SEI) provides a useful estimate of the relative social standing of the most recent job in comparison with the rankings of other jobs.[12] The extent to which occupational standing can be attributed to higher education can then be estimated.

There is abundant literature on the private (i.e., individual) rate of return to education. Pascarella and Terenzini provide a thorough set of references (1991, 503). Cohen and Geske review studies from 1940 to 1976 and estimate the average rate of return at 13.8 percent (1985, cited in Pascarella and Terenzini). Leslie and Brinkman (1988) deal exhaustively with economic rates of return to higher education, assessed in several different ways. For example, in their comprehensive meta-analysis of twenty-two studies they found that the mean estimates of the annualized rate of individual return on costs ranged, depending on the method employed, from 11.8 to 12.4 percent over the years 1939 to 1980 (47-48). The methodological issues are too extensive to be dealt with here. Our earnings differential figures, however, appear quite consistent with theirs, although we could not calculate a rate of return for individual investment costs with our data. Rates of return have historically fluctuated considerably, with lows of 11.6 and 11.7 percent around 1950 and the early 1970's (Leslie and Brinkman 1988, 47). The reader should be aware that the earnings differentials we report here are rates that do not fully take investments into account. We isolate, however, the earnings differentials net of the effects of the initial differences between individuals in terms of their initial background characteristics: gender, race, high school academic achievement, and original socioeconomic status. That is why we add to our focus on income other factors such as occupational standing, values, and goals as outcomes.[13] Indeed, none of the issues in this chapter can be divorced from the wider context of this book. For, as Adam Smith observed, "Wages of labor vary with ease or hardship, the cleanliness or dirtiness, the honorableness or dishonorableness" (*The Wealth of Nations*, quoted in Leslie and Brinkman 1985, 66).

There is much evidence that "honorableness," or occupational standing, is affected positively by the level of educational attainment (Pascarella and Terenzini 1991, 427). The evidence also points to the nonlinearity of the relationship, with the bachelor's degree yielding "the single largest incremental return in terms of occupational status" (Pascarella and Terenzini 1991, 427). Although the finding is in terms of 1961 Duncan SEI points, Jencks et al. (1979) showed that college completion seemed to give an occupational status bonus about double that for finishing high school. Will our data be in accord with this?

PROBABLE DIFFERENCES BETWEEN MEN AND WOMEN

Educational attainment may affect career success differently for men than for women. There are fundamentally different patterns of participation in education and work that have roots in men's and women's gender roles. Aggregate sex differences in schooling[14] and labor market behavior may underlie different effects of higher education on career outcomes.

In addition, there are persistent differences in the types of education young men and women obtain.[15] Differences in men's and women's college majors[16] have been estimated to explain 12 percent of the gender gap in economic returns to schooling among the college-educated (U.S. Bureau of the Census 1987).

Studying the instrumental work values and goals of women has special significance in the context of women's historical role in the labor force. Women's work motivations used to be seen predominantly as temporary or superficial and always less salient than their principal roles as mothers and wives.[17] Because extrinsic goals are primarily met in market rather than household work, occupational decisions that stress these goals tend to conflict with women's family role obligations. Women, it is clear, have tended to become increasingly interested in occupations and careers.[18] Yet, given the conflicting work and family roles of married women, it is reasonable to expect women to devalue job characteristics that conflict with family life. Specifically, these role conflicts may result in women's valuing instrumental factors like earnings and prestige less than men. This is precisely what Herzog found in surveys of the work values of high school seniors in 1976 through 1980 (1982).[19]

Women participate in the labor force (either employed or actively looking for work) at a lower rate than men. Since the middle of this century, men's labor force participation rate has remained steady between eight and nine of every ten men over age sixteen. In contrast, women's rate of labor market participation has risen steadily, from three of ten after World War II to more than five of ten by the early 1980s (U.S. Department of Labor 1983). This narrowing gap between participation rates has been most marked among women of childbearing years.[20]

Despite the trend toward converging men's and women's work roles, differences between their market roles patently persist, with women tending to be in work careers that are interrupted or diluted.[21] Consequently, women may not be able to derive maximum earnings from their schooling experiences (Hudis 1976). Women have also been concentrated in a relatively small number of predominantly female occupations, although they have become somewhat more evenly spread over the occupational distribution in recent decades.[22]

Measures of occupational prestige typically rank women's traditional jobs—teaching, nursing, librarian—relatively highly. Thus, female college graduates typically begin their work lives in higher-status jobs than their male counterparts, but—at least among the 1957 high school cohort—lost this advantage by mid-life (Sewell, Hauser, and Wolf 1980). There is some evidence that women in more recent cohorts are able to maintain this job status advantage through early mid-life (Lindsay, Knox, and Kolb 1988). Much more dramatic than higher education's rates of return are the bottom-line differences in men's and women's pay. At every level of educational attainment, women earn less than their male counterparts.[23]

Thus, as we examine the data on our major question of the impact of education on occupation, we shall be especially alert to gender differences.

CORRELATES OF EDUCATIONAL ATTAINMENT, GENDER, AND RACE

Median levels of both occupational status and earnings increase sharply with level of education completed (Table 2.1).[24] While half of those completing only high school achieved less than 29 on the Socioeconomic Index (a score typical of vehicle dispatchers and asbestos and insulation workers, for example),

Table 2.1
Median Annual Earnings and Occupational Status in 1986 by Educational Attainment, Gender, and Race

	Annual Earnings	Occupational Status[a]
Educational Attainment		
Only High School	$16,000	29
Less than Two Years College	$18,000	37
Two or More Years College	$20,000	45
Bachelor's Degree	$23,920	51
Advanced Degree	$27,000	69
Gender		
Men	$25,730	45
Women	$15,156	46
Race		
Black	$16,900	40
White	$20,000	46
Total	$20,000	46

N = 5409

[a]Stevens and Featherman (1981). See Appendix B.

half of advanced degree holders scored more than 69 (the standing of public relations workers and health administrators). Half of the high school-educated earned less than $16,000 in 1986, while half of the most highly educated reported yearly incomes of over $27,000. Earnings jumped markedly between the baccalaureate and advanced degree categories. However, both status and earnings climbed with each step up in education. Are there similar effects on work goals and activities?

Holding job security important clearly decreases with successive levels of educational attainment.[25](See Table 2.2.) Moreover, over 60 percent of those in the class of 1972 who completed no more than high school and those finishing less than two years of college considered eventual good income, job openings, and security "very important" in their work, contrasted to only 44 percent of advanced degree holders. On the other hand, the belief that intrinsically valuable work is important commands assent for nearly 90 percent of the sample, and it rises steadily with

Table 2.2
Importance of Work Goals and Activities in 1986 by Educational Attainment, Gender, and Race

	Opportunities for Advancement[a]	Occupational Groups[b]	Job Security[c]	Intrinsic Work Value[c]	Opportunities for My Children[a]	Success[a]	Money[a]
Educational Attainment							
Only High School	69	7	64	80	69	61	12
Less than Two Years College	63	8	65	86	64	64	15
Two or More Years College	64	9	60	88	56	68	14
Bachelor's Degree	62	14	53	91	46	71	15
Advanced Degree	56	27	44	95	37	78	16
Gender							
Men	63	14	55	86	56	73	18
Women	58	9	62	89	56	62	11
Race							
Black	75	9	74	82	87	74	23
White	60	12	58	88	54	67	13
Total	61	11	59	87	56	67	14

N = 5409

[a]Percent "Very Important."
[b]Percent "Active Participant."
[c]Percent in the two highest categories.

each increment of education from 80 to 95 percent. One can think of this, perhaps, as a central tenet of work ideology in the post–World War II years. The educational patterning of the importance of providing better opportunities for children is dramatic, with the proportion holding this goal declining steadily with educational attainment, from two-thirds of high school–educated adults to little over a third of advanced degree holders. The success goal rises, but nonsignificantly, with level of education. The importance of having a lot of money does not vary systematically with educational attainment. Indeed, the vast majority of this cohort rejects this as a goal. The importance of opportunities for advancement is significantly higher than the reference group for all those with some college experience except for those with advanced degrees.

The proportion actively participating in occupational groups rises sharply with educational level. Only 7 to 9 percent of those with two years of college or less participate, but this climbs to 14 percent of bachelor's degree holders and again to better than one-fourth of those with postbaccalaureate degrees. This may be more a function of fundamental differences between unions and professional organizations than an expression of people's instrumental orientation. Many occupations taken by those with less than a college education—blue-collar in particular—represented by labor unions defined by industry (e.g., United Auto Workers) that have a deteriorating record of inspiring membership in the United States in recent decades. In contrast, more educated—typically white-collar—workers join professional associations corresponding to well-defined areas of theory and practice (e.g., American College of Surgeons, National Education Association, American Psychological Association). Subscribing to job security does not increase with education whereas occupational group participation, valuing work for its intrinsic value, and the success goal do. Therefore, it seems reasonable to suppose that high-status workers participate in work-related organizations both for fulfillment and advancement while union participation, insofar as it is voluntary, may be largely a defensive tactic to maintain security. For example, participating in an occupational association may be integral to the job performance of knowledge-intensive work when it facilitates the flow of new information between specialists in isolated research endeavors.

Note that, without holding differences in education and background constant, women are somewhat more likely than men to emphasize job security as an extrinsic aspect of work in choosing an occupation (62 percent compared with 55 percent; see Table 2.2). However, they are somewhat less likely to count work success goals as very important in their lives (63 percent of women rate these as very important, compared with 73 percent of men). They are not much more likely than men to subscribe to the importance of intrinsically worthwhile work or to differ in other respects, except for their deemphasis on having a lot of money. The relatively low pay of women—only 59 percent of their male cohorts' 1986 earnings (Table 2.1)—corresponds to their lower levels of subscription to the goals of having lots of money and of being successful in their work. Emphatically, this does not imply that gender differences in these values *caused* the pay differences.

Black adults from the high school class of 1972 earned on the average markedly less—about 15 percent—than whites in 1986 (Table 2.1). Mean black occupational status was also lower than white—the equivalent of a building supervisor rather than a radiology technician. Blacks valued the security, success, and money goals of work much more than whites (Table 2.2). Hence, the blacks in our sample may be instrumentally more highly motivated than whites. These race differences in the theme of tangible success persist in the importance attributed to one's own advancement opportunities in deciding on a line of work. Such differences leap to more than 30 percent when the importance of giving their children better opportunities than they had is considered. Consistent with this, too, is the slight tendency for blacks to place a lower premium on the intrinsic rewards of work than whites. One should not, however, make overmuch of the above differences in view of the relatively high attrition of blacks from our panel. That is, more highly motivated blacks may have survived the forces of attrition.

How many of the differences between these educational categories persist when variations in background and initial disposition are held constant? How will men and women, blacks and whites, fare? Here, we can assess how educational attainment effects change in attitudes and activities and how it affects income and job standing. Most important, what are the consequences of educational attainment and variations in the school context and individual educational careers for outcomes?

EDUCATIONAL ATTAINMENT AND EFFECTS ON WORK LIFE

What if we now hold constant the differences in background—race, sex, socioeconomic status, and academic abilities—as well as earlier values, goals, and activities, where appropriate? Now, what are the relative effects of educational level, that is, of attaining less than two years of college, two or more years of college, a bachelor's degree, or a postbaccalaureate degree compared to finishing high school?

Attaining two years or more of higher education pays handsomely compared with merely completing high school. The first column of Table 2.3 shows the estimated effects of educational attainment on earnings. For clarity, we converted these estimates to percentages.[26] By their early thirties, then, attaining an

Table 2.3
Effects of Educational Attainment on Earnings and Occupational Status

	1986 Earnings		Occupational Status	
Postsecondary Educational Attainment				
Less than Two Years	.08 (.05)	.02 (.01)	4.31*** (.10)	5.53*** (.13)
Two Years or More	.13** (.07)	.02 (.01)	7.92*** (.16)	9.13*** (.18)
Bachelor's Degree	.26*** (.16)	.14* (.08)	18.52*** (.42)	23.32*** (.53)
Advanced Degree	.41*** (.18)	.25** (.11)	29.46*** (.48)	35.29*** (.57)
Background Factors				
Whites	-.07 (-.03)	-.07 (-.02)	-.22 (-.00)	-.35 (-.00)
Women	-.59*** (-.41)	-.74*** (-.52)	1.99** (.05)	6.49*** (.17)
Family Socioeconomic Status	.01*** (.08)	.01*** (.08)	.14* (.05)	.15* (.05)
Academic Abilities	.00 (.05)	.00* (.06)	.10*** (.15)	.10*** (.15)
Previous Goals	N.A.	N.A.	N.A.	N.A.
Interaction Effects				
Gender x Less than Two Years		.12 (.06)		-2.22 (-.04)
Gender x Two Years or More		.20* (.08)		-1.95 (-.03)
Gender x Bachelor's Degree		.22** (.10)		-9.28*** (-.16)
Gender x Advanced Degree		.33** (.10)		-12.13*** (-.13)
$R^2 =$	.24	.25	.37	.38

N = 5409
*p <.05   **p <.01   ***p <.001

advanced degree means for this cohort a 51 percent higher income than for high school classmates who got no post-high school schooling; those with a bachelor's degree gained a 30 percent edge; and even two years of college profited this cohort 14 percent annually.[27] In addition, each increment in higher

Table 2.3 (continued)

	Effects of Educational Attainment on Earnings and Occupational Status Conditional on Gender				
	1986 Earnings			Occupational Status	
	2 years or more	Bach. Degree	Advanced Degree	Bach. Degree	Advanced Degree
Men	.02	.14	.25	23.32	35.29
Women	.22	.36	.58	14.04	23.16
Only statistically significant conditional effects are included.					

NOTES: Figures in this table are unstandardized regression coefficients (standardized coefficients are in parentheses). Each category of educational attainment is compared with the reference category of those having no more than a high school education.

education yields higher occupational standing than that attained by high school graduates, ranging from an additional four SEI points for less than two years of college to a 30-point advantage for advanced degree holders.

Completing anywhere from less than two years of college through obtaining a bachelor's degree improves the odds[28] of placing greater weight on opportunities to get ahead, by 36 to 41 percent (Table 2.4). Attaining either a bachelor's or advanced degree results in nonsignificantly greater emphasis on the goals of career or making money (Table 2.3). This contrasts with the freedom from concern for these factors predicted by the arguments of Goldthorpe et al. (1968) and Kohn and Schooler (1983).[29] Education level, however, has profound effects on the importance of the intrinsic value of work. The odds of subscribing to this value are almost twice as great for those with two or more years of college as for those with no postsecondary education. These odds then increase to two and one-half times and nearly four and one-half times, respectively, for baccalaureate holders and advanced degree holders. Furthermore, the likelihood of participation in occupational groups follows a similar pattern. There are also no significant effects of educational level on the importance of job security.

The powerful effects of the level of education on both the intrinsic work value and participation in occupational groups suggest new interpretations. Higher education fosters commitment to career success to be understood in complex ways, as intrinsically rewarding but also as enhancing somewhat the perceived opportunity for advancement and depressing the importance of opportunities for children.[30] Although the relationships of educational level to career success and making lots of

Table 2.4
Effects of Educational Attainment on Values and Goals and Participation in Occupational Groups

	Opportunities for Advancement	Occupational Groups		Job Security	Intrinsic Work Value	Opportunities for My Children	Success	Money
Postsecondary Educational Attainment								
Less than Two Years	1.36*	1.36	1.26	.93	1.43	.91	.81	1.24
Two Years or More	1.37*	1.65**	1.48	.89	1.82**	.78	1.02	1.16
Bachelor's Degree	1.41*	2.63***	1.77*	.96	2.52***	.67*	1.20	1.42
Advanced Degree	1.12	5.54***	3.52*	.66	4.42***	.59**	1.82	1.45
Background Factors								
Whites	.55*	1.18	1.20	.98	1.53	.33***	.68	.94
Women	.89	.64***	.38***	1.26*	1.37*	.97	.67**	.86
Family Socioeconomic Status	1.02	.99	.99	.97	1.04	.96*	1.01	1.02
Academic Abilities	.98	1.04*	1.05*	.93**	.98	.89***	.97	.94*
Interaction Effects								
Gender x Less than Two Years			1.21					
Gender x Two Years or More			1.30					
Gender x Bachelor's Degree			2.46**					
Gender x Advanced Degree			2.87**					
Previous Activities								
Medium[a]	1.53**	2.00***	1.99***	1.36	1.12	1.80**	1.25***	2.27***
High[b]	2.48***	2.42***	2.37***	2.39**	2.03	4.03***	2.34***	6.64***
-2 Log Likelihood=	7948.50	7551.63	7511.91	5319.48	3743.53	8008.75	4419.58	5336.46

N = 5409
* p <.05   ** p <.01   *** p <.001

Table 2.4 (continued)

Effects of Educational Attainment on Participation in Occupational Groups Conditional on Gender		
	Bachelor's Degree	Advanced Degree
Men	1.77	3.52
Women	4.34	10.10
Only statistically significant effects are included.		

NOTES: Figures in this table are the effects on the odds of being higher rather than lower on a particular value or activity. Each category of educational attainment is compared with the reference category of those having no more than a high school education. Each category of previous activities or values is compared with the reference category of low on a scored variable or "Not Important," "Never," or "Not at All" on a trichotomous variable.

[a] Intermediate values on a scored variable: "Somewhat Important," "Sometimes," "Member Only."
[b] High values on a scored variable: "Very Important," "Frequently," "Active Participant."

money are nonsignificant, they are in the same direction and may suggest instrumental success as a concern dependent upon educational attainment.

Counter to expectations from a socialization model, educational attainment in itself does not change the importance of security as a goal (a score of the importance of openings available, starting income, and job security) (see Table 2.4). Instead of being a function of education, valuing job security, then, is a function of preexisting value differences and academic abilities.[31] In other words, those who ultimately attain higher education already held job security values different from their peers soon after high school, and these values largely persisted through college and beyond.

Greater opportunities for one's children is the only utilitarian value that the more educated tend to downgrade in contrast to those who do not go to college. Increases in utilitarian "selfishness," as to some degree reflected here, may well be a "cost" of higher education—a concern that permeates this book. This is almost certainly linked to the high proportion of children of the high school-educated as compared to their peers with more schooling. Given the unique pattern, the effect of educational attainment per se may be the culprit. Such effects reflect the deferred childbearing associated with educational attainment. The better educated also may simply tend to assume that their children will be successful and have good opportunities available to them and, hence, may not have much concern about such matters in their life decisions. Concern for children's opportunities becomes salient when one has a child. In fact, the addition of educational attainment variables to background factors and prior values does not substantially improve our understanding of the weight these individuals attribute to providing opportunities for their children.

Educational Attainment: The Work Lives of Men and Women

The impact of educational attainment on some work rewards, goals, and activities differs profoundly for men and women. The economic payoff derived from schooling is greater for women than men when educational attainment is two years or more of college. In the box at the end of Table 2.3 appear the effects of education on earnings conditional on gender. Again, converting to proportional effects, having two years or more of college nets women a 25 percent better wage than similar high school graduates, whereas this amount of education only pays men 2 percent more. A bachelor's degree profits women 46 percent, but men only 15 percent; and an advanced degree improves women's earnings by an enormous 78 percent and men's by only 28 percent. This does not contradict our earlier observation that women in this sample earn less than men. When we control for education, ability, and background factors, women earn 59 percent less than men (column one, Table 2.3). The dramatic payoff to postsecondary education for women is partly a function of the extremely low earnings of the high school-educated women who serve as the reference point.

If it is women who get an earnings dividend from higher education, it is men who reap a prestige dividend much greater than women's. Table 2.3 (third and fourth columns and conditional effects in box at bottom) shows the improvement in occupational standing men and women gain for each increment in education. Whereas male baccalaureates attain occupations 23 SEI points more prestigious than their high school-educated counterparts, female baccalaureates gain only 14 points. Only by holding an advanced degree do women find jobs 23 SEI points better than they would have found with a high school degree; men with advanced degrees have a yet greater advantage, at 35 SEI points. Thus, although the typical high school graduate of either sex attains the occupational standing of a motion picture projectionist, postbaccalaureate degrees enable women to take positions equivalent to health technicians or librarians whereas men attain the status of teachers or social workers.[32]

While women in general do not join occupationally related groups, educational attainment boosts the likelihood that they will do so much more than it does for men (Table 2.4). While the men who completed a four- or five-year program had nearly twice the odds of men with only a high school education of joining an occupational group, baccalaureate women had over four times the odds of their less-educated women classmates of doing the same. And for men with advanced degrees, the odds go to about three and one-half times while for women with postgraduate degrees the odds go to ten times that of the reference category.

The odds for women to prefer work for its intrinsic meaningfulness are one and a third those for men. Yet there is no interaction between gender and education here. Both men and women are powerfully affected, as previously discussed.

In sum, adults from the high school class of 1972 profit greatly from higher education in terms of both income and occupational status. Postsecondary schooling also produces persistent changes in occupational activities. However, the pattern of changes is not clearcut as that with occupational status and income. Rather than decreasing the prominence of instrumental considerations, completing some higher education does not affect the importance of job security as a factor in determining one's line of work. It only slightly and nonsignificantly increases the importance of the goal of economic success. However, that higher education, irrespective of initial background characteristics, powerfully enhances the intrinsic work value can be interpreted as supporting Kohn and Schooler. This finding also supports Meyer's allocation hypothesis, to the extent that college characteristics do not explain the outcome. The next section asks just that: whether differences in college characteristics and student careers explain these results.

EFFECTS OF COLLEGE CHARACTERISTICS AND STUDENT CAREERS

If outcomes in the domain of work depend on institutional differences, it may not be the gaining of educational credentials in itself, but the differences in college environments and student career factors that elicit certain increased emphases on work concerns or bring about instrumental payoffs.

Earnings and occupational status are the utilitarian outcomes most influenced by variations in student careers and college characteristics (Table 2.5). Yet no college characteristic by itself makes a significant difference in these outcomes. The institutional characteristics in our models are institutional size, selectivity, public versus private control, proportion of full-time students, proportion of students residing on campus, and cur-

Table 2.5
Effects of College Characteristics and Student Careers on Earnings and Occupational Status

	1986 Earnings		Occupational Status	
College Characteristics[a]				
Student Enrollment	.02 (.03)	.02 (.03)	.82 (.05)	.80 (.05)
Selectivity	.03 (.05)	.03 (.05)	.18 (.01)	.17 (.01)
Private Control	.04 (.03)	.05 (.03)	1.18 (.03)	.98 (.02)
Full-Time Students	-.09 (-.03)	-.08 (-.02)	-1.08 (-.01)	-1.20 (-.01)
Vocational Emphasis	-.02 (-.03)	-.02 (-.03)	-.35 (-.03)	-.35 (-.03)
Highly Residential	-.01 (-.01)	-.01 (-.01)	.07 (.00)	.08 (.00)
Student Careers				
Business Major	.12* (.07)	.13* (.07)	-.21 (.00)	-.38 (-.01)
Education Major	-.24*** (-.12)	-.26*** (-.13)	-4.19* (-.08)	-3.51 (-.07)
Arts and Sciences Major	-.20*** (-.12)	-.21*** (-.13)	-3.25* (-.07)	-3.09* (-.07)
Ever Lived on Campus	.03 (.02)	.03 (.02)	.49 (.01)	.41 (.01)
College Grades	.04 (.06)	.04 (.06)	1.18* (.07)	1.11 (.06)
Postsecondary Educational Attainment				
Two Years or More	.04 (.02)	-.10 (-.06)	2.76 (.06)	2.14 (.05)
Bachelor's Degree	.16* (.11)	.01 (.01)	12.66*** (.33)	14.92*** (.39)
Advanced Degree	.29** (.16)	*.12 (.07)	22.73*** (.48)	26.58*** (.56)

Table 2.5 (continued)

	1986 Earnings		Occupational Status	
Background Factors				
Whites	-.06	-.06	-1.05	-1.04
	(.02)	(-.02)	(-.01)	(-.01)
Women	-.51***	-.74***	-.56	2.58
	(-.36)	(-.52)	(-.01)	(.07
Family Socio economic Status	- .00	.00	.07	.08
	(.04)	(.04)	(.03)	(.03
Academic Abilities	.00	.00	.08**	.08**
	(.00)	(.00)	(.11)	(.11)
Previous Goals	N.A.	N.A.	N.A.	N.A.
Interaction Effects				
Gender x Two Years or More		.27*		1.12
		(.12)		(.02)
Gender x Bachelor's Degree		.29*		-4.58
		(.16)		(-.10)
Gender x Advanced Degree		.36**		-8.51*
		(.14)		(-.12)
R2 =	.24	.24	.30	.31

N = 2702
+p <.10   *p < .05   **p .01   ***p <.001

Effects of Educational Attainment on Earnings and Occupational Status, Conditional on Gender, Controlling for College Type and Student Careers				
	1986 Earnings			Occ. Status
	2 years or more	B.A. Degree	Adv. Degree	Adv. Degree
Men	-1.0	.01	.12	26.58
Women	.17	.30	.48	18.06
Only statistically significant conditional effects are included.				

NOTES: Figures in this table are unstandardized regression coefficients (standardized coefficients are in parentheses). Each category of college major is compared with the reference category of all other majors. Each category of educational attainment is compared with the reference category of those having less than two years of postsecondary education.

[a]For persons attending more than one institution, the one attended longest; in case of ties, the more recently attended.

ricular vocational emphasis; the student career factors are student's college major, grades, and having lived on campus.

As Leslie and Brinkman wisely observe, "Informed observers of higher education institutions can identify elite institutions; it is doubtful that they can make accurate subjective discriminations among the mass of institutions below this level" (1988, 67). It is likely, then, that the effects attributable to most institutions are quite weak, for Solmon (1975; 1985), whose analysis of quality and earnings is the most complete, concluded that quality makes a measurable difference in income only for institutions in the top quartile as compared to the bottom quartile.

Let us, however, look ahead and take all the college differences and student career factors simultaneously into account after we have removed the effects of both the initial 1972 values (race, gender, socioeconomic status, abilities, values, and activities) and educational attainment. Doing so adds significantly (beyond the variance accounted for by educational attainment, individual background factors, and prior values, goals, and activities) to our understanding of job security as a motive, participation in occupational groups, and the importance of opportunities for one's children and for one's own advancement (see Table 2.6).[33]

Student careers are particularly important for extrinsic rewards (Table 2.5). Majoring in education results in 22 percent lower annual pay[34] than others with similar educational attainment and background characteristics, while majoring in the arts and sciences yields a 19 percent pay shortfall. (All findings discussed in this section are *net*[35] of educational attainment, background factors and earlier levels of goals or activities.) In contrast, business majors profit 13 percent over alumni of other fields of study.

The wage benefits of attaining higher education persist but are somewhat diminished when college characteristics and student career factors are included. Variations in college environments and individual careers, then, explain part of the benefits earlier attributed to educational attainment. To reiterate, no particular dimension of institutional characteristics is, by itself, significantly related to any of the outcomes. As discussed in chapter 1, our method of analyzing colleges obscures any effects peculiar to schools with a special charter to legitimate the status identities of their graduates (Meyer 1970; Kamens 1971, 1974, 1977, 1979).

Furthermore, institutional characteristics and student careers definitely do not explain the divergent payoffs derived from educational attainment for men and women. Among those who attend college, women gain a greater increase in earnings from

Table 2.6
The Significance of Educational Attainment, College Characteristics, and Student Careers in Explaining Work Goals, Values, and Activities

1986 Earnings	Educational Attainment	College Characteristics and Student Careers
	**	**
Occupational Status	**	**
Intrinsic Work Value	*	n.s.
Success	**	n.s.
Money	n.s.	n.s.
Opportunities for Advancement	n.s.	*
Occupational Groups	**	*
Job Security	n.s.	*
Opportunities for Children	**	**
n.s. = not significant * p < .05 ** p < .01		

NOTES: Results are based on F-tests for linear regression or analogues in the case of logistic regression (see Appendix B). Column one reflects the improvement of fit achieved by adding the dummy variables for educational attainment over a model using only background variables and prior values of the dependent variable. Column two reflects improvement of fit when the college characteristics and individual experiences are added to the model tested in column one (i.e., background, previous characteristics, and educational attainment).
Previous (1972) earnings were not included in the base model.
Previous (1972) occupational status was not included in the base model.

additional schooling than their male counterparts from similar institutions and with similar backgrounds and college careers. Table 2.5 presents the effects of educational attainment contingent on gender when college characteristics and individual careers are controlled. Women with two or more years of college earn 18 percent more than women with fewer years of college, while baccalaureate women make 35 percent more and women with advanced degrees earn 62 percent more. In contrast, factors like choice of college major explain most of the payoff from educational attainment for men; when this is taken into account, college men earn essentially the same amount regardless of their educational attainment—even with advanced degrees they gain no more than 13 percent over the earnings of men with less than two years of college.

There is little evidence here for the claim that more selective colleges confer an earnings advantage when factors like family social class and amount of education attained are also considered.[36] Many scholars have observed an earnings gain for men from more selective colleges (Tinto 1977; Solmon 1975; James et al. 1989), and at least one has found such effects for women as well (Mueller 1988). From their comprehensive review of thirty studies, Pascarella and Terenzini believe that there is a small, positive net effect of college quality (especially selectivity) on earnings (1991, 508-509). A long-term reinforcement of the relationship between college quality and earnings found in some studies could be argued to support a human capital or socialization interpretation but does not rule out credentialing, either (Pascarella and Terenzini 1991, 510-511).

Why is the relationship observed here between college selectivity and earnings so tenuous? Several factors may help account for this. There are four major technical and measurement issues. First, research focusing on the effects of college selectivity typically examines only college graduates. College quality may be expected to play a larger role in the occupational attainments of baccalaureates or of advanced degree recipients than of those who do not complete their degree. Solmon (1975) finds empirical evidence of this. Second, median freshman Scholastic Aptitude Test (SAT) scores, although a common and convenient indicator of college selectivity, measure only one aspect of college quality— student academic aptitudes. Faculty quality and subjective ratings of institutions are interrelated, but distinct, indicators of college quality. Third, Solmon (1975) observes that college quality influences later incomes (his respondents had been in the labor force for twenty years) much more than earnings immediately after leaving school. Fourth, recall that our estimates of statistical significance are highly conservative.

In addition, simply controlling for individual background characteristics and facets of institutional differences may obscure processes involving these factors at earlier stages of educational careers involving these factors. For example, so much sorting goes into placement in colleges that attainment—which differs dramatically by college type—may also include some effects of type (see Solmon 1975; James et al. 1989). Individual ability is much more important for quality of college attended than ascribed characteristics like race, sex, or parental income (Hearn 1984). But considering the pervasive impact of ascribed factors on academic performance, the result is that, "the academically and socioeconomically 'rich' become richer (i.e., attend schools having superior intellectual and material resources) while the academically and socioeconomically 'poor' become poorer" (Hearn 1984, 28).

Also, differences between colleges have been linked to differences in occupational choices, supplying another indirect means by which college quality could affect later work rewards. Kamens (1979) found a small impact of college quality (measured in terms of academic resources) on men's and women's academic career plans five years after high school, and positive effects on women's choosing professional careers. Thus, to the extent that ascribed characteristics influence the quality of the institution attended and that, in turn, college quality results in unequal occupational outcomes, higher education perpetuates class differences in ways not visible in this analysis.

An individual's college major and grades affect earnings strongly, with arts and sciences majors and education majors significantly lower and business majors significantly higher than the rest of the college sample.[37] This is paralleled for occupational standing for the three major categories, although the relationship is not so strong as with income. Yet educational attainment affects occupational status most profoundly, and here we are in accord with many studies that demonstrate long-term effects throughout the lifespan (see Pascarella and Terenzini 1991, 427). By their early thirties, education majors held jobs about four SEI points lower than their peers—the difference between being an elementary school teacher and a stock and bond salesman. Arts and sciences majors also held lower-status positions by about three points—or the difference between librarians and airplane pilots. Good college grades contribute to adult occupational standing, however, at the rate of one point per grade increment.[38] Again, institutional differences and student careers mitigate the impact of educational attainment somewhat. As observed in the total sample, highly educated women do not gain as much occupational status as men from their educational attainment. This may no longer hold true—except for the advanced degree level—after differences between the institutions attended by men and women and their differing careers there are accounted for (Table 2.5).

One cannot claim with certitude any effects of specific college characteristics or individual careers on values and behaviors. However, as Table 2.6 illustrates, considering college environments and college careers explains significantly more for nearly all of these outcomes than considering educational attainment, background characteristics, and previous values, goals, and activities alone. Only success as a life goal and the intrinsic work value are entirely unaffected by college context. (As shown in Table 2.7, those with advanced degrees are about 250 percent more likely to support the intrinsic work value than those with less than two years of college and collegiate women, 70 percent more likely to do so than men.)

Table 2.7
Effects of College Characteristics and Student Careers on Values and Goals and Participation in Occupation Groups

	Opportunities for Advancement	Occupational Groups	Job Security	Intrinsic Work Value	Opportunities for My Children	Success	Money
College Characteristics[a]							
Student Enrollment	1.01	1.00	.90	1.00	1.00	1.01	1.01
Selectivity	.91	.98	.84	.93	.92	.94	1.03
Private Control	1.05	.72	.09	1.12	1.21	1.30	1.05
Full-Time Students	.93	1.01	.93	.93	1.03	.96	1.00
Vocational Emphasis	.93	1.01	.99	.93	.99	.98	1.00
Highly Residential	1.09	1.09	1.26	1.01	.87	1.06	.93
Student Careers							
Business Major	1.25	.68	1.04	1.12	1.05	1.24	1.12
Education Major	.67	1.20	.75	1.06	1.07	.90	.80
Arts and Sciences Major	.86	.79	.74	.92	.89	.74	.87
Ever Lived on Campus	.96	1.01	.92	1.08	.90	.98	.95
College Grades	.90	1.04	.88	.99	.96	1.12	1.01

Our criterion for evaluating the statistical significance of each variable is highly conservative. It seems appropriate to consider effects that have less than a 10 percent probability of being in error. Under this more relaxed rule, participation in occupational groups and the importance of promotion opportunities are affected by some college characteristics and individual collegiate careers (Table 2.7).

Under this less stringent criterion, business majors are 32 percent less likely than their peers to participate in occupational groups. And the chances of rating opportunities for advancement an important factor in determining one's line of work are decreased by attending a college with a high proportion of full-time

Table 2.7 (continued)

	Opportunities for Advancement	Occupational Groups	Job Security	Intrinsic Work Value	Opportunities for My Children	Success	Money
Postsecondary Educational Attainment							
Two Years or More	1.08	.90	1.13	1.32	.92	1.57	1.18
Bachelor's Degree	1.21	1.76*	1.66	1.94	.90	1.76*	1.42
Advanced Degree	1.05	3.34***	1.34	3.47*	.82	2.68**	1.55
Background Factors							
Whites	.49	1.14	1.08	2.00	.35	.83	1.03
Women	1.00	.67*	1.50*	1.70*	.98*	.71*	.91
Family Socioeconomic Status	1.03	.99	.95	1.04	.95	.99	1.05
Academic Abilities	.96	1.07*	.45	.98	.91***	.95	.91**
Previous Values, Goals, or Activities							
Medium[b]	1.34	1.74*	1.49	3.94	1.44	2.02	2.40***
High[c]	1.98***	2.28**	2.50**	7.27*	3.32***	3.76	6.91***
-2 Log Likelihood =	3529.27	3747.01	2515.91	1420.63	3750.25	2732.31	3335.46

N = 2702
p < .10   *p < .05   **p < .01   *** p < .001

NOTES: Figures in this table are the effects on the odds of being higher rather than lower on a particular value or activity. Each category of college major is compared with the reference category of all other majors. Each category of educational attainment is compared with the reference category of those having less than two years of postsecondary education. Each category of previous values, goals, or activities is compared with the reference category of low on a scored variable or "Not Important" or "Not at All" on a trichotomous variable.

[a]For persons attending more than one institution, the one attended longest; in case of ties, the more recently attended.
[b]Intermediate values on a scored variable: "Somewhat Important," "Member Only."
[c]High values on a scored variable: "Very Important," "Active Participant."

students, by 7 percent for each 10 percent increment in students attending full time. Similarly, majoring in education results in a 33 percent lower probability of valuing opportunities for advancement. The decision to major in education is likely to entail a self-conscious decision to deemphasize utilitarian ends. It is, after all, a commonplace that one does not enter teaching or educational careers to make money.

Of the college characteristics and individual career factors examined, the student's choice of college major appears to have the most wide-ranging impact on successful instrumental outcomes. Yet only the extrinsic rewards of the jobs they hold in their early thirties can be declared, within the customary margins of error, to be influenced by course grades and choice of college major. Instrumental life goals, the wish for job security, the intrinsic work value and subsequent associational participation are affected little by the college student career. And even the rewards of job earnings and occupational status are largely unaffected by institutional differences. Moreover, educational attainment conveys considerably more about the outcomes than could have been garnered from the background variables and the previous goals and activities alone for the following items: the prominence of instrumental life goals, the importance of intrinsically valuable work, participation in occupational groups, and valuing better opportunities for children (see Table 2.6).

CONCLUSIONS

Our society clearly rewards educational attainment with higher pay and occupations of greater status. These benefits are distributed somewhat more generously to alumni of business programs than to education or arts and sciences majors. Postsecondary education is economically rewarded more among women than among men, although the absolute levels of women's earnings lag substantially behind men's. And academic abilities and good grades in college are rewarded by placement in more prestigious occupations. Yet the rewards from educational attainment itself overshadow these minor variations.

Completing some higher education also influences the instrumental values and goals of students, even several years after leaving school. It affects, as well, the importance of intrinsically rewarding work. These changes are not explained by student careers in college or by particular aspects of college environments. Earlier research on subsets of the high school class of 1972 also found little effect of variations in college career on values and goals even in the period most immediately following college attendance. Anderson (1985), observing only those who attained about four years of college, found little evidence of differential socialization in different types of higher education institutions.[39] After controlling for individual careers at these institutions, differences between the colleges and universities accounted for very little change in occupational goals and work.[40] Only attending a religiously affiliated college or studying at a research university lowered men's extrinsic work values shortly after college. Neither Anderson's findings nor ours support the hypothesis that colleges differentially socialize their charges for distinct types of positions in the work world. However, caution certainly is in order, since the data she and we have available do not allow the assessment of work skills, habits, and attitudes.

That attainment of higher education in itself induces changes in values, goals, and behaviors is consistent with Meyer's portrayal of postsecondary institutions' allocative role; so is the content of the shifts in values and goals that accompany further schooling. Educational attainment is slightly (nonsignificantly) associated with greater concern for issues one might assume to be less problematic in white-collar jobs than in the jobs the high school educated take: the importance of being successful and making lots of money, and opportunities for advancement. On the other hand, level of education also sharply enhances the importance of intrinsically rewarding work. Accordingly, we may tentatively conclude that today it is a case of "both/and," with education creating a concern with success not only in the sense of income and status but also meaningful work with a measure of autonomy.

This fits well with the idea that identities are being transformed through the process of higher education. These changes appear compatible with allocation arguments. Instrumental success as a work value may become more, not less, salient for the great majority of college-educated workers. Job security as a motive cuts across all strata and does not differentiate between them. Postsecondary schooling has been observed so often to enhance expectations of work rewards (e.g., Quinn and Mandilovitch 1977) that it is practically a truism. With large proportions of the population now completing at least some higher education, a college degree no longer guarantees a secure, well-remunerated and highly regarded career. Setting instrumental life goals may have been particularly problematic for the class of 1972 because they reached adulthood at a time when there was a glut of college graduates without college-graduate jobs (Smith 1986; Freeman 1976), a time when their newly developed work goals might well be frustrated. With an oversupply of college graduates, higher education does not guarantee freedom from concern about extrinsic factors. Given the vagaries of supply and demand, then, the question of whether the instrumental life goals and work values engendered by higher education are appropriate to ensuing occupational roles cannot be resolved with a cohort study. Less susceptible to economic fluctuations, perhaps, is the thesis that colleges prepare students to value intrinsically rewarding jobs.

Our findings on earnings are consonant with those of many other studies. Pascarella and Terenzini determined, after examining seventeen such studies employing various research designs and methods, "One of the safest generalizations one can make about the structure of nearly all highly developed (as well as less developed) societies is that formal education has a strong positive association with earnings, even when such factors as age, gender, and occupational category are held constant" (1991, 500). Citing our 1988 paper and one by Goodman (1979), they also surmise that attaining the baccalaureate "may be the single most important educational step in the occupational and economic attainment process" (1991, 501). The socialization and human capital hypothesis cannot be rejected out of hand on the basis of the data in this chapter. Nonetheless, there is a marked impact of both bachelor's and advanced degrees on earnings, on occupational status, on work values, and on participation in occupational associations, coupled with the relatively slight impact of particular educational milieux. For those reasons, the certification-allocation hypothesis appears the superior alternative, and besides, it also encompasses the socialization and human capital explanations.[41]

There is a compelling and demonstrable connection between higher education and the work lives of young adults and their utilitarian successes, goals, and values. So strong is the connection that it is tempting to believe the socially critical view that education is largely preparing students for their future economic roles, perhaps to the neglect of other future roles. One may think of this as a mixed blessing, with many social costs accompanying the social benefits. To conclude this now would be premature, for it remains a major issue throughout the remainder of this book. The role that higher education plays in molding the quest for self expression and the commitment to community then becomes the more intriguing, and that will concern us in the next two chapters.

NOTES

1. These notions have been foreshadowed in chapter 1 and will be elaborated below in this chapter and throughout this book as well.

2. The status attainment research popularized by Wisconsin sociologists established that educational attainment is the vehicle by which individuals' background (such as family socioeconomic status, race, and sex) and abilities are translated into occupational attainment (Sewell and Hauser 1975; Tinto 1977). These individual attributes and educational attainment also partially explain earnings, but less completely than occupational standing does. These models, while useful, unfortunately cannot address how or why postsecondary schooling results in occupational rewards. This shortcoming, resulting in underestimates of the impact of education and its quality, has been frequently noted (Griffin and Alexander 1978; Kerckhoff, Campbell, and Trott 1982).

3. However, education's part in certifying young people to take particular roles in society goes beyond simply allocating individuals to existing places in the social structure. Meyer (1976) expounds a more general institutional theory—legitimation theory—that highlights the impact of educational systems on defining and constructing social statuses and fields of expertise.

4. For example, Dore (1976) presents a detailed logical classification of education-earnings mechanisms, including several not covered here. Indeed, employers may operate under some combination of assumptions. For example, in hiring a highly educated worker, an employer may believe both that the general knowledge will make a more productive worker and also that the intelligence necessary for students to achieve such educational levels will make for a saving in training (human capital and screening). Also, the organizational and economic context in which decisions are made to hire, promote, or give more pay determines the nature of the relationship between education and jobs or earnings.

5. Cultural capital arguments, especially, would be highly consistent with the idea that institutional characteristics make a difference. However, that rewards to cultural capital depend on organization-level differences, like product sector, company size, and leadership attitudes, may obscure gross differences in individuals' pay and job status.

6. Most students at a Princeton University or a Mills College know that they are having a distinctive and privileged set of educational and social experiences and that the difference, at

the root, is the prestige of the institutions mandated through a clear charter. We contend that, if one sets these institutions to one side, the effects of socialization traceable to the particular setting pale by comparison with educational attainment and certification. In particular, Solmon (1975) notes that college quality has a measurable impact on earnings only for the top prestige quartile of four-year colleges. Kingston and Lewis (1990) elaborate upon the relationship between elite schools and the stratification order but do not deal with the full gamut of post-secondary education institutions.

7. These values are not mutually exclusive, as Weber shows in acknowledging both the concept of a calling and the profit-motive as operating in all but a few occupations (Parsons 1947).

8. By a Marxist line of reasoning, manual wage workers, having sold their labor power, are "*constrained* to regard work primarily as a means to an end, and to be primarily concerned with its economic return" (Goldthorpe et al. 1968, 38, emphasis theirs). Although we have rightfully included occupational pres-tige among the factors not integral to the work itself, we do not equate it with the instrumental orientation to work discussed here. In contradiction to the patterns of economic motivation described here, Weber asserts that valuing high-prestige work is characteristic of the privileged—the wealthy and the highly educated (Weber 1947, 214). Thus, white-collar jobs are much more likely sources of self-realization and other intrinsic re-wards. See the classic studies of British blue-collar workers (Goldthorpe et al. 1968, 1969). Kohn and Schooler (1983) find that, for American men, the lower their positions the more importance they attach to extrinsic factors; and the higher their positions the more salient are aspects intrinsic to the work itself. However, as opposed to many scholars, we differentiate between two kinds of extrinsic factors: seeking success and avoiding failure by seeking security.

9. The Cronbach's (1951) Alpha coefficients indicate quite high reliability (.73 and .63 for 1972 and 1986).

10. The broad variations in pay within occupational categories means that earned wages do not accurately represent job status, despite the fact that earnings are a component in the calculation of occupational standing through the Socioeconomic Index. Con-sequently these two rewards will be treated distinctly.

11. However, rather than simply assuming that earnings are indicators of work productivity—and Little (1984) argues persua-sively that they are not—to examine a broad range of mecha-nisms by which education can affect rewards and values for individuals is useful.

12. Stevens and Featherman (1981) provided improved ways of conceptualizing and computing Duncan's Socioeconomic Index, one of which we used. See both appendixes for a complete discussion of the issues involved.

13. Leslie and Brinkman (1988) point out that there are benefits beyond the conventional individual rates of return, such as consumption benefits, investment benefits (66-67) and a whole congeries of social returns (69-103).

14. Until the late 1970s, male students outnumbered females in institutions of higher education (National Center for Education Statistics [NCES] 1989). Now, female students outnumber their male classmates, and sixteen to thirty-five year old students are half male and half female (NCES 1990). The proportions of each sex completing four or more years of college in the twenty-five to twenty-nine age group had very nearly converged at around 26 percent by the late 1980s (NCES 1990). Women in graduate programs outnumbered men by the mid-1980s, but the more numerous (and more lucrative) professional programs continued to be heavily dominated by men.

15. Women of traditional college age (sixteen to twenty-four) are less likely than men to enroll in four-year colleges (NCES 1990) and more likely to enroll only part-time (NCES 1989). In four-year colleges in 1986, the number of men and women undergraduates in business and management fields and life sciences were equivalent, but men substantially outnumbered women in engineering, mathematics, and physical sciences (NCES 1989). For example, in the NLS-72, one-fourth of the men majored in business compared with only 13 percent of the women, while 21 percent of the women majored in education compared with only 8 percent of the men. The segregation of men and women into different fields of study is about as great as the occupational segregation between black and white men: in 1984, about a third of college women would have had to change majors to be distributed across fields like their male classmates (Jacobs 1989).

16. The choice of college major appears to be at least as powerfully affected by gender and sex-role conformity pressure as by aptitudes or previous course work (Wagenaar 1984; Jacobs 1989). Women's high rate of attrition from male-dominated fields (Jacobs 1989) is at least partially attributable to the social environment of these major departments (Hearn and Olzack 1981). Jacobs (1989) argues persuasively that the "revolving door" pattern of movement between fields of study and occupations dominated by men and those dominated by women reflects

the exercise of social controls over individuals' gender roles throughout the life cycle.

17. Until recent decades, it was assumed that women who worked did so only in family emergencies when the husband or father was disabled or absent, or for extra spending money, or to serve society (for example, as a teacher or nurse).

18. Changes in individual women's work values over time depend on a number of factors, including the timing of marriage and childbearing in relation to work experience and postsecondary education. For example, women from the class of 1972 who remained single through 1979 were more likely to have an instrumental view of work (valuing career success, money, and stable work) than those who had married seven years after high school (Baker and Bootcheck 1985). These single—in contrast to married—women were also more likely to have become *increasingly* instrumental in their views of work over this time period. The number of years college women completed prior to marrying were also related to an instrumental orientation toward work. Attending college *after* marrying contributed to instrumental work values, as well, but not as much. Although it is difficult to disentangle preexisting differences from maturational and educational effects, women's views of work appear to differ from men's both in anticipation of and in response to parental responsibilities (Waite, Haggstrom, and Kanouse 1986).

19. These surveys show that young women value intrinsic aspects of work (interpersonal and altruistic elements, as well as a job's stimulation and potential for self-actualization) more than young men, but are less concerned with extrinsic aspects (such as pay, status, and vacation time). Over the five-year span, successive cohorts of high school seniors of both sexes increasingly valued extrinsic dimensions of work (possibly a reflection of the contracting national economy in this time period), but there was no indication of convergence between young men's and women's work values.

20. Until the early 1970s, women between the ages of twenty-four and thirty-five participated at lower levels than younger and older women, resulting in an "M" shaped age distribution of women workers (Shank 1988). By the late 1980s, however, dramatic increases in the labor market participation of women with young children has resulted in an age distribution of women workers that closely resembles the inverted "U" of their male counterparts.

These shifting patterns have been attributed to a number of factors, including reductions in the birth rate in the 1960s, growth in demand for workers, particularly in the service and public sectors where women are often employed, increasing levels of education, and changing views of women's work and family roles (Shank 1988).

21. Although more than half of the women in the U.S. labor force work full-time and year-round (Shank 1988), few maintain the continuous full-time employment characteristic of men's employment histories (Moen and Smith 1986). Differences in market participation stem largely from families continuing to divide responsibilities along gender lines,˙with women taking primary responsibility for the household and child rearing (Hochschild 1989). Strategies designed to accommodate family obligations—dropping out of work or taking part-time or seasonal employment, for example—result in reduced seniority and impede occupational success, especially in professional fields.

22. Yet, 57 percent of working women would have to change occupations in order to approximate the occupational distribution of men, down from over two-thirds in 1970 (Jacobs 1989). Economists argue that people who take typically female jobs seek the advantages these jobs offer: higher starting wages, less deterioration of human capital when not employed (especially attractive for interrupted employment), and better working conditions (England et al. 1988). But England and her colleagues find no evidence that female occupations provide either high initial wages or negligible penalties for interrupted employment. Instead, they found that workers—both male and female—in predominantly female occupations experience pay discrimination. In fact, women enter male-dominated occupations when opportunities are available, but high rates of attrition from these occupations suggest that male coworkers and management exert social control to maintain a masculine sex role and economic advantages in the occupation (Jacobs 1989).

23. Sex differences in type of education, the amount and type of work, and life-long labor force participation patterns all contribute to the earnings gap (Hudis 1976; Waite 1981). But even among full-time workers, on the average, men earn significantly more than women with similar seniority and education, or equal productivity (Waite 1981). And only a fraction of the differences between the hourly pay of working men and women is due to their choice of college major (Angle and Wissman 1981). Instead, the gender earnings gap persists in part as a function of the sex segregation of jobs and employer discrimination in women's job assignments (Waite 1981). The 1990 money income for all full-time employed women was $20,586, while for all men it was $29,172 (U.S. Bureau of the Census 1992, 452). Of course, this comparison does not take occupation into account.

24. The reader should note that we are merely discussing correlates of educational attainment, gender, and race as a way of introducing the topic. Since we are examining zero-order correlations, we will be noting only associations between factors and not causal connections. The discussion of causality starts in the following section.

25. This finding confirms the pattern the NLS-72 already exhibited in 1979 (Lindsay and Knox 1984), although we then called job security, "extrinsic work goal."

26. We converted regression coefficient estimates to percentages following Halvorsen and Palmquist (1980, 474–75). See how income was measured and the various steps in the measurement process in Appendix B.

27. See Gujarati (1988) for details on the treatment and interpretation of *semilog models* such as this, where only the dependent variable is in logged form.

28. Here the categorical nature of the data necessitate using logistic regression. Results from logistic regression can be expressed in terms of the effects on the odds of an outcome, that is, the likelihood that each given increase in the causal factor will be accompanied by a different outcome (e.g., voting or not). Thus, for each change in the category of an ordered antecedent factor the odds of falling into a given category of an outcome become higher or lower. See the full discussions in Appendix B, Choosing Linear or Logistic Regression, and Interpreting Linear and Logistic Regression.

29. The Goldthorpe and Kohn and Schooler predictions pertain clearly to those already from advantaged circumstances.

30. This is either because higher educational attainment creates a sense of security about the future or undermines commitment to the next generation or because the salience of children is not great for the more highly educated whose fertility is lower (and delayed) than those with lesser educational attainments.

31. It is somewhat surprising to observe a relative decline in the goal of job security motive with academic abilities. It would be reasonable to suppose that academic abilities actually have this effect partly through their impact on the type of job obtained. As shown in Table 2.3, greater academic abilities indeed do result in the attainment of higher-status occupations in addition to affecting educational attainment. The better jobs attained by the more academically able—being stable, with high status and reasonable pay—may free incumbents to focus on intrinsic work goals.

32. The reader should take these as *illustrating* differences in occupational standing, *not* as literal realities.

33. That these rewards appear to be more affected by college experiences and institutional types is likely. We cannot control for earnings and occupational status prior to postsecondary education. As a consequence, the effects of unmeasured factors that predispose individuals to earn a lot or achieve prestige (such as interpersonal skills, physical appearance, or determination, for example) are absorbed by their educational attainments, experiences, and choices of institutions, to which these factors are also related. Thus, in observing differences between the breadth and magnitude of higher education effects on extrinsic rewards as compared to values, goals, and activities, the reader should keep in mind this fundamental difference in the explanatory models.

34. As we did with Table 2.3, we converted the estimates from Table 2.5 into percentages, following Halvorsen and Palmquist (1980, 474-75).

35. That is, we control for the effects of attaining two or more years of college, a bachelor's degree, or a postbaccalaureate degree rather than less than two years of college and for background factors—including race, socioeconomic status, gender, and academic abilities—as well as earlier values, goals, and activities.

36. Only when men in this cohort are studied apart from their female classmates does attending a more selective college improve later earnings—by about 6 percent per 100-point increase in the college's median freshman Scholastic Aptitude Test (SAT) score. There is as much as a 10 percent chance that this finding is in error—that the selectivity of the college attended does not affect men's earnings when considered apart from their female classmates. And this effect does not appear when both sexes are included. Nevertheless, given the findings of others, it is likely that a relationship between college selectivity and later earnings does exist, at least for the most highly selective colleges.

37. Our findings appear quite consistent with those from the many other studies that deal with the effects of field of study, although our findings are only roughly comparable with them (See Pascarella and Terenzini 1991, 515-17).

38. Smart (1986) identifies the failure of most studies to include multiple measures of college characteristics and undergraduate experience as a primary cause of null findings of college effects on status attainment. We have complied with his recommendations in considering a variety of college characteristics and individual college careers. We included the same institutional

characteristics covered by Smart, and some similar individual experiences: grade point average, major, but somewhat different indicators of integration. Smart used grade point average and membership in an honor society to indicate academic integration and items assessing students' involvement with peers and faculty.

39. The young people were included in her study only if they enrolled in academic college programs each fall from 1972 through 1975, and in a four-year program at least during the final year. She does not control for educational credentials received, a critical factor in distinguishing between socialization and credentialing types of arguments.

40. Her institutional characteristics include selectivity (Astin's seven-category index developed in 1965), private versus public control, religious affiliation (yes or no), and four of the Carnegie groupings (Carnegie Commission on Higher Education 1973): research universities, doctoral-granting universities, comprehensive colleges, and liberal arts colleges. Individual factors consist of whether students were transfer students, residence on campus, work experience, college grade point average, college satisfaction, and contact with faculty.

41. Pascarella and Terenzini's conclusion (1991, 428-30) flows from a thorough overview of much of the literature. Their interpretation is roughly similar to ours, but they attribute more independent explanatory power to the socialization-human capital theory than we do.

3

In Pursuit of Self-Expression

*He would certainly . . . produce excellent motor cars; he would
make impressive speeches to the salesmen; but he would never
love passionately, lose tragically, nor sit in contented idleness
upon tropic shores.*

Sinclair Lewis, *Dodsworth*

By the end of the novel Sam Dodsworth has experienced all three:
love, loss, and loafing on a Mediterranean island. Dodsworth's
dilemma, captured so succinctly, is the ambivalence of Americans over work and leisure and the clash between instrumental
and expressive individualism. There is earnest, "selfless" labor[1]
in the pursuit of success as opposed to self-fulfillment that
perhaps may transcend mere self-indulgent escape.

In the preceding chapter we have seen that higher education
today works far-reaching, profound, and lasting effects as young
adults embark on their occupational careers. The realm of
self-expression will occupy us in this chapter and civic commitments in the next.

Most Americans expect to have a "good life" that goes beyond
monetary success and attaining status. Leisure patterns may
vary by class (Goldthorpe et al. 1968, 1969; DiMaggio and Useem
1978a, 1978b), across cultures and in many other ways (Cheek
and Burch 1976), but they are integral to human life. As the
latter authors observe, "Participation in the economy of a social
order does not constitute the totality of existence . . . . Perhaps
leisure is as necessary as nonleisure to an understanding of the
human condition" (Cheek and Burch 1976, 6).

The penetrating words of Bellah and his associates in *Habits
of the Heart* radically qualify the foregoing and cut with a

poignant and nostalgic edge: "In a period when work is seldom a calling and few of us find a sense of who we are in public participation as citizens, the lifestyle enclave, fragile and shallow though it often is, fulfills that function for us all" (1985, 75).

The lifestyle enclave is the heart of what Bellah and his coauthors call *expressive individualism*. Cocooned in this private interpersonal world, "we are supposed to be able to find a group of sympathetic people, or at least one such person, with whom we can spend our leisure time in an atmosphere of acceptance, happiness, and love" (Bellah et al. 1985, 83). Yet the very notion of lifestyle "is fundamentally segmental and celebrates the narcissism of similarity," whereas community "celebrates interdependence" (Bellah et al. 1985, 72). The rise of an imagery of networks and networking heralds the collapse of community as we have known it.

Does higher education have as profound an impact on individual self-expressive values and activities as it does on those having to do with individual success? If the major function of education is to confer status (as Meyer's theory states), educational attainment, especially the completion of certificates and degrees, will have stronger long-term effects on students than differences in the characteristics of colleges they attend or their individual educational careers. Thus, educational status levels and the behavioral expectations that go with them will influence changes in expressive attitudes and activities. But, under a status conferral argument, differences in college environments are less likely to be associated with these changes. How does higher education affect the values of marriage and family, of friendship, of the importance of leisure, and of reported participation in several leisure activities: sports and recreation, literary and cultural groups, and avocational groups?

We shall see whether we are justified in considering the effects of higher education on expressive factors as distinct from the utilitarian arena. The separation of the world of work and home created the initial disjuncture. Weber emphasized this as part of the process of rationalization and disenchantment of the world. The separation received its greatest impetus with the development of large-scale industrial production requiring the cooperation of large numbers of persons at a central location. Yet the separation of work and home has been further complicated by other related events. Once it took place, the individual pursuit of hedonic gain during hours when one was not working became possible. Indeed, the modern conception of leisure primarily means time not committed to work and, secondarily, not obligated for other duties, civic and familial. The fragmentation of all these spheres is at the crux of the "privatization" or "loneliness" critique advanced by so many socially concerned students who anticipate Bellah. The autonomous man of de Tocqueville's penetrating analysis becomes part of Riesman's lonely crowd (Riesman, Glazer, and Denny 1955) and perhaps, as Lasch (1978) has observed, narcissistically self-absorbed.

Robin M. Williams's celebrated list of dominant American value-orientations (1963) includes freedom, economic success, and the worth of the individual personality, but not meaningful leisure or fun. This was probably less a sin of omission on Williams's part than it was a blind spot in American culture itself. However, the pursuit of meaningful leisure has emerged as a theme with some legitimacy for large numbers of people with a variety of lifestyles since World War II. The many lifestyles renew segments of society but do not knit the whole together. The publication of Cheek and Burch's text, *The Social Organization of Leisure in Human Society* (1976), marked a growing scholarly recognition of the importance of leisure. The modern American dream can involve intimacy and an escape from busyness—expressive fulfillment that sometimes represents a longing for the perfection of privatized withdrawal from work and community commitment. This craving for a moral holiday of irresponsibility is catered to and encouraged by a booming recreational industry. For example, a promotional flier for an island vacation targets the key values inherent in expressive individualism:

USEPPA . . . A true island experience

The activities and recreational pursuits on Useppa are as endless as the moods of the waters that surround her. But, equally important, Useppa is uniquely capable of offering you the luxury of doing nothing at all . . . of being gently and happily alone with someone you love, or with yourself. This invaluable commodity can only be achieved through the privacy to which we are so deeply and irrevocably committed.

Robert N. Wilson gives a more intellectualized, creative, and less vulgarly self-indulgent expression to some of the above themes in his brilliant and evocative "The Courage to Be Leisured" (1981). At the heart of his discussion is the contention that we have impoverished vocabularies for leisure fulfillment and that we ought to learn to be leisured as an end in itself. This includes, for Wilson, friendships, intimate attachments, and love relationships—all experiences to be intrinsically valued.

One cannot use survey data to exhaust the elaborations of the individual's private world and the variety of available lifestyles. The survey does not encompass the subtleties and richness of people's lives and their reflections on them. A more clinical, biographical, or ethnographic approach, like Riesman's or Bellah's, is appropriate for that. Nonetheless, survey data can map out the main strands of people's expressive commitments and activities. More important for our purposes, we can see how higher education affects these. We can start rounding out our understanding of what education does for society and how it does it.[2]

The expressive and lifestyle items of NLS-72 themselves are literally documents of the American ethos (see the Expressive Individualism variables listed in Appendix A). The expressive individualism is transparent, not just in subject matter alone but in question wording, research design, and research instrument. Questionnaire methodology itself asserts this ideology, for the typical questionnaire, like the NLS-72, asks for the private views of the individual. The questions reinforce this further by aiming to elicit opinions and reports about individual preferences and activities.[3]

EXPRESSIVE GOALS AND ACTIVITIES OF THE NLS SAMPLE

We selected from NLS-72 a variety of items bearing on individual self-expressive goals and on activities (see Expressive Individualism in Appendix A). The individual life goals dealt with education, leisure, friendship, and marriage and family. The activities were group or club participation in sports, in various cultural interests, and in an avocation or recreation. How higher education and type of educational institution and individual careers effect changes in these lifestyle goals and activities occupies us now.

The goals included "having a good education" on the assumption that, when stated in this manner, education is more an end than a means to more instrumental goals. In view of the close articulation of education, occupation, and social status, this item certainly could have been considered in the preceding chapter.

The goals of "meeting and working with friendly, sociable people" in work throughout one's life and "having strong friendships" as a life goal were also included as two dimensions of orientation to friendliness and friendship. The final item with directly interpersonal content was "finding the right person to marry and having a happy family life." By 1986 most of the sample had been married at least once. One exception is the category of women with advanced degrees, the majority of whom were still unmarried in 1986.

In addition, we included the goal of "having leisure time to enjoy my own interests" and data on three self-expressive leisure activities as behavioral indicators of that value. These are reported levels of participation in "sports teams or sports clubs," "a literary, art, discussion, music, or study group," and "social, hobby, garden, or card playing group." Though these latter three are group activities, the role of voluntary individual choice is great. These activities are clearly distinct from those directly and obviously connected with the worlds either of work or civic and political engagement. They result from the individual exercise of choice and represent community anchorages less than they do attachments to micro-communities or quasi-communities centered around lifestyles. The activities are relatively purely self-expressive in themselves and are not evidently means to some other end. Even though these items are broad indicators, they can give us a valuable first approximation of the centrality of a taste for leisure and leisure activities among young adults.

EXPRESSIVE RESPONSES OF THE SAMPLE IN 1986

How the total sample responded to the items in 1986 shows some quite strong normative tendencies that may be instructive on American life, and provides a backdrop against which we can examine some of the changes this sample of young adults is undergoing. (The reader should read the bottom row, entitled "Total" in Table 3.1 to follow this discussion.) To almost everybody in the sample all of the goals have at least some importance in both 1972 and 1986, varying primarily in the relative strength of importance.

In 1986, finding the right person to marry and having a happy family life receives overwhelming assent, with 86 percent of respondents concurring that these are very important. America continues to be a "marrying country" in ideal and fact, in spite of the emergence of serial monogamy and living arrangements and relationships short of formal marital commitments. The sweeping subscription is somewhat surprising in view of the

Table 3.1
Importance of Expressive Values, Goals, and Activities in 1986
by Educational Attainment, Gender, and Race

	Strong Friend- ships[a]	Marriage & Family[a]	Leisure[a]	Sports Clubs[b]	Cultural Groups[b]	Social Groups[b]	Working with Friendly People[c]	Good Educa- tion[c]
Educational Attainment								
High School Only	70	87	57	23	3	16	59	45
Less than Two Years College	70	85	60	27	4	17	55	52
Two or More Years College	68	87	62	24	6	17	53	54
Bachelor's Degree	73	86	63	29	8	20	54	69
Advanced Degree	70	85	59	29	11	17	50	81
Gender								
Men	66	85	61	33	5	15	48	56
Women	75	87	60	19	7	20	61	61
Race								
Black	54	80	52	16	8	17	55	76
White	72	86	61	27	6	18	57	57
Total	71	86	61	26	6	17	55	58

N = 5409

[a]Percent "Very Important."
[b]Percent "Active Participant."
[c]Percent with scores of 5 or 6.

obvious spread of partially legitimated means for people to pursue the joys and responsibilities of intimacy outside of marriage. Both deep and enduring intimate familial attachments and work that one finds inherently rewarding are, then, central modes of expression in America. Forming enduring and strong friendships is not quite as highly valued, with 71 percent holding it very important. Yet, it still ranked higher than all the items not yet discussed. The three items concerning having leisure time to pursue one's own interests, good education, and working with sociable, friendly people all had about 60 percent agreeing that they were very important.

Along with the set of goals in Table 3.1 is the set of three types of leisure activities. The highest levels of participation are in organized sports groups, with 26 percent reporting active participation. Seventeen percent report active participation in some form of social or avocational group. Only 6 percent report active involvement in a "cultural" group. Those reporting active participation fell from 9 percent in 1972 to 6 percent in 1986. Indeed, in 1986, 91 percent of the sample reported no participation in these groups at all. Perhaps such bumper sticker slogans as "Arts Are Basic" are quixotic expressions of the saving remnant of the liberally educated with the courage to be leisured. Access to the high arts as consumers is limited to the highly educated, for reasons we discuss in the concluding section of this chapter.

EFFECTS OF EDUCATIONAL LEVEL
ON EXPRESSIVE FACTORS

Level of education is highly related to all expressive goals and reported activities, although the pattern is sometimes inconsistent. (See the first five rows in Table 3.1.) The clearest of these patterns is the relationship between educational level and enhanced goals of getting a good education. Participation in cultural groups also becomes regularly greater with more educational attainment. However, while participation in sports and recreational activities and avocational social groups varies significantly between educational levels, the pattern is not linear.

Gender and race also have consequences. Women appear particularly likely to believe in the importance of strong friendships, working with friendly people, and getting a good education, and they are significantly more likely than men to report active participation in both cultural and avocational groups. Men report higher levels of participation in sports clubs than women. Blacks differ significantly from whites on several items. They are less likely than whites to value strong friendships, to value leisure time, and participate frequently in sports clubs; yet more likely to report frequent participation in both cultural and avocational groups and to regard getting a good education as important.

However, we cannot reduce our uncertainty about the long-term effects of such background factors as race, gender, socioeconomic status of the family of origin, and abilities—much less within-cohort changes—without looking explicitly at change and controlling for all the effects in the same analysis. Accordingly, our strategy is to see how the introduction of the background factors affects connections between educational level and the outcomes.

EDUCATION AND EXPRESSIVE GOALS
AND ACTIVITIES

We have sketched the life goals and leisure activities through which the members of our young adult sample are essaying self-expression in 1986. Whether and how higher education attainment and educational settings and careers effect change is our chief purpose in this book. In this chapter our main task is to examine changes in self-expressive matters. Since the frequencies of the expressive goals and activities data are in discrete categories and quite skewed, all of the analyses for the rest of this chapter are expressed in terms of odds derived from a logistic regression analysis (see Appendix B under Causal Modeling). For clarity we will first discuss changes in outcomes for the entire sample which includes those of all educational levels, including those who did not go on to postsecondary education. Only then will we deal with the college sample, consisting of those with at least some postsecondary education, to seek the effects of college characteristics and student careers.

GENDER AND RACE:
CHANGES IN ATTACHMENT AND LEISURE GOALS

Educational attainment has no effects on the goals of intimate attachments and leisure, once background characteristics and earlier values are held constant (Table 3.2).[4] Nonetheless, this age cohort undergoes major changes as it moves from adolescence to young adulthood. While family socioeconomic status and high school academic abilities, like educational attainment, do not have significant effects, race and gender do.

Women have odds 75 percent higher than men of valuing strong and lasting friendships as important, but there are no other significant gender differences here. Thus, women have changed significantly more than men by early mid-life.

Race has quite consistent effects on attachment and leisure goals on all three items. Whites have almost twice the odds (1.84 times) of blacks of placing a greater premium on life-long strong friendships in their early thirties than they did shortly after high school. During that time they also became 73 percent more likely than blacks to increase their rating of the goal of finding the right person to marry and having a happy family life as very important or important. In addition, whites also tend increasingly to subscribe to the goal of having enough time to pursue leisure goals with odds about one and one-half times those for blacks. While the effects of educational attainment do not differ by race, nonetheless the different effects of race on change in these expressive factors remains once the effects of gender, social class origin, abilities, and educational attainment are removed.

From this, it appears that blacks experience contracting interpersonal horizons while whites experience relatively undiminished ones.[5] One can speculate that the quality of life available to the typical black high school graduate may increasingly erode as the person reaches young adulthood. Cumulative limitations on possibilities and opportunities might compel a realistic downward revision of leisure, family, and friendship goals. A lowering of aspirations to strong primary relationships as they become less certain may go hand-in-hand with the fragmentation of black families. Life chances may continue to be relatively open for many young whites as they reach early adulthood. The possible race differences in horizons here may reflect differences in the ease of solidifying a tolerable and possible life plan in the realm of intimate attachments and meaningful leisure pursuits. Unfortunately, educational attainments appear not to alter this picture.

EDUCATIONAL ATTAINMENT: ATTACHMENT AND LEISURE GOALS

As can be seen in Table 3.2, going to college does not appreciably alter the odds of holding important the goals of strong life-long friendships, marriage and family commitments, or time to pursue leisure interests. We will advance some reasons why educational level does not affect attitudes about the importance of primary group attachments in the discussion concluding this chapter.

Table 3.2
Effects of Educational Attainment on Expressive Goals and Activities

	Strong Friend-ships	Marriage & Family	Leisure	Sports Clubs	Cultural Groups	Social Groups	Working with Friendly People	Good Educa-tion
Postsecondary Educational Attainment								
Less than Two Years	1.03	.83	1.17	1.24	1.4	1.00	.93	1.28
Two Years or More	.95	1.01	1.25	.92	2.10*	1.12	.94	1.34
Bachelor's Degree	1.14	1.01	1.30	1.10	2.15*	1.26	1.13	2.75***
Advanced Degree	1.02	1.03	1.14	.99	2.87*	.98	1.08	.59***
Background Factors								
Whites	1.84**	1.73*	1.55*	1.79*	.56	1.04	1.24	.60*
Women	1.74***	1.12	1.08	.63***	1.47*	1.23	1.58***	1.35*
Family Socioeconomic Status	1.03	.98	1.03	1.02	1.03	1.02	1.00	.96*
Academic Abilities	.94	.98	.97	.98	1.03	1.01	.94**	.97
Previous Values, Goals, and Activities								
Medium[a]	1.95	1.13	1.03	2.30***	2.31*	1.93**	1.70**	1.31
High[b]	4.52***	2.66***	2.67**	3.51***	4.72***	2.17	2.85***	3.28***
- 2 Log Likelihood = N = 5409	6284.76	4565.70	6755.19	7044.86	3253.77	6498.67	7946.02	6959.12

* p < .05   **p < .01   *** p < .001

NOTES: Figures in this table are the effects on the odds of being higher rather than lower on a particular value, goal, or activity.
Each category of educational attainment is compared with the reference category of those having no more than a high school education.
Each category of previous values, goals or activities is compared with the reference category "Not Important" or "Not at All."

[a]Intermediate values on a scored variable: "Somewhat Important," "Member Only."
[b]High values on a scored variable: "Very Important," "Active Participant."

EDUCATIONAL ATTAINMENT
AND EXPRESSIVE ACTIVITIES

If educational attainment has no significant effects on the goals of intimate attachments and leisure time, it does on reports of increasing participation in "a literary, art, discussion, music, or study group." Those with two or more years beyond high school and those with bachelor's degrees are slightly more than twice as likely to report participation than the baseline group, those with no education beyond high school. The advanced degree holders are almost three times as likely as those with no education beyond high school to increase in reported involvement in these cultural groups. College educators may take some solace that they are making some difference at each level, a difference that becomes significant with more than two years of college and that becomes most pronounced at the graduate level.[6] However, as we have already noted, for no higher education category does the absolute level of reported participation in cultural groups become very high.

Educational attainment has no significant effects upon the other types of group participation, that is, sports clubs and teams and various kinds of avocational and social groups. Educational level, then, specifically enlarges those activities that are most closely related to the academic domain proper. For the other reported activities and the life goals thus far discussed, amount of schooling matters hardly at all. Whites are more likely than blacks to have substantially increased odds of participation on sports teams and clubs. The persistence of de facto segregation in many communities may continue to militate against black participation,[7] especially as blacks become young adults and no longer have access to the recreational facilities of educational institutions.

There are also two major gender differences. Women have much lower odds than men of increased sports and team participation—about 40 percent lower. On the other hand, the women in our study are half again as likely as men—or 50 percent more likely—to report an increase in participation in some kind of cultural group. The last two findings are consistent with what we know about traditional gender differences. What is interesting is that the passage of time, net of educational attainment and other factors, has enhanced gender differences in these respects.

EDUCATIONAL ATTAINMENT:
GOOD EDUCATION AS A GOAL

Educational attainment has extremely powerful effects on holding education as a goal. At the highest educational levels the odds of subscribing to the importance of a good education are dramatically higher than for the lower levels. The odds for those with bachelor's degrees of increasingly valuing a good education as intrinsically important are almost three times greater than for their classmates who did not go beyond high school. The odds are almost six times greater for those with advanced degrees.

For all those with less than a bachelor's degree, the patterns persist, for the odds remain positive. Clearly, however, obtaining a bachelor's or graduate degree is most strongly associated with the goal of a good education.

Higher education as an increasingly dominant set of institutionalized relations is in the business of creating a self-fulfilling prophecy in its own behalf. Our own idealism led us to treat education in this chapter on self-expression. The relationships, however, strikingly parallel those for the intrinsic work value in the previous chapter. Therefore, we should think of good education as a means to instrumental success, not as an end in itself. In modern societies the institution of education has the power to invent and control the symbols of a moral reality of instrumental success. Education as an institution goes largely unchallenged in the process. It builds a framework of legitimacy that induces inductees to enter into the process of legitimation. It can do this precisely because of its gatekeeping or credentialing role. The educated become like a church hierarchy—in general, the higher the educational status, the more orthodox and legitimating the opinions of beneficiaries become. As Meyer notes, "Education is, as has often been noted, a secular religion in modern societies: as religions do, it provides a legitimating account of the competence of citizens, the authority of elites, and the sources of adequacy of the social system to maintain itself in the face of uncertainty" (1977, 72). This complements Bourdieu's analyses but stresses the role of higher education in creating knowledge, which can, of course, be thought of as cultural capital.

Women, especially, may perceive education as providing them an avenue to work that carries with it a promise of freedom and equality. Women, indeed, are about one and a third times as likely as men to have shifted in the fourteen years in the direction of saying that a good education is important or very important. Now higher education *appears* to women to be a disproportionately good bargain, no matter that the objective payoffs show large gender biases. Today women gain against the historical background of greater relative deprivation in the past and in contrast to those women who do not get as much education. They believe in the relative benefits of the process of higher education more than men do. So, too, do blacks more than whites. Another way of looking at this is that whites in general may be more likely than blacks to take equality of educational opportunity for granted.[8] The historical and still remaining relative differences in college attendance among members of one's own race and social class provide baselines for social comparisons. To those who succeed, these are salient to the extent that their reference groups have triumphed over obstacles to upward mobility. Whites have only six-tenths the odds of blacks of increasing their appraisal of the importance of a good education.

But what of the long-established fact that blacks tend to be of lower socioeconomic status than whites? Remember that the effect for blacks is *net* of those of other statuses, including social class origins and 1972 values. Regardless of all other factors, does socioeconomic origin play a part, too? Do those whose families are relatively lower in socioeconomic status differ from those from more advantaged families? For each decile higher in the socioeconomic status of the family of origin, there is a slight reduction of 4 percent in the odds of saying a good education is important. The overall effect from top to bottom of the socioeconomic ladder is considerable. Thus, among high school graduates, relative family standing in 1972 is inversely related to the upward reappraisal of the importance of education. The token of increased attitudinal legitimation of higher education is in rough proportion to the value in status enhancement[9] to be gained in the educational process. Can we conclude that the lower one's social origins, the more the praise for higher education? Only when we examine reported satisfactions with education in chapter 6 can we address this question squarely.

EDUCATIONAL ATTAINMENT AND SOCIABILITY AT WORK

The last expressive goal to be considered here is "meeting and working with friendly, sociable people." Level of education has

no significant bearing on this goal. However, three of the background factors do. The odds of the intensification of this goal for
women over the years are about one and one-half those of men.
Each increase in family socioeconomic status also elevates the
odds by 1 percent of an increase in valuing working with friendly
people. And each increase in academic abilities is matched by
a considerable drop of about 6 percent in the odds of increasingly
valuing work relations—as though to the degree that they are
bright, people become increasingly alienated from the interpersonal rewards of friendly collegiality in their work lives.

EFFECTS OF INSTITUTIONAL CHARACTERISTICS
AND STUDENT CAREERS

In this discussion we limit the sample to those who had some
postsecondary education. As shown in Table 3.3 the effects of
institutional characteristics and educational careers on the odds
of expressive goals and activities are few, but may be meaningful.
However, there are no statistically significant effects of college
characteristics or careers on the items appearing in the first three
columns—strong friendships, leisure time, and marriage and
family—and in the sixth and seventh columns—social groups
and working with friendly people.

The size of the student body slightly enhances the odds of
increased involvement in activities in sports clubs. However,
this is statistically significant only if we relax our confidence level
to $p < .10$. Is it the presence of more adequate facilities in large
institutions that is reflected here? If so, students should be more
satisfied with sports and recreation facilities in large institutions
(see chapter 6). Size of the student body has no other effects.
Selectivity, however, uniformly reduces the odds of subscribing
to any of the expressive life goals or reporting any of the leisure
activities. Although none of the relationships is significant, the
pattern is tantalizing. Schools with "bright"[10] student bodies
may be places to critique typical values and activities. Apparently, the more selective the school, the more intellectual and
critical the student body and the less the credence in generally
accepted values. Correlatively, such schools also have student
bodies with the financial wherewithal to take atypical, even
alienated stances, with less proportionate risk. Neither the
proportion of full-time students nor the degree to which an
institution is residential yields any pattern.

Table 3.3
Effects of College Characteristics and Student Careers on Expressive Values, Goals, and Activities

	Strong Friend-ships	Marriage & Family	Leisurea	Sports Clubs	Cultural Groups	Social Groups	Working with Friendly People	Good Educa-tion
College Characteristics[a]								
Student Enrollment	1.00	.99	1.00	1.01	1.02	1.01	1.00	1.01
Selectivity	.91	.98.	95	.98	.92	.97	.90	.88
Private Control	1.23	.85	1.01	.99	1.42	.99	.96	1.26
Full-Time Students	1.02	1.02	.93	.99	1.92	1.92	1.01	1.00
Vocational Emphasis	1.81	1.94	.96	.97	.94	.94	1.06	1.01
Highly Residential	.94	1.10	1.03	.91	.90	1.04	1.09	1.07
Student Careers								
Business Major	1.13	1.00	.98	.99	.69	.94	.93	.69
Education Major	1.17	1.14	.88	.95	1.00	1.12	1.06	1.15
Arts & Sciences Major	1.05	.79	.95	.93	1.41	1.08	.80	.90
Ever Lived on Campus	1.00	1.05	1.05	.83	1.03	1.10	1.01	1.02
College Grades	1.00	1.10	.96	1.01	1.19	.97	.97	1.04
Postsecondary Educational Attainment								
Two Years or More College	1.17	1.19	1.02	.71	1.52	.97	.95	1.03
Bachelor's Degree	1.19	1.19	1.14	.94	1.38	1.02	1.30	2.16**
Advanced Degree	1.26	1.34	1.02	.86	1.54	.84	1.41	4.51***
Background Factors								
Whites	2.26*	1.71	1.54	1.65	.58	1.23	1.32	.59
Women	2.04***	1.07	1.19	.61**	1.46	1.05	1.66***	1.48*
Family Socioeconomic Status	1.05	.99	1.02	1.00	1.04	.99	1.00	.97
Academic Abilities	.95	.98	.96	.95	1.01	.98	.96	.98

Table 3.3 (continued)

	Strong Friendships	Marriage & Family	Leisure	Sports Clubs	Cultural Groups	Social Groups	Working with Friendly People	Good Education
Previous Values, Goals, and Activities								
Medium^b	2.63	1.23	1.37	2.82**	2.05	1.49	1.62	1.88
High^c	6.09**	2.82**	3.75*	3.55***	3.96*	2.26***	2.83**	4.26**
- 2 Log Likelihood =	2648.71	1992.03	2980.67	3199.21	1750.61	2959.23	3483.22	2906.62

N = 2702
* p < .05   ** p <.01   *** p <.001

NOTES: Figures in this table are the effects on the odds of being higher rather than lower on a particular value or activity.
Each category of college major is compared with the reference category of all other majors.
Each category of educational attainment is compared with the reference category of those having less than two years of postsecondary education.
Each category of previous values, goals, or activities is compared with the reference category of low on a scored variable or "Not Important" or "Not at All" on a trichotomous variable.

^{a}For persons attending more than one institution, the one most frequently attended; in case of ties, the one more recently attended.
^{b}Intermediate values on a scored variable: "Somewhat Important," "Member Only."
^{c}High values on a scored variable: "Very Important," "Active Participant."

The proportion of full-time students and the proportion of students in residence may simply not be good indicators of solidarity or cohesiveness, but it is more to the point that there is no particular theoretical basis for expecting them to have a bearing on the self-expressive realm as measured here. The effect of the proportion of full-time students on elevating the odds of valuing leisure is slight.[11]

Variations in college career, like college characteristics, also have no significant effects. However, college grades and majoring either in business or in the arts and sciences appear to have meaningful changes associated with them. Having majored in business lowers the odds of holding getting a good education as important. Having majored in business also results in lower odds of participating in a literary, art, discussion, music, or study group, while, in contrast to the residual reference category, arts and sciences majors have higher odds of increasing participation in such groups. The reported average of college grades, too, has a similar effect on such participation. For each upward increment in grades the odds seem to change somewhat in favor of such participation.

What may be most significant is the lack of statistical significance of the relationships between both college characteristics and individual careers and these expressive outcomes—and, hence, this is a connection that remains not proven.

EFFECTS OF EDUCATIONAL ATTAINMENT BEYOND HIGH SCHOOL

The effects of educational attainment among those who went to college are nearly identical to those for the total sample (Table 3.3). This redundancy helps support the hypothesis that educational attainment is the most powerful explanatory factor in this study. Since the college sample is much more homogeneous than the whole sample, this remains interesting, for the effects persist, though diminished.

For the most part the odds do not attain significance because of the reduced sample size and its greater homogeneity. Despite this, the odds of subscribing to the goal of getting a good education remain markedly improved by educational attainment. A bachelor's degree holder has about double the odds of the reference category (those with less than two years of postsecondary education) of strengthening their assent to the value of getting a good education. For the advanced degree holders these odds are about four and one-half times. The credentialing effect remains even when we change the reference category to those who have completed "some college" and after we have controlled for whatever impact college characteristics and careers might have had. Among those with some higher education, the effects of the characteristics of higher educational institutions or individual careers on expressive outcomes are rare.

EFFECTS OF BACKGROUND FACTORS AMONG THE COLLEGE SAMPLE

Gender has quite strong and consistent effects among those who have gone to college (see Table 3.3). College women, like the sample of all women, have more than double the odds of increasingly holding the interpersonal domain of friendships and friendliness at work to be important. College women's odds of increased subscription to the value of a good education (1.48) are significantly higher than for college men. On the other hand, college women have only about three-fifths the chance of college men of increasing their level of organized sports activities.

The odds that college-going whites will become more favorable to strong friendships are more than twice those of otherwise identical blacks. Enhanced chances of subscription to marriage and family and leisure for whites in contrast to blacks continue, but are no longer statistically significant.[12] Whites have higher odds of increases in reporting organized sports participation than blacks, but have only about six-tenths the odds of change in support of the importance of getting a good education. Although only the first finding in this paragraph is significant, results parallel those for the total sample.

Finally, among those who went to college, there were no significant relationships between either measured abilities or socioeconomic status, on the one hand, and other outcomes.

OVERVIEW OF FINDINGS

What is striking about this chapter is how few significant findings level of education accounts for in the realm of expressive goals and activities. Level of educational attainment, as an important, if not the principal, criterion for social standing, only effects change in one of the goals in the domain of individual self-expression: the goal of getting a good education. Educational attainment also strongly enhances an expressive aspect of work, the intrinsic work value, as we showed in chapter 2. Educational attainment does appear to facilitate the attainment of occupational status by creating attitudes—indeed, an ideology—appropriate to the occupational roles people will play after graduation.

Table 3.4 shows that educational attainment improves goodness of fit over a model using only background characteristics and initial values of the outcome variables. It does so, however, only for the goal of getting a good education.

In addition, when thoroughly examined, the power of education to carry over into changes in group activities having a cultural content proves illusory, for such effects are explained by initial individual characteristics. Thus, higher education may only appear to prepare students for participation in culturally elite activities.[13] Even among those with graduate degrees, who report the highest levels of active participation in cultural groups, only 11 percent report they are now active participants in such groups. Education has scarcely transformed them into avid consumers of high culture, and they may be turning out the way they would have anyway.

We found that amount of schooling did not affect many changes in reported life goals and leisure activities. This does not mean that education is not associated with great differences in the particular contents of activities and goals and great stylistic nuances that we cannot capture with the items and analytical models available. Education may directly and indirectly facilitate particular leisure elaborations and inhibit others.[14] There are, no doubt, large differences in leisure behavior that are functions of social class, and educational institutions may well play their part in maintaining the differences. For example, the elite liberal arts college often includes such carry-over sports as tennis and golf among physical education requirements for graduation and, thus, buttress the claim to upper-middle-class identity of the graduate. Of course, deliberate tutelage is probably less important than informal socialization in peer groups. This study's method of aggregation is not sensitive to the elite schools and how they might pass on the culture of elites.

Table 3.4
The Significance of Educational Attainment, College Characteristics, and Student Careers in Explaining Expressive Goals, Values, and Activities

	Educational Attainment	College Characteristics and Student Careers
Strong Friendships	n.s.	n.s.
Marriage and Family	n.s.	n.s.
Leisure	n.s.	n.s.
Sports Clubs	n.s.	n.s.
Literary Clubs	n.s.	n.s.
Social Groups	n.s.	n.s.
Working with Friendly People	n.s.	n.s.
Good Education	**	n.s.
n.s. = not significant	* $p < .05$ ** $p < .01$	

NOTE: Results are based on F-tests for linear regression or analogues in the case of logistic regression (see Appendix B). Column one reflects the improvement of fit achieved by adding the dummy variables for educational attainment over a model using only background variables and prior values of the dependent variable. Column two reflects improvement of fit when the college characteristics and individual experiences are added to the model tested in column one (i.e., background, previous characteristics, and educational attainment).

In the main, the workings of education appear largely irrelevant to shifts in other expressive goals and activities—especially the interpersonal ones. This may result largely from cultural continuities in general goals and values. For example, broad accord on the importance of marriage and the family and friendship goals that we find here in young adulthood[15] surely has had a long historical existence in American—not to mention Western European—culture. Such goals preceded the rise of mass education and mass higher education. In the domain of intimate attachments, then, many cultural values have tended to persist irrespective of higher education's mushrooming growth in this century.

There are minor effects of college characteristics and student careers. Institutional size is accompanied by slightly enhanced participation in sports clubs. Business majors are slightly less likely than others to value getting a good education. They also are less likely to report participation in cultural or literary groups. Arts and sciences majors are less likely than others to value getting good college grades.

Some gender differences are not surprising, given traditional gender-role differences: enhanced tendencies to value a good education, lower levels of participation in sports clubs, higher levels of participation in cultural and literary groups and an enhanced premium on friendship. Blacks value education much more than do whites; also, the lower the socioeconomic origins, the more good education is valued. Blacks appear to change in the direction of downgrading aspirations in the realms of friendship and marriage and happy family life.

Is education, then, curiously irrelevant to much else that goes on in the realm of self-expression? Perhaps. Or does the large-scale omnibus survey fail to capture much that is going on? As noted above, there might be much informal tutelage in lifestyles, especially in residential collegiate settings. Alternatively, perhaps any influence that educational institutions per se might have is now drowned out by an ocean of voices from the mass entertainment and mass leisure industries—voices well-calculated to attract attention.

It is perhaps not surprising in view of capitalism's emphasis on work, acquisition, and saving that our educational institutions even now devote so little attention and study to leisure, the emotions, and self-expression. At any rate, educational institutions at all levels seem to do little beyond athletics—and a minor, saving emphasis on "high" culture—to inculcate leisure tastes and lifestyles. Consistent with the instrumental traditions[16] that maintain the legitimacy of the link between higher education as an institutionalized process and the society, education by and large does not do much to help people cultivate cultured leisure pursuits. This may well suit the interests of the elite strata, as we discuss below. In this context, Wilson's "The Courage to Be Leisured" (1981) is a radical exhortation not readily legitimized in most educational circles. We would argue that educational institutions largely leave students to their own devices in the voluntaristic world of leisure consumption and that whatever tutelage takes place is haphazard and informal.

College characteristics and college careers are weak and sporadic in their effects. These nonsignificant socialization effects, however, pale in contrast to the effects of educational attainment itself, confirming Meyer's thesis that status conferral is the fundamental force of education. But educational attainment has only selective effects, for it has no effects on the domain of the interpersonal and intimate. The credentialing and certifying process that bestows a new identity and a new status on graduates does not affect nearly unquestioned and ancient cultural values. However, the specific items incorporated in NLS-72 are so general that they do not capture concrete lifestyle elaborations. Thus, they have severe limitations in illuminating socialization and allocation issues.

SOCIETY, CULTURE, AND LEISURE CONSUMPTION

Higher education may also not have much to do with the domain of expressive behavior and values, broadly considered. In the Western world, intimate interpersonal relationships are largely compartmentalized from the realms of education and work.[17] Indeed, fulfillment in intimate attachments is an important cultural value that is universal, not just Western. And certainly it is an old Western value, too. Striving for love and self-expression may be a profound part of our human condition, antedating modern societies and often repressed by the alienating demands of work. Sinclair Lewis's Dodsworth found that his success in work had left him an incomplete person, and he tried to become authentic by becoming committed to another person and by experiencing a Useppa-like moral holiday. Love, marriage, friendship, and even leisure and play may be such elemental forces that formal educational processes and attainments can only channel and make for stylistic modifications and elaborations.

The direction of such elaborations may be partly collective, especially in ethnic collectivities in which self-expression is to be muted. When we discussed the island of Useppa above, we noted that the direction can be highly privatized and individualistic.[18] Flamboyant and more collective modes of individualistic self-expression—like an absorption in The Grateful Dead—can also be just as privatized as the ideal life on Useppa.

Higher education may affect personal choices of how to realize these basic commitments in a lifestyle, but the tutelage may be largely indirect and unintentional. It can indirectly provide an arena for students to hone specific criteria of taste and social acceptance in particular groups.[19] Bourdieu and Passeron have clearly shown how elite groups use the educational system to maintain their dominance. As discussed in chapter 1, there are powerful selection effects, with the children of the elite having a great advantage in terms of their cultural capital. The educational process, especially higher education, plays its part in creating cultural capital by morally legitimating approved symbols and inculcating students in their correct use and display. Of course, this flies in the face of a democratic ethos. How different is America with its de Tocquevillean egalitarian ethos from that presented by Bourdieu and Passeron (1977, 1979)? Their analysis, however profound, may be less pertinent to the more open, permeable class structure of the United States than to more closed stratification systems with relatively clear elites. Note, for example, Allan Bloom's shrill elitist complaint, an atypical voice crying in the wilderness against democratic pluralism and relativism in *The Closing of the American Mind* (1987): a book that one has difficulty applying to France.

As regards education and social elites, the more fluid case of the United States may not be so clearcut as that of France. For example, Wilensky concluded in 1964 that there was a significant degree of cultural homogenization, with television playing a pervasive role. He notes that educated strata—even products of graduate and professional schools—are becoming full participants in mass culture" (190), but adds, "The educated display, on balance, a mild tendency toward more discriminating tastes" (191). Both college quality and educational attainment mattered: "For the avoidance of big slugs of poor TV, sheer level of education counts slightly more than quality (188). Yet, the use of "quality print" was declining, even among the graduates of quality institutions. Wilensky suggests that, the rising average level of education will protect against enervating amounts of the very shoddiest media content but it will not cause large populations to break the mediocrity barrier" (188). Wilensky's prescience appears unassailable: with ever more students slated to go to college after the 1960s and with smaller proportions attending "quality institutions," even most of the more highly educated would not be distinctively insulated from middlebrow media.

More recently, DiMaggio has been the major contributor to the literature on the social organization of the consumption of high art and the consumers of art in the United States. High culture as cultural capital still legitimizes elite status. Its consumption still appears reasonably vigorous for the few, despite the onslaught of mass consumption alternatives. For example, DiMaggio and Useem found those consuming the high arts are "dominated by the wealthy and well-educated, most of whom are professionals and managers" (1978a, 156). Of all the dimensions of social class, education was "the most salient determinant of arts involvement." The consumption of popular arts (e.g., movies, jazz, rock music) cuts across all classes, perhaps providing a relatively classless lingua franca, and this development is traceable to changes in social structure, especially the growth of far-ranging networks and the diminished control of local, discrete groups. DiMaggio and Useem argue: "Participation in the world of the arts may be most crucial to the upper-middle class, the group whose status is most marginal to the elite, in that arts consumption provides this group with the opportunity for symbolic identification with the upper class and may even yield socially useful contacts" (1978b, 195). It is not in the interests of an elite, however, to increase access to and consumption of high art, for that would diminish its ability to control the means of cultural reproduction and undermine its symbolic justification.[20] The reality is one of pluralistic and overlapping consumption for elite groups, with, however, lower educational strata excluded from the world of high culture. This is entirely consistent with the dearth of high cultural participation in general and the slight positive boost to such participation received as a consequence of educational attainment.

Education may, in general, have a largely unplanned bearing on the norms of expressive consumption and fulfillment. In a broad sense, Bellah and his associates are close to the mark by linking expressive individualism to the hegemony of individualism in the utilitarian realm. However, as Cheek and Burch observe so artfully, there remain methodological difficulties in examining such elusive subjects as lifestyles and leisure: "Just as we think we have found the uniting variable that accounts for complex behavior, the subjects under observation slip into another level of their personal and social dimension" (1976, 56).

Does the loose connection of higher education with most aspects of expressive pursuits, except those related to the world of work, also characterize the realm of concern for community and society? Or is higher education serving to buttress civic and political engagement? The next chapter will deal with these questions.

NOTES

1. It is selfless in the sense that, while work is often seen as self-expressive, it also frequently entails, blunting of many self-expressive possibilities.

2. It is highly likely that the social organization of occupations will have a decisive effect on non-work behavior and that any effects education might have are mediated by attachments, groups, and organizations. Unfortunately, the data will not allow us to assess the extent to which patterns and contents of leisure behavior are reinforced by the character of the occupation in addition to educational attainment or experience. For a useful discussion of the connection between occupation and leisure, see Cheek and Burch (1976, 54-71).

3. Of course, the social survey may have other units of analysis, like organizational, societal, or cultural characteristics. Thus, the technology need not be limited to the individual and individual responses as the primary object of study.

4. Most of the items were present in the 1972 wave of the survey. However, all of the reports of social participation were added in 1974, as were items on the importance of leisure time for oneself and getting a good education.

5. To be sure, the sample of blacks is too small and unrepresentative for this to be a definitive statement. However, if anything, the sample of blacks represented here may have more stable patterns of attachment, for they survived successive survey waves.

6. See the discussions of DiMaggio and Useem (1978a, 1978b) at the conclusion of this chapter.

7. This interpretation assumes that blacks have only limited resources to mount organized sports and recreational activities on their own.

8. Cautious interpretation is required, for the black sample suffers from biases that affect the differences between blacks and whites in unknown ways.

9. The gain is in expressive terms, that is, access to more highly approved symbols and experiences, as much as it is in narrowly utilitarian ones.

10. Read, if you will, "higher socioeconomic status," since selectivity and median family income of student body are highly correlated (Pearsonian R = +.60).

11. It, too, is significant at the <.10 level.

12. We repeat the earlier caveats about the nonrepresentativeness of the black sample.

13. Nevertheless, since in the early waves of the survey educational level is also correlated with such activities, much of the groundwork has already been laid.

14. See the discussions of the interplay of education and occupation with leisure behavior in Cheek and Burch (1976, 54-72).

15. These values are fundamentally the same in the early waves of the survey. Hence, there is no great shift between adolescence and the early middle years.

16. We refer here to the cooptation of education by the economically productive institutions of the society and its increasing dedication to servicing their needs.

17. The data do not really allow us to evaluate Kohn's spillover hypothesis, that qualitative differences in lifestyles stem from both occupational and educational experiences (1969, 190). From this perspective nonwork behavior is similar to or congruent with occupational style. An alternative view that our data also do not allow us to assess is Wilensky's compensatory hypothesis, that nonwork is diametrically opposed to work and compensates for its limitations. See the discussion in Cheek and Burch (1976, 54).

18. One doubts that there could actually be that much privacy on a small island thickly settled with like-minded people. Even in highly individualistic societies, people have group attachments.

19. Our uncertain findings regarding the effects of college characteristics and individual experiences do not support the idea of arenas differing broadly in expressive values, goals, and acts. That does not mean that they cannot be identified and measured with appropriate research techniques.

20. For a fascinating specification of how cultural capital affects school success in high school most especially for girls,

see DiMaggio (1982). In addition, DiMaggio and Mohr (1985) found significant net effects of cultural capital on educational attainment, college attendance, college completion, graduate attendance, and marital selection for both men and women.

4

In Pursuit of the Common Good

*I don't think about politics.... That's one of my Goddam precious
American rights, not to think about politics.*

Rabbit, in John Updike, *Rabbit Redux*

Developing citizens who are committed to the common good is
one of the fundamental goals of higher education. Plato, Thomas
Jefferson, John Dewey, as well as educational reformers of the
1990s all affirm this purpose. Ernest Boyer is a major advocate
today: "In the end, the quality of the undergraduate experience
is to be measured by the willingness of graduates to be socially
and civically engaged" (1987, 278-79). Active citizenship in a
democracy requires educated persons who can read, write, think,
and participate critically. President Jefferson and many others
have believed that schools and colleges ought to provide the
knowledge and skills that make such citizenship possible. We
have seen how higher education intensifies the pursuit of individual success and is only loosely connected with the form and
content of personal happiness. Does it also fulfill the social
expectations of philosophers and educators? What did college
do for the civic commitment of the members of the high school
class of 1972?

In modern Western democracies including the United States,
only a tiny proportion of the population actually participates in
civic affairs. Education seems to breed participation—the more
years of education, the more likely people are to vote, discuss
politics, and take part in political, community, and voluntary
activities (Almond and Verba 1963; Verba and Nie 1972; Verba,
Nie, and Kim 1978). With respect to civic attitudes and values,
research of the last twenty years shows that persons attaining

higher educational levels are somewhat higher than high school graduates on measures of altruism, humanitarianism, social conscience, political interest and support for civil rights and liberties (Hyman, Wright, and Reed 1975; Hyman and Wright 1979; Pascarella and Terenzini 1991).[1]

The evidence is mixed, however, on the crucial question of the net effects of higher education—what difference does college itself make apart from maturation and other influences? Effects of college are modest and not consistent across all studies—in sum, "disappointingly foggy" (Pascarella and Terenzini 1991, 330). As Weil (1985) argues, using the cases of the United States, France, Germany, and Austria, higher education may not always be liberalizing in its effects. His analysis suggests that it may be most liberalizing where there is both religious heterogeneity and an established tradition of democratic rule, as in the United States. Jackman and Muha (1984) found that educational attainment is associated with commitment to individual rights but not to equality. Far from enhancing moral enlightenment or even increasing superficial commitment to democratic values, Jackman and Muha contend that education encourages development of ideologies that justify the interests of dominant classes. These effects of education differ with regard to intergroup attitudes concerning race, gender, and social class. Education, they find, has little effect on men's attitudes toward women, positive effects on whites' tolerance of blacks, and negative effects on attitudes toward the poor. Education, then, enhances the ability of those who achieve more education "to protect dominant interests without unduly antagonizing subordinates" (765).

The data we examine here do not justify our choosing among these competing theories and approaches. They do, however, permit us to explore the more general formulation of Meyer (1977) that education allocates persons to new statuses, and at the same time socializes them in attitudes, values, and motivation to play the appropriate roles associated with those statuses. With our broad national sample including two-year and four-year colleges, we expect to find a modest positive effect of educational attainment on socialization into citizenship roles, what Meyer calls diffuse socialization. Specific institutional differences and variations in student careers will be less likely to affect these civic commitments. First, we examine how civic commitment changes during early adulthood. That leads us to consider how educational attainment affects, in turn, political involvement, participation in voluntary community activities, and civic goals. Finally, we analyze the effects of college characteristics and student careers on these changes.

CHANGING CIVIC COMMITMENTS AMONG YOUNG ADULTS

How did the civic commitment of these young adults evolve from their 1972 high school graduation until 1986? We examine changes in an array of attitudes and activities. We begin with voting and other types of political involvement. Then we consider four kinds of community activities. Finally, we examine two life goals on which our respondents expressed their attitudes in their senior year in high school and again fourteen years later. In Table 4.1 we present a summary of the responses discussed in this section.

Political interest and activity can occur on several levels involving different degrees of commitment: voting; political discussion with family, friends, and work associates; and engaging in such political activities as contacting public officials, canvassing voters, contributing money to campaigns, attending political meetings, working for candidates, and participating in political organizations.

Voting is the elementary political act in a democracy, but is only a small step toward what Bellah and his colleagues mean by civic commitment. Voting is relatively easy; it is an intermittent and infrequent rather than a sustained activity. One may make it to the polls to vote on election day, even if one is not very invested in the outcome. During their first two years after high school, 67 percent of our respondents reported voting at least once. Fourteen years later, during a two-year period, 76 percent reported voting.[2] This increase was expected, since there is usually a rise in voting rates as people grow older, become settled in communities, raise families, and become more experienced politically, as demonstrated by Verba and Nie (1972) and Wolfinger and Rosenstone (1980).

A further step toward civic engagement is political discussion, which requires more interest, knowledge, and time than voting. In 1986, 43 percent of the adults in our sample discussed politics frequently with family, friends, and fellow workers. This represents a slight decrease from 1974, with the proportion of women declining more than men. The third indicator of civic commitment in politics requires even more interest, energy, and time, and consequently, fewer people are involved. Only one out of twenty took part frequently in political campaigns and contacting public officials—about the same as in 1974. With the exception of voting, the men of the high school class of 1972 were slightly more active politically than the women, but the gap is small.[3]

Table 4.1
The Importance of Civic Goals and Activities in 1986 by Educational Attainment, Gender, and Race

	Voted[a]	Political Discussion[b]	Political Activities[c]	Community Groups[d]	Volunteer Work[d]	Youth Organizations[d]	Non-Worship Church Activities[d]	Social Justice[e]	Community Leadership[e]
Educational Attainment									
Only High School	61	32	4	3	3	17	18	8	2
Less than Two Years College	73	40	4	4	5	17	23	7	3
Two or More Years College	77	44	4	5	6	13	26	8	2
Bachelor's Degree	85	47	7	9	7	11	28	8	4
Advanced Degree	89	59	11	9	8	9	29	12	7
Gender									
Men	75	45	6	5	4	11	20	7	4
Women	77	40	5	7	7	17	29	9	2
Total	76	43	6	6	6	14	25	8	3
Race									
Black	75	50	7	12	7	11	36	21	7
White	76	42	5	5	6	14	24	7	3

N = 5409

[a]Voted in last two years.
[b]Score of 7 or more.
[c]Score of 12 or more.
[d]"Active Participant."
[e]"Very Important."

In the local community, voluntary associations offer many opportunities for civic participation. People join with others in particular activities that are more personal than the political party, the state, or the nation. These provide an experience of acting and governing within smaller groups—but outside the circle of family and friends. This is more than privatized self-expression, although the activity may be fulfilling. It expresses social and public values and commitments. The organizations considered here are not explicitly political. Sometimes, however, they engage in social or political action; sometimes they provide services for people. Since de Tocqueville, observers have noticed that the United States is a nation of joiners. Compared to other nations, voluntary association membership in the United States is high. Even so, only a minority are so engaged (Hyman and Wright 1971; Kemper 1980; Smith 1975). In a recent national survey, 12 percent of Americans reported volunteering five hours per week or more (Independent Sector 1988).

The NLS-72 High School Class of 1972 participated in four diverse types of community organizations. Most similar conceptually to political activities is participation in "community centers, neighborhood improvement, or social-action associations or groups." The latter two activities include efforts to change the community or to resist change, while community centers usually provide services rather than agitate for change. This kind of participation, then, may or may not have explicit political implications. Almost 6 percent of the respondents reported active participation in such groups in 1986, a slight increase from 1974.

Even less political or controversial, but still contributing to the community, is organized volunteer work (e.g., in a hospital). Again, in 1986 about 6 percent of the respondents did organized volunteer work, a slight increase from 1974, with women doing volunteer work at a higher rate than men.

Thus far, apart from the expected increase in voting activity, we have discovered only slight change in levels of political and community involvement. Moreover, the differences between men and women are small. In contrast, participation in youth organizations and church-related activities as well as life goals undergo major changes and vary strikingly with gender. Two years after high school, women are actively engaged in youth organizations at only half the rate of men. By 1986, while the men's rate has increased slightly, women's activity has tripled. Seventeen percent of women were now participating actively, one and one-half times the rate for men. Of all the activities discussed here, youth organizations seem most likely to be related to having children. By the age of thirty-two, many of our respondents had children old enough to participate in youth activities. This is especially true of those who married soon after high school. We would expect these parents, then, to have become more active in youth organizations.

Church-related activities (other than worship) are difficult to classify in our framework. We recognize that such participation usually has expressive elements and also often has the utilitarian motive of status improvement. Frequently, however, church-related activities include community service or broadly defined social action. We classify them here, then, as a type of civic engagement. Active participation is higher for both men and women than in any other civic activities. Women participated at a higher rate two years after high school than men. Both groups participated increasingly during the intervening time, with women increasing more than men. As with voting, we expect young adults to take part more as they settle down in communities and begin raising children. By 1986, 29 percent of women and 20 percent of men took part actively.

Finally, on the two life goals expressing civic commitment, the young adults changed considerably after high school. How important in your life, they were asked, is "working to correct social and economic inequalities"? We call this goal "commitment to social justice." As the authors of *Habits of the Heart* argued, the common language of Americans does not typically include such phrases. Even when people engage in community and political activities, they tend to articulate their participation in terms, not of civic commitment, but rather of utilitarian or expressive individualism. They lack the kind of "second language" of Biblical or republican social ethics that was part of the culture of colonial America (Bellah et al. 1985, 20–22). It is more common in the United States today, even among social activists, to hear this commitment defined in terms of expressive individualism: "I am in the struggle because it means a lot to me. It's where I'm at" (Bellah et al. 1985, 133). But this commitment is rare enough at all, for only 8 percent of the young adults rated working to correct social and economic inequalities a very important goal, with women more likely to do so than men. In contrast, as we have seen in previous chapters, goals like opportunities for advancement, having strong friendships, and finding the right person to marry are very important for a great majority of the respondents.

The low level of commitment to social justice among these adults is a dramatic change from their attitudes in high school. In twelfth grade, 20 percent of men and 30 percent of women had said this was a very important goal, while by 1986 only 7 percent of men and 9 percent of women gave this response.[4] We will explore later in this chapter the relationship of higher education to these changes. Have fourteen years of life experience suppressed the idealism of these people? Have trends in American culture from the early 1970s to the late 1980s influenced their thinking? While our data cannot provide the last word, both individual life cycles and societal context have probably had an impact.

Another dimension of civic commitment is belief in the importance of "being a leader in the community," which is similar to Verba and Nie's (1972) concept of civic mindedness. It implies commitment to make a contribution to the larger community, beyond one's own political or interest group. It does not connote social criticism or conflict. These are associated with the previous goal of commitment to social justice. On the other hand, to be a community leader is to stand apart from the crowd in a way that many Americans do not welcome. Riesman et al., describing the "other-directed" character of modern Americans, put it graphically: "The effort is to cut everyone down to size who stands up or stands out in any direction. . . . Overt vanity is treated as one of the worst offenses, as perhaps dishonesty would have been in an earlier day. Being high-hat is forbidden" (Riesman, Glazer, and Denny 1955, 93). Indeed, people may not feel competent to act as community leaders. This may help to explain why only 3 percent said this goal is very important. This, too, represents a significant change from the attitudes expressed during the senior year in high school, when 10 percent rated this goal very important. While women were more committed to social justice, men were more committed to being community leaders. Both in high school and fourteen years later, men are almost twice as likely as women to rate community leadership very important.[5] This reflects traditional role expectations for men and women. Men are supposed to be concerned with leadership and power and women with helping others.

We have seen, then, varying patterns during the first fourteen years after high school. Voting rates rose, political discussion decreased slightly, and political activities remained about the same. Work in community organizations and volunteer activities increased only slightly. By 1986, there was considerably more engagement in church activities and youth organizations. But commitment to social justice and community leadership—the explicit statements of civic commitment—declined, changing more than any of the other indicators of concern for the common good.

Women and men exhibited diverse patterns and changes in civic commitment, but what trends are apparent between blacks and whites? Some tendencies are similar: in the fourteen years after high school both blacks and whites became more likely to vote and to work in community groups, youth and volunteer organizations and church activities. People of both races became less committed to social justice and community leadership. Political discussion and political activism, in contrast, declined slightly among whites but not among blacks. Only in youth organizations did white participation increase more than black. Most striking are differences in the starting and most recent levels of commitment. In both 1974 and 1986 blacks were more than twice as likely as whites to be active in community groups, although the activism of both blacks and whites increased slightly. Similarly, in 1972 and again in 1986, blacks were over twice as likely as whites to choose commitment to social justice and community leadership as very important life goals. Blacks in 1974 were less likely to vote than whites but had caught up by 1986. These differences suggest that the development of civic commitment varies for black and white young adults as it does for men and women. In general, blacks are more likely than whites to maintain or increase their level of commitment.[6] How higher education is related to these changes is our next concern.

For all but one of the forms of civic commitment discussed so far, the more postsecondary education, the more commitment. The pattern is especially strong in voting and political discussion. Each successive level of education is associated with higher levels of voting, from 61 percent of people with only high school to 89 percent of those with advanced degrees. Similarly, for political discussion, the range of those highly engaged is from 32 to 59 percent. Even in political activities, community groups, and volunteer work, where total participation is only 6 percent, people with advanced degrees are over twice as active as those with only high school. Patterns are similar for church-related activities and commitment to social justice and community leadership; the only exception is work in youth organizations. The sharp contrast between people of differing educational levels suggests that higher education has a particularly strong impact on civic commitment. We will assess this influence in our analyses throughout the rest of the chapter.

EDUCATIONAL ATTAINMENT
AND POLITICAL INVOLVEMENT

How does higher education affect political participation? The level of engagement in politics is highly stable. Tables 4.2 (columns one and two) and 4.3 show that people who were more involved than others right after high school were more active in 1986 as well, as indicated by the large coefficients for "previous activities." For example, with effects of differences in education and background removed, people who voted in 1974 were over two and one-half times as likely to vote in 1986 as those who had not. Similarly, all else being equal, those frequently involved in political discussion in 1974 were almost four times as likely to be more involved in 1986 as those who were not.

Does higher education modify these tendencies? Level of educational attainment has strong independent effects on voting, political discussion, and activism, when we control for background factors and previous participation. The odds that a person with an advanced degree will vote are over three times the odds for a person with only a high school education. The bachelor's degree creates odds two and one-half times those of high school graduates. Having less than two years of postsecondary education produces odds one and one-half times as high. Educational attainment is clearly related to this modest act of participation in the political system.

Political discussion—with family, friends, and fellow workers—reflects a higher level of political awareness and interest, evidencing at least the beginnings of "civic consciousness" (Janowitz 1983). Educational level clearly affects political discussion, for the higher the educational attainment, the more likely respondents were to increase their level of political discussion during these years. However, beyond political discussion, we have seen that only 5 percent of the thirty-two year old respondents participated actively in politics. Higher education again makes a difference, but only in the case of advanced degrees.

Why does higher education have these effects? It is conventional to attribute the greater participation of more educated persons to knowledge and skills gained in schooling. Presumably, education increases abilities to read, write, think, and participate critically. Even if we can assume this—and there is little empirical evidence to go on—it is possible that the relevant knowledge and skills are learned outside the classroom. For example, a student who has overcome typical college registration obstacles for four, six, or eight semesters may be better prepared to deal with the difficulties of voter registration. One who has

Table 4.2
Effects of Educational Attainment on Civic Goals and Activities

	Voted	Political Discussion	Political Activities	Community Groups	Volunteer Work	Youth Organizations	Non-Worship Church Activities	Commitment to Social Justice	Commitment to Community Leadership
Postsecondary Educational Attainment									
Less than Two Years College	1.55**	1.25**	1.22	1.75	1.01	1.18	1.19	.95	1.19
Two or More Years College	1.68**	1.39*	1.40	1.86	.73	.89	1.26	1.04	1.23
Bachelor's Degree	2.46**	1.52*	1.82*	2.38**	.53**	.74	1.43	1.09	1.82***
Advanced Degree	3.17***	2.27***	1.96*	2.76**	.51*	.93	1.42	1.54*	2.63***
Background Factors									
Whites	.75	.61*	.47**	.67**	1.60	1.58	.71	.38***	.59**
Women	1.18	.83*	1.36*	1.56*	1.47**	2.09*	1.47*	1.40***	.74**
Family Socioeconomic Status	1.02	1.03	1.04	1.04	.99	.99	.96*	1.00	1.02
Academic Abilities	1.05	1.03	1.00	1.00	1.01	1.00	1.01	.99	.94**
Interaction Effects									
Gender x Less than Two Years						.77			
Gender x Two or More Years						.73			

	N.A.								
Gender x Bachelor's Degree							.57		
Gender x Advanced Degree						.27*			
Previous Activities and Goals									
Medium[a]	N.A.	1.39	2.36**	2.54	2.10*	2.14*	2.27***	2.05***	2.62***
High[b]	2.56***	3.89**	2.71***	1.65	1.98***	1.97**	6.01***	3.85***	5.85***
-2 Log Likelihood	4930.90	6980.82	4566.97	3000.74	5627.06	5607.03	8915.28	8306.73	6673.86

N = 5409

* p< .05   ** p < .01   *** p < .001

NOTES: Figures in this table are the effects on the odds of being higher rather than lower on a particular goal or activity based on logistic regression. Each category of educational attainment is compared with the reference category of those having no more than a high school education. Each category of previous goals or activities is compared with the reference category of low on a scored variable or "Not Important" or "Not at All" on a trichotomous variable. Voting is compared with not voting.

[a]Intermediate values on a scored variable: "Somewhat Important," "Member Only."
[b]High values on a scored variable: "Very Important," "Active Participant"; voted.

Effects of Educational Attainment on Participants in Youth Organizations Conditional on Gender	
	Advanced Degree
Men	.93
Women	.25
Only statistically significant conditional effects are included.	

Table 4.3
Effects of Educational Attainment on Political Activities

	Political Activities
Postsecondary Educational Attainment	
Less than Two Years	.17 (.04)
Two Years or More	.15 (.03)
Bachelor's Degree	.29 (.06)
Advanced Degree	.68*** (.10)
Background Factors	
Whites	-.37 (-.04)
Women	-.23* (-.06)
Family Socio-economic Status	.00 (.01)
Academic Abilities	-.00 (-.02)
Previous Activities	.36*** (.37)
R^2 =	.16

N = 5409
* p < .05   ** p < .01   *** p < .001

NOTES: Figures in this table are unstandardized regression coefficients (standardized coefficients are in parentheses).
Each category of educational attainment is compared with the reference category of those having no more than a high school education.

learned to socialize with diverse groups of people may be better prepared to take part in political discussions as a young adult. Students who find out how to ask for what they need from faculty or administrators may be more able, as adults, to approach civic officials. These skills, of course, might be learned in noneducational settings, too.

More important than knowledge or skills, however, may be attitudes, including a sense of political efficacy. As Meyer (1977) suggests, students adopt the personal and social qualities appropriate to the status their degree confers upon them. Adults behave as people of their educational status are supposed to.

People with higher degrees are expected to be responsible citizens. And as Meyer further points out, more education could affect the sense of political efficacy by making people in fact more politically influential.

In any case, we can observe here how higher education separates people into statuses, affecting subtly their expectations and behavior and thus their access to political power. This illuminates a paradox of American politics discussed by Verba and Nie (1972). On the one hand, political participation in the United States does not take place in terms of explicit class-based ideologies. Political parties are broad coalitions of diverse groups cutting across social class lines. Class conflict and class interests are seldom discussed openly in political campaigns. On the other hand, the association between social class and level of participation is stronger in the United States than in six other democracies they studied.[7] Working-class persons are more likely to vote and be active in politics in those nations with parties and ideologies clearly representing their interests. Where inequality is seldom discussed openly, political participation is more unequal than in societies with class-based political parties. In the United States, people of high educational status participate more, consequently gaining more material benefits from the political system.

Apart from these issues, striking gender differences appear. We expect women's political activity to be slightly less than men's, partly because their educational attainment is slightly lower. Recall that among this high school class 38 percent of men achieved bachelor's degrees or higher, while 33 percent of women did so. However, when the influence of educational attainment and other background factors are separated out, women are still less likely to engage in political discussion and activities than men. The influence of being female is independent of the effects of educational attainment. This finding is entirely consistent with data gathered twenty years earlier in the United States and six other nations (Verba, Nie, and Kim 1978). At that time, women took part in politics less than men, but the gap was smallest in the United States. This gender gap, while still small, persists. In this respect, the pace of social and cultural change is glacial. In spite of the activity of women's movements in the 1970s and 1980s, in spite of continuing gains in educational attainment for women, gender differences persist. Many women apparently still think of themselves as less appropriately involved in political action. Simultaneously, the expectations and behavior of men in positions of power and in the voting booth may limit the activity of women. The pervasive inhibiting factors limiting the political role of women postulated by Verba, Nie, and Kim continue to operate.

Does higher education affect men and women differently with respect to their later political interest and activity? Our finding of no significant gender differences here differs from that of Verba, Nie, and Kim who found women converting their education into all three types of political commitment (voting, discussion, and activism) at higher rates than men. Age differences between the samples may explain the variations in results. While our respondents are all about thirty-two years old, Verba, Nie, and Kim studied adults of all ages. Political participation tends to increase until middle age or beyond (Verba and Nie 1972). Educational attainment may enhance women's political activity increasingly as they move beyond the stage of child rearing. College may have delayed effects on women's voting and other political activity that become apparent only as they grow older.

Race differences are also present here. Blacks are more likely than whites of equal educational attainment to engage in political discussion.[8] As a consequence of their experience as a deprived group, blacks in the United States develop a self-conscious awareness of their group membership. This becomes an increasingly important resource for political involvement in adulthood (Verba and Nie 1972; Ellison and London 1992). Black members of our sample are also more likely than whites to believe that forces outside themselves are directing their lives, as we will show in chapter 5. Awareness of constraining social conditions may motivate blacks to pay close attention to what is going on in politics, in contrast to the indifference of relatively satisfied whites.

EDUCATIONAL ATTAINMENT AND COMMUNITY ACTIVITIES

How did higher education affect participation in other community activities? With respect to community centers, neighborhood improvement, and social action groups, persons with bachelor's and advanced degrees were twice as likely as the reference group of those with no postsecondary education to increase their involvement (Table 4.2, column three). Higher education also enhances participation in volunteer work, such as work in hospitals. Respondents with bachelor's and advanced degrees are over twice as likely as those who did not go to college to join volunteer efforts (Table 4.2, column four). Apart from educational level and other background factors, women are more likely than men to participate in both community organizations and volunteer work.

Youth organization work, such as leadership in Scouts and Little League, is different from the other measures of civic engagement in two respects. First, this is the one civic activity in this study in which the higher the level of education, the less the participation. Members of the class of 1972 who did not obtain any postsecondary education and those who finished less than two years of college were most likely to do youth work—17 percent of them were active (Table 4.1). As level of education increased, participation decreased, with only 9 percent of advanced degree graduates taking part. When we take account of background factors and previous youth work, we observe that bachelor's and advanced degree holders are still only half as likely to do youth work as those who did not go to college (Table 4.2, column five).

Youth organization participation is also unique among the civic activities we consider because the effects of higher education, especially obtaining advanced degrees, are significantly different for men and women. Earlier in this chapter we pointed out the increase in youth work among women during the fourteen years after high school. By 1986, women were half again as likely to participate as men. However, for women the effect of obtaining advanced degrees is dramatic—women with advanced degrees are only about one-fourth as likely as women with high school education to participate, while men with advanced degrees are not significantly different from high school graduates. (See Table 4.2, column six and effects conditional on gender at the bottom of table). The dramatically lower rate of youth group participation for people with more education is primarily due then, to differences among women.

Why is the relationship of this activity to higher education so different from that of other civic activities? People are almost certainly more likely to be youth leaders when they have children in these groups. The timing of marriage and the number and ages of children are also related strongly to the amount of higher education. Members of the class of 1972 who did not go to college married and began having children earlier; in the fourteen years after high school they were consistently more likely to have children than those who enrolled in postsecondary institutions (Eagle et al. 1988). One year after high school, 6 percent of this non-college group had children; four years after high school, 32 percent; and by 1986, 74 percent had children. In contrast, by 1986 only 42 percent of those with bachelor's degrees had children and generally the children were younger than those of non-college parents. Thus, by age thirty-two, people with less education are more likely to have school age children participating in youth groups.

Among women and men with advanced degrees, why are women less likely than men to work in youth organizations, a gender difference that does not appear in other types of civic activities? We suspect subtle differences in gender role expectations may play a part. Among unmarried people and people without children, we would expect men to volunteer as youth leaders more than women. Men may accept youth group responsibilities as part of their community leadership role, as expressions of their interest and skill in sports (see chapter 3), or even as extensions of their business and professional goals. Women without children may hesitate to work with mothers and their children, choosing other activities instead. Among married people with children, on the other hand, while men may work in youth groups for the reasons just mentioned, women, more oriented to the activities of their own children, are more likely to wait and do so when their children are old enough to participate. Most children of thirty-two year old women with advanced degrees have not yet reached this stage. These factors may explain why, among people with advanced degrees, men are more likely than women to volunteer for leadership in youth organizations.

Church-related activities bear a unique relationship to civic commitment. Bellah et al. argue that even when middle-class Americans are involved in political or community service activities, they lack a language to talk about their commitments apart from the dominant utilitarian or expressive individualism. Among the activities we analyze, non-worship church-related activities are most likely to be accompanied by a "second language," acknowledgement of goals and values beyond the individual. Church-related activities, we have seen, have a higher rate of participation than any other activity discussed in this chapter. Participation is higher at each successive level of post-secondary education (Table 4.1). Educational attainment, however, is not the crucial factor fostering participation. When we control for background factors and previous church-related activities, levels of education do not make a significant difference (Table 4.2, column seven).[9] The only influences that affect engagement in these activities are gender, family socioeconomic background, and previous participation. Women participate more than men in church-related activities; persons from families of higher socioeconomic status are less active than those from lower-status families. The most important factor, however, is previous level of participation. Those who were active soon after high school were six times more likely to be active in 1986. Church-related activities, presumably based on early commitments, are the most stable of the civic activities. Previous research showed that college-educated persons became more liberal religiously (Feldman and Newcomb 1969) and less likely to keep their traditional denominational affiliations (Astin 1977). There is no evidence in our data, however, that higher education diminishes participation in church-related activities themselves.

EDUCATIONAL ATTAINMENT AND CIVIC GOALS

Earlier we described the decline in commitment to civic goals of young adults during the fourteen years after high school. We now inquire how higher education affects these changes.

Only people with advanced degrees are significantly more committed to working to correct social and economic inequalities than high school graduates (Table 4.2, column eight). At the level of bachelor's degrees and below, educational attainment makes little difference. Professional norms, ideally, include a concern for serving society. Some observers contend that professions are those occupations that have been able to persuade the public that they serve society, thus gaining enough prestige to achieve their real underlying goals of wealth and power (e.g., Ritzer and Walczak 1986). Our data indicate that, at least on the individual level, professional and graduate education may perform some of this ideal function. It appears to foster an underlying commitment to service goals and ethical concerns. Undergraduate education, on the other hand, has no apparent effect on this goal.

Just as important as advanced degrees for commitment to social justice are race and gender. The odds of whites becoming more concerned about social justice are only about a third those of blacks. Women are almost one and one-half times as likely as men to become more committed. For blacks, early socialization as part of a minority ethnic group that has experienced a history of discrimination may in itself promote sensitivity to injustice. Our data indicate that in the years of early adulthood blacks, more than whites, continue to respond to social justice concerns, apart from their educational level or earlier degree of interest in such issues. While the effect of gender is not as strong as that of race, women also develop or maintain in these years more commitment than men to social justice. That this is due, as for blacks, to consciousness of being discriminated against is possible. But women's socialization into caring for others as opposed to men's socialization for achievement may be a better explanation for this difference.

Commitment to being a leader in the community, we have seen, also declined for our whole sample in the years of young adulthood. Yet those who do retain greater civic-mindedness in this sense are more likely to be people with bachelor's and advanced degrees (Table 4.2, column nine). The patterns in the data are clear and strong. Compared to high school graduates, the odds of being more committed to this goal are almost twice as high for bachelor's degree holders and even higher for those with advanced degrees. We see in these life goal changes the process described by Meyer (1977) in which young adults come to recognize the educational status they have achieved. They begin to define themselves in these terms and anticipate acting appropriately for people of their status. People with less education lower their expectations and accept their place as followers rather than leaders. Those with college degrees are not as likely to reduce their commitment to community leadership. People at all levels accept the definitions of themselves conferred by the educational system they have accepted as fair and legitimate.

Race and gender are important factors in commitment to community leadership. Blacks are more likely than whites to sustain or increase their commitment. As with the goal of social justice, we believe this is a result of their being part of a self-conscious minority group. While we have no direct evidence, we suspect many blacks think of "community" in more senses than do most whites. For blacks there is the wider community (town, city) and there is also the black community. Leadership in the community may refer to either. Blacks have two communities to be involved in, while whites who are not part of other ethnic enclaves have only one. While blacks suffer the consequences of lower status in the wider society (see chapter 2), they often have more encouragement to be leaders and more accessible leadership positions in the smaller ethnic community. What is most interesting is that, in spite of their continuing belief that their lives are constrained by external forces (see chapter 5), blacks have not given up either on working for social betterment or assuming leadership positions.

Women, on the other hand, are less likely than men to retain their commitment to community leadership during the young adult years. That as high school seniors, women were less likely than men to want to be community leaders reflected the traditional idea of their subordinate roles in society. Beyond these initial attitudinal differences, the conditions of women's lives at this time of the life cycle may also have influenced their outlook on community leadership. Multiple roles and responsibilities, especially working outside the home while at the same time bearing and rearing children, may reduce motivation to seek additional community responsibilities.

EFFECTS OF COLLEGE CHARACTERISTICS AND STUDENT CAREERS

Throughout this study we have found that attaining credentials in higher education has significant effects on changes in utilitarian, expressive, and civic goals and activities. Yet, institutional characteristics and student career differences only occasionally have any noticeable influence. Those isolated effects that do appear are tantalizing and suggestive. In this section, we examine the effects of college characteristics and student careers, which are presented in Tables 4.4 and 4.5.

The only college characteristic with statistically significant effects on any of the civic commitment outcomes is the proportion of students who are enrolled full time. This is an indicator of the intensity of campus life. The more full-time students, the more the campus environment involves and affects its students. Such campuses are more likely to schedule activities in the afternoons, and evenings and on weekends. Students have a better chance to spend their leisure time within the context of a campus community. There is more potential for involvement in extracurricular activities including sports and on-campus jobs, more social support and encouragement for participation, and more opportunity to exercise leadership in campus groups. As Astin (1985) argues, such environments are more likely to have a long-term impact on students. More involvement leads to more learning, more "value added" by the college experience. Although Astin stresses the individual student's residence on campus, we simply find no evidence of this difference. However, we do find that having higher proportions of full-time students significantly increases non-worship church activities. The college context, then, apparently makes a difference. This finding is especially remarkable when one remembers that we have controlled here for size of the student body and proportion of students who live on campus, as well as individual residence. The proportion of full-time students also has positive, but not statistically significant, effects on six of the other eight civic outcomes. This is in contrast to the apparently random and nonsignificant effects of other college characteristics.

Table 4.4
Effects of College Characteristics and Student Careers on Civic Goals and Activities

	Voted	Political Discussion	Community Groups	Volunteer Work	Youth Organizations	Non-Worship Church Activities	Social Justice	Community Leadership
College Characteristics[a]								
Student Enrollment	1.01	1.00	1.00	.99	1.00	1.00	1.00	1.00
Selectivity	.90	.98	.99	1.10	.92	1.04	.94	.99
Private Control	1.05	.79	.88	1.04	1.01	1.05	1.12	1.02
Full-Time Students	1.05	.97	1.05	1.09	1.04	1.09*	1.01	1.08
Vocational Emphasis	1.04	.91	.94	.95	1.01	1.03	.98	.95
Highly Residential	.91	1.14	.86	.84	.98	.91	.97	.96
Student Careers								
Business Major	1.02	.89	.86	1.00	1.13	1.02	.79	.99
Education Major	1.15	.83	1.03	1.10	1.69	1.25	1.24	1.02
Arts & Sciences Major	1.32	.98	.90	.55	1.05	.82	1.32	.78
Ever Lived on Campus	.98	.93	1.01	.79	.92	1.14	.97	.96
College Grades	1.03	1.03	1.14	1.13	1.13	1.17	.94	1.03
Postsecondary Educational Attainment								
Two Years or More	1.02	1.06	.92	1.26	.56*	.96	1.15	.95
Bachelor's Degree	1.68	1.24	1.27	1.25	.47**	.92	1.09	1.27
Advanced Degree	2.24*	1.76*	1.34	1.43	.92*	.88	1.51	2.18**

Background Factors

Whites	.76	.74	.51	.71	1.43	.83	.40***	.69
Women	1.18	.83	1.18	1.46	1.16	1.31	1.53**	.79
Family Socioeconomic Status	1.03	.99	1.04	1.02	.96	.96	1.02	1.03
Academic Abilities	1.00	1.27	.97	.99	.97	.98	.99	.93
Interaction Effects								
Gender x Less than Two Years						.77		
Gender x Two or More Years						.73		
Gender x Bachelor's Degree						.57		
Gender x Advanced Degree						.27*		
Previous Activities and Goals								
Medium[b]	N.A.	.67	1.89	2.78	2.17	2.32***	2.12***	2.52***
High[c]	2.35***	1.87	2.55**	1.06	1.86	6.43***	4.31***	5.98***
-2 Log Likelihood	1953.31	3047.41	2235.16	1515.96	2237.05	3913.06	3619.64	3071.22

N = 5409

* p < .05   ** p < .01   *** p < .001

NOTES: Figures in this table are the effects on the odds of being higher rather than lower on a particular value or activity. Each category of college major is compared with the reference category of all other majors. Each category of educational attainment is compared with the reference category of those having less than two years of postsecondary education. Each category of previous goals or activities is compared with the reference category of low on a scored variable, or "Not Important" or "Not at All" on a trichotomous variable. Voting is compared with not voting.

[a]For persons attending more than one institution, the one attended longest; in case of ties, the more recently attended.
[b]Intermediate values on a scored variable: "Somewhat Important," "Member Only."
[c]High values on a scored variable: "Very Important," "Active Participant," "Voted."

Table 4.5
Effects of College Characteristics and Student Careers on Political Activities

	Political Activities
College Characteristics[a]	
Student Enrollment	.04 (.02)
Selectivity	-.05 (-.02)
Private Control	.14 (.03)
Full-Time Students	-.03 (-.00)
Vocational Emphasis	-.01 (-.01)
Highly Residential	-.12 (-.02)
Student Careers	
Business Major	-.06 (-.01)
Education Major	-.13 (-.02)
Arts & Sciences Major	-.08 (.02)
Ever Lived on Campus	-.14 (-.03)
College Grades	.10 (.05)
Postsecondary Educational Attainment	
Two Years or More	-.09 (-.02)
Bachelor's Degree	.10 (.02)
Advanced Degree	.44 (.08)

Only one type of student career experience has significant effects on civic commitment—college grades make a difference in church-related activities. Each increment in the seven-step scale of college grades increases the odds of being involved in such activities 1.17 times. One might speculate that higher grades lead to higher self-esteem and a greater sense of personal

Table 4.5 (continued)

	Political Activities
Background Factors	
Whites	-.53
	(-.05)
Women	-.33*
	(-.07)
Family Socioeconomic	.01
Status	(.03)
Academic	-.00
Abilities	(-.05)
Previous	.37***
Activities	(.38)

$R^2 = .17$
$N = 2702$
* $p < .05$ ** $p < .01$ *** $p < .001$

NOTES: Figures in this table are unstandardized regression coefficients (standardized coefficients are in parentheses).
Each category of college major is compared with the reference category of all other majors.
Each category of educational attainment is compared with the reference category of those having less than two years of postsecondary education.

[a]For persons attending more than one institution, the one attended longest; in case of ties, the more recently attended.

efficacy, which, in turn, lead to higher rates of participation. However, as chapter 5 will show, the relationship of grades to these personality outcomes, while positive, is not statistically significant. College grades, of course, reflect not only academic skills, but motivation and self-discipline as well. The association between grades and church activities suggests that individual characteristics that lead to higher grades may also motivate greater participation in some kinds of civic activity.

Other student career differences have no significant effects on civic commitment. However, majoring in education does influence participation in youth organization leadership to a degree that is of substantive interest.[10] Education majors are more likely than business, arts and sciences, and other majors to engage in youth organization leadership. Education majors, trained to work with children and youth, have the skills and predisposition to be involved in this kind of volunteer work. Moreover, many of their activities are probably extensions of their responsibilities as teachers.

CONCLUSIONS: HIGHER EDUCATION, GENDER, RACE AND CIVIC COMMITMENT

What can we conclude, then, about higher education and the willingness of graduates to be socially and civically engaged? How do the facts about higher education and young adulthood illuminate the hopes of Jefferson, Dewey, and Boyer? And does American higher education in the late twentieth century contribute to the solution of the problems defined by *Habits of the Heart* (Bellah et al. 1985)?

It is abundantly clear that achieving bachelor's and advanced degrees enhances participation in political and community activities. With respect to the two civic goals—social justice and community leadership—college education slows down the general decline in commitment. Our analysis, controlling for earlier commitments, strengthens the evidence for these conclusions. Only participation in youth organizations is an exception, a phenomenon apparently related to marital status and number and age of children.

Moreover, it is primarily certificates and degrees, that is, educational status, rather than college characteristics or student careers, that enhance civic commitment. Meyer is right about this. The far stronger influence of educational attainment is shown clearly in Table 4.6. The first column shows that educational attainment adds significantly to background factors and previous goals and activities in explaining participation in voting, political discussion, youth organizations, and the goal of community leadership. In contrast, college characteristics and student experiences add significant explanatory power only for church-related activities. Apart from the characteristics of institutions and the different educational experiences of students, educational level has powerful effects. The educational status of these adults carries with it certain roles and expectations and the graduates adopted the appropriate qualities.

The enhancement of civic commitment by higher education is substantially the same for women and men. Only for participation in youth organizations is there a gender difference in education effects. Women with advanced degrees are considerably less likely than men with advanced degrees to volunteer as leaders in youth organizations. Apart from education effects, however, women are more active and more committed than men on five of the outcomes analyzed in this chapter; men are more committed than women on only three. In community group participation, volunteer work, and the goal of social justice, women start at higher levels than men as high school seniors and remain ahead as they climb the educational ladder. Rising educational status increases civic commitment for both gender groups, but it does not change the gap. College seems to reinforce rather than alter early socialization and traditional group structures and norms that make volunteer and community work and espousing idealistic social goals part of women's roles.

In contrast, political activities, political discussion, and the goal of community leadership tend to be masculine commitments. Upon high school graduation, women are as likely as men to be involved in political activities and discussion. By the age of thirty-two, however, men have become more politically engaged. Community leadership is a goal more often valued by men at high school graduation and this pattern continues into adulthood.

We have seen that race figures significantly in civic commitment. On five indicators, blacks are more committed than whites to civic goals and activities; whites are more committed than blacks on none.[11] This persistent race effect, like the influence of gender, has implications for the concerns we share with Bellah et al. about civic commitment in American society.

Ironically, it is just those groups excluded from civic participation in colonial America, blacks and women, who may have most to offer in reviving civic commitment in the future. Bellah and his coauthors use the civil rights movement as one example of the kind of social commitment they espouse. The civil rights movement was not concerned merely with individual rights and privileges. It was also a movement to transform the moral or social ecology of the society "the web of moral understandings and commitments that tie people together in community" (1985, 335).

One black scholar criticized the authors of *Habits of the Heart* for limiting themselves to the civil rights movement of the 1960s (Harding 1988). This approach, he says, ignores many earlier contributions of black scholars and writers to American cultural consciousness. Harding also points out that by emphasizing middle-class whites, they fail to recognize the contributions to civic commitment of middle-class blacks, with their "razor-sharp memories of poverty, joblessness, protest, and despair" (1988, 80).

Similarly, feminist scholars have noted the brief treatment of the women's movement in *Habits of the Heart* (Albert 1988). Bellah et al. do grant that women exhibit moral sensibilities that have much to contribute to the common good. But the women's movement, at least so far, has stressed the need and right of women to be individualistic, assertive, and autonomous. Bellah

Table 4.6
The Significance of Educational Attainment, College Characteristics, and Student Careers in Explaining Civic Goals and Activities

Voting	Educational Attainment	College Characteristics and Student Careers
	*	n.s.
Political Discussion	*	n.s.
Political Activities	n.s.	n.s.
Community Groups	n.s.	n.s.
Volunteer Work	n.s.	n.s.
Youth Organizations	*	n.s.
Non-Worship Church Activities	n.s.	*
Social Justice	n.s.	n.s.
Community Leadership	**	n.s.
n.s. – not significant * p < .05 ** p < .01		

NOTE: Results are based on f-tests for linear regression or analogues in the case of logistic regression (see Appendix B). Column one reflects the improvement of fit achieved by adding the dummy variables for educational attainment over a model using only background variables and prior values of the dependent variable. Column two reflects improvement of fit when the college characteristics and individual experiences are added to the model tested in column one (i.e., background, previous characteristics, and educational attainment).

and his colleagues emphasize social movements that go beyond individualism to an emphasis on the common good. They could take hope from these American women who were high school seniors in 1972. Most of these women probably do not consider themselves feminists. They are committed to the values of home and family (see chapter 3). In some respects they are traditional in outlook, for they are less involved in political discussion and activities and are less committed to being community leaders than men—at least at this age. Nevertheless, more than men, they are involved in a wide range of civic activities and they are more committed to working for social justice. These women are more likely sources of the kind of civic commitment that would sustain new social movements for changing American society.

Similarly, the black high school graduates of 1972, conscious of their group membership and of the traditions of the black community and the civil rights movement, are more committed to the civic goals and activities we examine here. Blacks more than whites have a recent and vigorous tradition of advocating social reform. We believe that, emerging from the rich ethnic diversity of the United States today, other minorities also will contribute to currents of social change. They will probably resemble blacks in their general patterns of commitment, though there will be variations in detail.[12]

While a few years of higher education are unlikely to change deeply embedded personality traits, values, or commitments, we have seen that educational attainment does, in fact, make a difference in civic commitment. This became clear after we took account of gender, race, family background, academic abilities, and earlier goals and activities. Bachelor's and advanced degrees, especially, are linked with higher levels of civic commitment. People who achieved these statuses do behave as more responsible citizens. They are two to three times more likely than those with no college education to vote, discuss politics, join community groups, and do volunteer work. Moreover, higher education slowed down the decline of idealism in the early adult years. Graduates with advanced degrees are over twice as likely to value community leadership and are half again more likely to want to work for social justice than persons with no postsecondary schooling. The high hopes of educational philosophers are not completely fulfilled, since so few persons are actually engaged in civic life. Yet the system of higher education, conferring new status upon its graduates, enhances their commitment as adults to the common good.

NOTES

1. For a thorough review of this literature, see Pascarella and Terenzini, Chapter 7 (1991).

2. For several reasons, these voting rates are higher than statistics often quoted in the national media. For example, it is often reported that 53.1 percent of American adults voted in the 1984 presidential election. The first two reasons have to do with the nature of the NLS-72 sample and questionnaire wording; the others are endemic to research on voting.

First, our sample excludes about 16 percent of the age group, all those who dropped out of high school before the spring of their senior year. Those with less than a high school education would be less likely to vote.

Second, the questionnaire item in both 1974 and 1986 asked not just about one presidential election, but whether respondents had voted in any local, state, or national election during the two previous years. In both years this would have included, for most respondents, one presidential election, one off-year general election, and two primary elections.

Third, voting rates in sample surveys are always higher than those based on population estimates and official vote counts. The latter tend to underestimate voting, because they are based on the total voting age population, including those institutionalized, people in the Armed Forces, persons who cast spoiled ballots that are not counted, people who vote but not for president, and people whose votes for write-in candidates are not counted. Wolfinger and Rosenstone (1980) discuss this thoroughly. In 1984, for example, the Current Population Survey of the United States Census reported 59.9 percent voting for president, while the U.S. Census figures based on population estimates were 53.1 percent (U.S. Bureau of the Census 1989).

Fourth, some people, reluctant to admit they have not been good citizens, might report that they voted even if they have not. Wolfinger and Rosenstone (1980) discuss this phenomenon. However, their data are from personal interview surveys rather than anonymous mail questionnaire surveys. In the latter, the social pressure for respondents to say they have voted would be considerably less. Still, there may be some degree of misreporting in our data. If so, ironically, this would give further support to our theory that people think they should adopt behavior commensurate with the status conferred by their schooling.

3. For political discussion the difference between men and women is statistically significant, but not for voting or political activities. Respondents were also asked if they ever held an office in a political party or were elected to a government job. Only 1 percent of the respondents had ever held either kind of office. Although higher education was related to this in the expected direction, the results were not statistically significant.

4. The differences in 1972 were statistically significant; in 1986, they were not.

5. Again, the difference is statistically significant in 1972, but not in 1986.

6. The sample of blacks, however, suffered from considerable attrition and, hence, biases of unknown magnitude. Perhaps those blacks not reachable in 1986 were more likely to become politically disengaged.

7. Verba and Nie use a combined measure of income, occupational prestige and educational level as their indicator of social class.

8. Blacks are also more likely than whites, with all else equal, to participate in voting and political activities, but the difference is not statistically significant.

9. People with postsecondary education are more likely to participate in church-related activities than those without post-

secondary education, but the differences are not statistically significant.

10. The effect of majoring in education on youth organization leadership has less than 10 percent probability of occurring by chance, rather than the 5 percent level we have used as our criterion elsewhere.

11. Blacks who graduate from high school do not represent all blacks, however. And as we discuss in Appendix B, attrition of blacks from the study sample leads us to be cautious in generalizing. Nevertheless, we can say that a significant segment of black high school graduates are socially committed as young adults and even increase this commitment.

12. This does not mean that minority groups will not clash with one another under economic conditions fostering conflict. Of course, on sampling and methodological grounds we have had to omit attention to groups of new immigrants—such as those of Hispanic and Asiatic background—who were not represented in sufficient numbers in the early 1970s when members of our sample were high school seniors.

5

In Pursuit of Self

I could've had class and been somebody. Real class. Instead of a bum, let's face it, which is what I am. It was you, Charley.

Budd Schulberg, *On the Waterfront*

The taxicab ride of Marlon Brando as Terry Malloy and Rod Steiger as his brother, Charley, is probably the most memorable scene of the film, *On the Waterfront*. Destroying the dignity of the individual through betrayal has sure-fire box-office appeal and made it one of the most celebrated scenes in cinematic history. The pathos of the scene seared itself into the imaginations of viewers of all strata by starkly dramatizing Terry's crushed aspirations, his loss of self-respect, and his impotence in the face of the powerful mob.

How we conceive ourselves is vital, especially in America. Two dimensions of self-conception are salient cultural preoccupations: how positive is the individual's self-regard and how effective does the individual believe self-choice to be in determining his future?

If college attendance and, especially, graduation bestow a new status and identity, changing attitudes toward both one's self and one's educational institution ought to echo these transitions clearly. In this chapter we look inward, toward effects on self-perceptions. Meyer never deals with the issue directly, but improving self-concept as a consequence of increasing levels of educational attainment is certainly consistent with his allocation-credentialing theory. In the next chapter we look outward, toward how individuals respond to their educational experiences.

In this chapter we first deal with conceptual issues and earlier research on self-concept. Second, we describe how educational attainment, gender, and race are related to self-esteem and self-direction as two major components of self-concept. Third, holding constant all four background factors and the 1972 values of self-esteem and self-direction, we see whether educational attainment works changes in self-esteem and self-direction for the total sample. (Throughout, we also continue to seek out the differences between men and women, blacks and whites, and those with differing academic abilities and socioeconomic origins.) Fourth comes a search for the effects of college characteristics and academic careers. Fifth, we place the findings in the general context of such issues as socialization and allocation. Finally, our chapter epilogue critiques the individualistic nature of these concepts and their cultural origins.

EDUCATION AND SELF-CONCEPT

Smart and Pascarella epitomize the research agenda for almost all American educational psychologists and educators: "Knowledge of the extent to which the collegiate experience contributes to the positive development of students' self-concept and the degree to which those contributions persist when students leave the campus setting is essential to informed assessments of the effectiveness of American higher education" (1986, 4). Thus, the mandate of the student of higher education is to ascertain how education, educational institutions, and educational experiences may function for the individual. Students presumably become happier and better adjusted while they become more competent and more effective. Higher education, then, should enhance both the individual's self-evaluation and sense of control over what happens.

Some statements are much more sweeping and holistic than Smart and Pascarella's. For instance, Bowen maintains that the goals of American higher education are "directed toward the growth of the whole person through the cultivation not only of the intellect and of practical competence but also of the affective dispositions, including the moral, religious, emotional, social, and aesthetic aspects of the personality" (1977, 33). An examination of the catalogs and promotional materials of virtually any four-year college convinces us that such claims for well-roundedness are typical. Since present data pertaining to self-concept are limited, we cannot possibly deal specifically with all these outcomes.

Self-esteem[1] and self-direction[2] are two dimensions of self-concept that have increasingly appeared over the last generation in studies aimed at understanding the relations between self and social context.[3] Corresponding to them in popular consciousness and self-help publications, respectively, are the all-too-familiar concepts of "feeling good about yourself" and "taking charge of your own life." Self-esteem is a general evaluation of one's self, while self-direction is the belief that the self, not other factors, controls one's future.

Both themes are clearly individualistic. They figure into the extensive discussion of the self and the rise of the therapeutic by Bellah and his associates, following Philip Reif's *The Triumph of the Therapeutic* (1966). However, self-esteem and self-direction, reduced to nearly contentless opinion about the self, is one aspect of the issue. Witness the following profound, acerbic critique: "Judgments of character as 'self-esteem' and of action as what 'works for me now' only dimly depict the meaning of work well done, a family well raised, and a life well lived, as if all such judgments were merely a matter of subjective feeling" (Bellah et al. 1985, 137).

EARLIER FINDINGS

Much systematic empirical work on self-esteem and self-direction among college students has taken place since the publication of Feldman and Newcomb's exhaustive overview of the effects of higher education in 1969. In addition, most of the work useful in assessing change over time has been conducted since then.

Alexander Astin's large landmark study analyzed more than two hundred thousand college students at the beginning and end of the four undergraduate years (1967-1971) at three hundred schools. Astin concluded that there are changes in students' self-concept[4] after entering college, specifically "a more positive self-image" (1977, 67).[5] Since the sample included only those going to college and since the time period was only four years and restricted to the college years, Astin does not deal entirely successfully, as he himself admits, with the possibility of maturation effects or the durability of the changes for the long term.

Using NLS-72 data, Smart, Ethington, and McLaughlin found that those who went to college were initially higher in self-image and self-confidence[6] than those who did not (1985, 14). They also found that the self-image scores of all respondents became more positive with each wave from 1972 and 1979. The latter suggested to them a maturational effect. Yet, with each wave of the survey, the gap in self-image widened between educational attainment levels. Smart and his associates inferred that collegiate experience *"tended to reinforce and increase the more positive self-image held initially by college-bound youth"* (1985, 14; emphasis theirs). However, that this effect was most clearly enhanced for those receiving college degrees suggests to us a credentialing effect. In general, the changes observed in self-confidence were all more modest. That self-confidence increased for all respondents over the seven-year time span again seemed a maturational effect. As with self-image, to the degree that students are exposed to the collegiate experience, self-confidence increases, but not by very much, and the effect is greatest for those attaining the bachelor's degree.

Kanouse et al. (1980) found similar generally rising trends in self-esteem over the first four years of the NLS-72 study, as others had with earlier studies (Bachman and O'Malley 1977; Carlson 1965; Engel 1959; Kaplan 1975). But they also found that most of the small initial differences between types of post-secondary activities[7] tended to disappear as time went by. With self-direction they found that scores also increased over the four-year period but that they increased much less than did the self-esteem scores.[8]

Using NLS-72 data, Behuniak and Gable found that both self-esteem and self-direction scores rose throughout the four college years,[9] but that there was a "consistently large jump in scores just prior to graduation" (1979, 5). They interpret this as stemming from "even the expectation of advancing status and earnings, and the perception of increased competencies associated with graduation" (1979, 5). It does not make much sense to expect competencies themselves to have increased dramatically immediately before graduation, and to explain this in terms of *perceived* competencies is a circular use of the self-esteem and self-direction concepts. However, we wholeheartedly endorse the other half of their explanation, that of an anticipatory effect of certifying and allocation and the status-identity transformation.

Smart and McLaughlin (1985) examined a large national sample of those entering college and receiving a degree by 1980. This study used self-esteem to predict changes rather than solely as an outcome. They concluded that graduation from different types of colleges[10] had, other things being equal, differential effects on values, academic and social self-concepts, and early career satisfaction, that was significant but of merely "modest magnitude." In all, however, type of college accounted for less than 1 percent of the variation in outcomes (1985, 11), while the repeated measures of self-concept accounted for 14 percent.

Based on a longitudinal study of college students, Smart and Pascarella (1986, 12) concluded that there was a "clear and consistent" association between students' "educational degree attainment and their development of a more positive self-concept over a nine year period."[11] However, males consistently gained more than females on the three dimensions of self-concept they examined. To Smart and Pascarella, this was "especially unsettling" in view of increased female enrollments and Astin and Kent's plea to provide female students with "a sense of autonomy and self-worth that will enable them to overcome any handicaps stemming from their earlier socialization for dependence and conformity" (Astin and Kent 1983, 309). Smart and Pascarella also concluded that the characteristics of undergraduate institutions played a part in producing long-term changes in students' self-concepts. In particular, institutional selectivity enhanced academic and artistic self-concept scores for both sexes. In contrast, increases in the size of an institution helped increase social self-concept scores for both sexes, but did so for academic self-concepts only for men. Student goal and institutional commitment and their academic and social integration into the institutions (1986, 13) promoted positive changes in self-concept.

Pascarella and Terenzini conclude in their massive, thorough, and judicious synthesis of the many studies since Feldman and Newcomb that the studies employing statistical controls converge on the finding that self-esteem increases somewhat as a consequence not only of maturation but also of attending college (1991, 181-182). The effects of higher education on self-direction also indicate a somewhat enhanced perception of self-control. Thus, Pascarella and Terenzini conclude that attending college has significant and positive effects on self-direction but that the direct effect is small (1991, 231). They also conclude that, for the last generation, there is for self-direction "strong evidence of the presence of college effects independent of changes in the population" (1991, 231).

SELF-CONCEPTS IN 1986

Before the causal analysis, we show 1986 data describing how level of education, gender, and race correspond with self-concept. Table 5.1 presents these effects.

Table 5.1
Self-Esteem and Self-Direction in 1986 by Educational Attainment, Gender, and Race

	Self-Esteem	Self-Direction
Educational Attainment		
High School Only	-.16	-.16
Less than Two Years College	-.04	-.04
Two Years or More College	.04	.11
Bachelor's Degree	.12	.25
Advanced Degree	.23	.36
Gender		
Men	.09	.04
Women	-.06	.11
Race		
Black	.09	-.26
White	.01	.10
Total	.01	.08

N - 5409

NOTE: Mean scores.

Educational attainment is highly correlated with both sets of scores for 1986, but is, however, somewhat more highly related to self-direction than self-esteem.[12] Women differ from men in both self-esteem and self-direction, for they are lower on self-esteem and higher on self-direction. While blacks' self-esteem scores are higher than those of whites, their self-direction scores are dramatically lower. We shall expand on this below.

CHANGES IN SELF-CONCEPT FOR THE WHOLE SAMPLE

When appropriate controls are used, what affects self-concept for the whole sample and, then, for the college sample? First, what changes are there in self-esteem and self-direction between 1972 and 1986? Second, how are level of education, gender, and race related to self-esteem and self-direction in 1972 and 1986?

How do abilities and socioeconomic origins figure in? How are the findings to be interpreted?

For the whole sample, none of the categories of educational attainment significantly affects perceptions of self-esteem, although the direction of the relationship is, as expected, consistently positive (Table 5.2). Women, however, are much more likely than men to have shifted in a negative direction on the self-esteem scale, all else equal. Emergence into adulthood in America in many respects favors men in contrast to women. For example, occupational success has long contributed to adult self-esteem, and men can pursue it without being hampered by responsibility for housework and child rearing. Even with regard to the aging process, attitudes are more negative toward women than toward men. These gross findings may reflect that disparity.

However, when we take interactions of educational level and gender into account, our findings also call into question Smart and Pascarella's (1986) notion of "unsettling findings" concerning the decline in college women's self-confidence and the increase in men's. There is one significant interaction between gender and educational attainment category, that for women who have had two years or more of postsecondary education. However, all the gender differences are in the same direction, with women benefiting more than men at each level of education. Women with bachelor's degrees also fare significantly better than men with such degrees if we relax the confidence level to $P < .10$. There is a tantalizingly modest suggestion in the data that college women gain more in feeling good about themselves, whereas men gain more in the more specific aspects of the self-concept that Smart and Pascarella studied. As we noted in chapter 2, for each educational increment beyond high school women gain more than men in earnings. If money isn't everything and can't buy happiness, in the aggregate it does accompany increments of self-esteem for women, with educational attainment having enhanced them both. Neither race nor family socioeconomic status[13] nor academic ability has a significant impact on changes in self-esteem, but the 1972 measure of self-esteem is reasonably highly correlated with the 1986 measure.

Educational level is highly related to positive changes in self-direction, and this relationship is highly significant statistically for each group with two years or more of college.[14] Educational attainment is more highly related to changes in self-direction than in self-esteem. In addition, academic abilities as measured in high school play a surprisingly prominent role in enhancing perceptions of one's own self-direction over the fourteen-year period for the whole sample.[15] Do such measures become self-fulfilling prophecies through a process that includes labeling either by others or by oneself? Or, do the abilities they are supposed to measure manifest themselves in successful actions—especially in academic context—actions that then become a basis for the enhanced belief that one is controlling one's own destiny? Race,[16] gender,[17] and the socioeconomic status of the family of origin[18] have no effects on changes in self-direction.

For 1986 and 1972 the before-after measures of both self-direction and self-esteem are about equally highly correlated. There are no significant changes between 1972 and 1986 on either of the two measures of self-concept, for the average scores were virtually identical. This may mean that the changes observed by some other researchers may not be maturational-developmental effects for the whole cohort. Although our analysis does not reveal possible changes within different groups that may essentially cancel each other out in the aggregate, we also are examining a much longer time period than most observers, and consequently, effects may become attenuated.

Table 5.2
Effects of Educational Attainment on Self-Esteem and Self-Direction

	Self-Esteem		Self-Direction
Postsecondary Educational Attainment			
Less than Two Years	.07 (.04)	.03 (.01)	.04 (.02)
Two Years or More	.10 (.05)	-.02 (-.01)	-.14** (.07)
Bachelor's degree	.14 (.07)	.04 (.02)	.16** (.09)
Advanced degree	.20 (.07)	.13 (.05)	.22** (.09)
Background Factors			
Whites	-.14 (-.04)	-.14 (-.04)	.14 (.04)
Women	-.12 (-.07)	-.25** (-.14)	.03 (.02)
Family Socio-economic Status	.01 (.04)	.01 (.14)	.01 (.05)
Academic Abilities	.00 (.04)	.00 (.04)	.00*** (.12)

Table 5.2 (continued)

	Self-Esteem		Self-Direction
Interaction Effects			
Gender x Less than Two Years		.08 (.03)	
Gender x Two Years or More		.24* (.08)	
Gender x Bachelor's Degree		.04 (.02)	
Gender x Advanced Degree		.12 (.03)	
Previous Measurement	.28 (.26)	.28 (.26)	.25*** (.24)
R^2 =	.10	.10	.15
N = 5409			

* p < .05   ** p < .01   *** p < .001

NOTES: Figures in this table are unstandardized regression coefficients (standardized coefficients are in parentheses).
Each category of educational attainment is compared with the reference category of those having no more than a high school education.

Effects of Postsecondary Educational Attainment on Self-Esteem Conditional on Gender	
	Two Years or More
Men	-.01
Women	.07
Only statistically significant conditional effects are included.	

Whites and blacks do not change appreciably in either aspect of self-concept. Blacks are, however, significantly lower than whites in perceiving themselves as responsible for events affecting them positively while they are much higher in self-esteem. As we suggested in chapter 3, blacks may realistically perceive neither their acts nor their situations as created by themselves, but by social constraints. This viewpoint encourages blacks to be realistic about the locus of power in society and may lead to greater civic commitment among blacks, as we have seen in chapter 4. The 1970s were the high point of the overt collective expression of black resentment and rage. It is worth speculating that the declining self-direction scores for blacks may reflect additional obstacles thrown in the way of blacks, many or most of which are racism in one of its guises, especially the institutional racism of the era following the civil rights struggle.

CHANGES IN SELF-CONCEPT
AMONG THE COLLEGE SAMPLE

For those pursuing education after high school there are no strong relationships between *any* educational factor and the self-concept dimensions. Thus, characteristics of postsecondary institution and student careers have no effects.

Indeed, for the two self-concept measures for the college sample there were only three substantial relationships (accordingly, we do not present tables). Abilities are again related to college-goers' growing perception of self-direction as they were for the whole sample.[19] With the college sample, however, increases in abilities are slightly associated with decreases in self-direction, whereas with the total sample the relationship was slightly positive. Perhaps abilities play a part in admission to postsecondary education and thereby enhance the sense of self-direction, but abilities have little influence on self-direction once one is enrolled. Furthermore, it is not surprising that the pre- and post-measures of the self-concept measures are themselves quite highly related, as they were for the whole sample, appearing to indicate substantial stability or continuity in self-concept over an extended time period.[20]

However, there are a few modest hints of relationships between student careers and college characteristics and the outcome measures (if we relax the requirement for significance to P < .10). Grades affect self-direction positively, while majoring in arts and sciences does so negatively. Getting good grades may boost modestly a sense of empowerment. The arts and sciences milieu may slightly weaken the individual's sense of effective control over the future. It may be surprising that this effect is not greater in view of what we saw in chapter 2: the very real objective shortcomings of arts and sciences majors in the game of utilitarian success in the short term.

The relationships between educational attainment and the self-concept measures among those who went to college are, at least, in the expected direction and show successive small increases for both self-esteem and self-direction with each increment in attainment. However, none of these relationships is significant even at the .10 level. Despite the lack of substantial differences in self-concept among those with various levels of postsecondary education, the expected enhancement of self-esteem and self-direction we observe agrees with the findings of Smart and Pascarella (1986). Since our study deals with a considerably longer time span than theirs, a diminished strength of the relationships is not surprising.

Among those who went to college, the evidence of a credentialing effect on these global self-concept measures is unconvincing. The connection between higher educational processes, on the one hand, and self-esteem and self-direction, on the other, appears minimal. There may be two mechanisms operating, one a selection effect and the other, an effect of social comparison. First, the individuals have already been sorted into different educational institutions—one reason why college environments do not influence self-concept and individual student career factors barely do so. Second, when called upon to make a self-appraisal, people tend to select others like themselves as points of reference. They are, then, most likely implicitly to choose others similarly situated in the social structure.[21] If self-esteem measures are subject to these sorts of social influences, this should also be the case with self-direction measures, because of the complex internal-external judgment entailed. Thus, for reasons of selection and social comparison, one is likely to come out neither appreciably better nor worse on a global assessment scale than persons in categories objectively higher or lower than one's own.[22]

College women decline on both self-measures, but the decline is slight. College blacks show a slightly enhanced sense of self-direction, but slightly reduced self-esteem. The socioeconomic status of the family of origin confers a slight benefit in terms of enhanced scores on both of the measures.

Among those who went to college we have found, then, largely trifling differences in the effects of college characteristics, student careers, and background on self-concept. Adding educational attainment to a model that already incorporates background characteristics does not improve our ability to predict self-concept outcomes. In turn, adding college characteristics and student career factors to this model taking background factors, initial values on self-concept measures, and educational attainment into account also produces no significant improvement in the predictability of outcomes. In neither case is the model appreciably improved. Among those who went to college, neither educational attainment nor the characteristics of the college nor student careers make a difference. Only individuals' abilities significantly bring about positive change in the sense of self-direction.[23]

CONCLUSION

On balance, the findings for self-esteem and self-direction are less pertinent to the Meyer hypothesis than outcomes in other chapters. Concerning allocation, the findings are, then, not as convincing as for the effects reported elsewhere in this book. Yet, completing the bachelor's degree and an advanced degree yields major benefits to self-direction when the contrast is between either of these categories and the reference category of those with no postsecondary education. Such attainments may represent a critical threshold. Those with two years or more of college, though, suffer a net loss in self-direction. Could their eyes be on the, perhaps yet elusive, prize of a bachelor's degree in the face of obstacles to its attainment? That could explain their increased sense of loss of control over their destinies. College has one other effect: completing two years or more of college has a positive impact on women's self-esteem. Furthermore, neither college characteristics nor student career accounted for any major differences in outcomes.

Does any kind of education or training beyond high school help define an identity differentiating the person from those who only finished high school? Does "going on" become distinctive in itself? That is dubious. It is more likely that unmeasured initial factors explain this difference. Either environmental characteristics—such as family expectations and supportiveness—or personality characteristics—such as need for achievement—may well explain both the tendencies to go on and to grow in self-concept. The evidence presented in this chapter does not confirm the socialization hypothesis, though it does provide modest emphasis that those with college degrees are clearly more likely to perceive themselves as self-directed than those who have never attended college or who attended only to stop short of degree attainment.

In general, educational attainment interacts with gender such that women experience a greater boost to self-esteem than men for completing more than two years of college or the baccalaureate. Academic abilities have an enduring effect on sense of self-direction. Distinctive changes between men and women appear to be more a result of life experiences in the society that do not stem essentially from education. Since the blacks in our sample appear relatively successful, they do not necessarily have to shield themselves from a sense of self-blame for failure. The attribution of causal obstacles to the external environment suggests a collectively shared vocabulary of lack of personal control.

EPILOGUE: AMERICAN VALUES AND RESEARCH ON THE SELF

Self-concept research is intrinsically individualistic and reflects cultural preoccupations. Implicitly in social science study of self-esteem and self-direction is the belief that everyone should experience a positive self-evaluation as an end in itself. This perceptual and evaluational framework is highly individualistic. "Know no boundaries! Let yourself run free!" is how one Wall Street firm in the 1980s glorified untrammeled individual economic freedom on television. Robert Bellah and his associates (1985) have strong critical reservations about the overriding predominance of this vocabulary. We share them. We should not be surprised that these cultural values have invaded American social science, which now frequently sports the same vocabulary, albeit in more sophisticated form.

NOTES

1. Among the most influential discussions of self-esteem are those of Wylie (1974, 1979) and Rosenberg (1979, 1981). Also see Gecas (1982).

2. Self-direction will be more familiar to many readers as "locus of control," but we chose not to use that term, because the measure of self-direction we use is only roughly comparable to various locus of control measures. However, psychometricians typically have the luxury of working with small samples of individuals so that they are able more conclusively to demonstrate validity and reliability. The numbers of reliable and more or less validated measures of locus of control are many and the numbers of studies using them are large. Julian B. Rotter is the father of the concept in his seminal work (1966, 1975). See also Lefcourt (1981, 1983, 1984) for a comprehensive treatment of this concept and all the attendant issues, including the prodigious amount of research inspired by the concept.

3. Both of these factors have face validity, considerable empirical demonstration of validity, and a long history of frequent use. Most scholars treat self-esteem as an effect while they treat self-direction (or locus of control) as a cause. This is partly a matter both of disciplinary orientation and of ideology. Educational researchers and psychologists have tended to assume that the motives of individuals affect subsequent attainments. Some have argued for reversing the direction of causation, that is, for

holding educational attainment a consequence of self-concept. Yet others have argued for two-way causation and the development of reciprocal models incorporating time lags. To do so is necessary to establish a complete model of the causal process, but it would carry us far afield from our main purpose. The appropriateness of the assumptions regarding direction of causality is, of course, difficult to test. Indeed, both concepts can be both cause and consequence. Accordingly, baseline measurements of both are controls in our analysis so that we can isolate how educational factors affect self-evaluative outcomes apart from the initial values of these factors.

Assessment of these concepts and change in their empirical indicators has become a major component of educational research. To be sure, we have reservations about such measures themselves, emblematic as they are of the cultural preoccupation with the individual. The sociocultural context always affects, indeed permeates, the tests and measurement of psychological traits and processes. Such measures may succeed as contemporaneous reflections of people's responses to their situations as much as they serve as indicators of enduring internal states. Many researchers using these psychological measures take educational and occupational structures as "givens" for individuals to tackle by their own efforts. These concerns reflect our own disciplinary orientation and ideology.

Richards (1983) questioned the validity of both self-concept measures on the ground that they do not predict future achievements well. His argument has considerable merit and, consequently, we believe that less global measures are clearly indicated for prediction. Here, however, we are using them provisionally as indicators of outcomes.

In Appendix B we consider the scales of both concepts, and the reader may wish to consult the somewhat technical discussion there under Self-Esteem and Self-Direction.

4. Astin's measurements of self-concept differed from ours in that changes in self-ratings as above average or below average on a number of specified items is the criterion of change. Through factor analysis he isolated interpersonal self-esteem and intellectual self-esteem as components. The former included the items, leadership ability, popularity with the opposite sex, public speaking ability, social self-confidence, and popularity. The latter included intellectual self-confidence, academic ability, and mathematical ability. Since these are all more concrete than the global self-esteem and self-direction measures in NLS-72 and since the designs of the two studies are so different, direct comparisons are not possible.

5. As Astin acknowledges, however, "The absence of residence and other involvement variables in the 1967–1971 data precluded any direct examination of the relative importance of maturational and college effects" (1977, 66). With our data we will be able to address such matters. He found that interpersonal self-esteem increased among blacks and those with strong athletic interests at entry, while it declined for those with high academic ability. Residing in a dormitory during the freshman year also had positive effects, as did majoring in social sciences and persistence in college. High-ability students showed smaller increases than others in interpersonal self-esteem, but larger changes on almost all other measures, including intellectual self-esteem. He found positive effects on self-esteem only at private colleges or universities, and interprets this and the similar findings of others (Nichols 1967) as a result of the less impersonal environments of private institutions (Astin and Lee 1972). Astin also found no relation between an institution's selectivity and its effect on student's "ability self-concept," thus calling into question the notion that selective schools would negatively affect students with average ability but with an outstanding high school record.

6. Smart, Ethington, and McLaughlin's "self-image" and "self-confidence" are their two factors. The former is our "self-esteem," for the items comprising their "self-image" are indeed the familiar Rosenberg self-esteem items that we used. Their "self-confidence" factor, however, includes not only those comprising our self-direction measure but also items on some life goals. They do not present the factor loadings of items. While their sample and ours are both subsets of the NLS-72 sample, they are not identical. Accordingly, the comparability is crude, especially between our "self-direction" and their "self-confidence."

The inclusion of life goals items in their self-confidence measure creates some difficulties, particularly in terms of validity. As we shall see below, we found greater effects on self-direction than on self-esteem, while, in contrast, Smart and his coauthors found greater effects on self-image than on self-confidence. Probably the inclusion of life goals in the measure of self-confidence confounded measurements, for it is quite well established that life goals and values change at a decelerating rate as one grows older. Thus, one would expect a measure in which life goals and values were major components to change less than a more global and general measure of self-direction.

7. The specific activities or "tracks" are student (four-year, two-year, and vocational-technical); worker (full-time and part-time); military; homemaker; unemployed; and unclassified.

8. There were "sharp differences associated with postsecondary track [activity]" (Kanouse et al. 1980, 41). Students were much more highly "internal" than part-time workers and the unemployed, but these differences narrowed when initial background differences were taken into account. Among males, those entering the labor force or the military gained in internality of locus of control in the first year after high school more rapidly than those who continued their studies, as did males of high ability. To paraphrase Kanouse et al.'s interpretation, for some it may be a relief to get out of school and think they are exercising more control over their life than previously. Among women these effects were not found, but women with relatively low rank in the high school class showed stronger initial gains in self-direction than those whose rank was higher. Ability among women was not related to changes in locus of control. Ability was, however, strongly related to self-direction for the sample as a whole in each wave of the survey. Blacks started out displaying a slightly lower sense of self-direction than whites. They also showed weaker gains than whites in this regard so that a significant gap opens up between the races for both men and women over the first four years after high school.

9. Tomala and Behuniak, using the same data, found that females were consistently higher in self-direction and that males who dropped out of college were initially lower in self-direction than those who persisted, but that eventually this gap closed (1981).

10. They used a modified Carnegie Classification (Carnegie Commission on Higher Education 1973): major research university, doctoral-granting university, comprehensive college or university, selective liberal arts college, and general liberal arts college.

11. Smart and Pascarella used a sample composed only of those going to college and, from a set of items quite distinct from ours, defined through factor analysis three dimensions of "self-concept": "social," "academic," and "artistic."

12. Eagle et al. made a descriptive survey parallel to ours as a Contractor Report for the Center for Education Statistics (1988, 48-53). While they report their findings for each year of the survey, their observations pertain to self-esteem and self-direction for the total NLS-72 sample and lack the controls and other refinements we have invoked. They also do not include academic

abilities as a control baseline for analysis. Thus, their report is largely descriptive.

The self-esteem scores of men, higher than those of women in 1972, tend to rise consistently over the years, while those for women tend to fall, such that the gap in scores about doubles by 1986 (Eagle et al. 1988, 48). Socioeconomic status of NLS-72 students' families of origin is positively associated with their self-esteem scores for each survey year and this gap widens somewhat as time goes by, suggesting the persistent influence of social class. Educational attainment is also correlated positively with self-esteem. By 1986 there is some suggestive descriptive evidence of a certification-allocation effect. The racial categories, black, white, and Hispanic, do not differ significantly throughout all the follow-up waves of the survey, but the black self-esteem scores start out significantly higher than whites' in 1972. Our data show a similar difference between blacks and whites in 1972, but it is not statistically significant.

Blacks are, however, consistently lower in scores of self-direction than whites, with the gap widening between 1972 and 1974 and remaining fairly wide, but narrowing slightly in 1979 and 1986. High socioeconomic status of the family of origin seems to confer a persisting sense of self-direction from the very outset throughout all waves. Women start off higher than men in self-direction perceptions in 1972, but each year the gap tends to narrow, such that there is almost no gender difference in 1986. Finally, educational attainment makes for an almost identical pattern of differences with self-direction as it did for self-esteem, with highest self-direction scores accompanying a bachelor's or advanced degree—yet another suggestion of a certification-placement process.

13. Eagle et al. (1988) found that the socioeconomic status of NLS-72 students' families of origin is positively associated with their self-esteem scores for each survey year and that the differences increased somewhat with time, suggesting the persistent influence of social class. Our finding suggests that the effect of class origin is not direct, for it disappears once other factors are controlled.

14. Eagle and her associates (1988) found that educational attainment has an almost identical pattern of effects on self-direction as it did on self-esteem, with highest self-direction scores accompanying a bachelor's or advanced degree. The disparities we found between the effects of education on self-esteem and those on self-direction occurred after we used controls.

15. Both socioeconomic status and academic abilities are highly related to self-concept in both 1972 and 1986. Both

factors are related about twice as strongly to self-direction as to self-esteem. However, these factors are controls in this study, and complete examination of their consequences would carry us far afield. The inclusion of these controls would seem to allow qualified use of self-esteem and self-direction measures in multivariate models. Richards's (1983) attack on those who, without controlling for background factors, have used these measures as predictors of subsequent outcomes does not appear entirely applicable here. Here we are invoking appropriate background measures as controls, and we are not attempting to predict future educational or career aspirations or actual outcomes with self-concept measures. Our reservations about these measures are, unlike Richards's, only in part technical.

16. In Eagle et al.'s report (1988), blacks are consistently lower in scores of self-direction than whites, with the gap widening between 1972 and 1974 and remaining fairly wide, but narrowing slightly in 1979 and 1986. Our data with our sample suggests a highly significant difference between blacks and whites in both years, with a slight widening of the gap by 1986. However, the reasons for the widening of the gap are not discernable in our analysis.

17. According to Eagle and her associates, women start off higher than men in self-direction perceptions in 1972, but each year the gap tends to narrow such that there is almost no gender difference in 1986 (Eagle et al. 1988). Our data confirm this, for there is no significant difference between men and women by 1986, even when the influence of other factors is controlled.

18. High socioeconomic status of the families of origin seems to confer a persisting sense of self-direction from the very outset throughout all waves of Eagle et al.'s report (1988). However, it does not directly affect change in self-direction.

19. Both standardized and unstandardized Betas were -.01, with a significance of $P < .05$.

20. For self-esteem the Betas, respectively unstandardized and standardized, are .25 and .24, with $P < .001$. The corresponding figures for self-direction are .24 and .23, $P < .001$.

21. While this may be generally so, there may be exceptions. See Singer's thorough discussion (1981, 78-81). See also Rosenberg (1981, 593-624).

22. This parallels the small differences that background factors typically make in self-esteem in most other studies. One factor that may reduce such relationships is the very global nature of the scales themselves. Another is the greater homogeneity of a sample that all had some postsecondary education or training. Finally, there may be compelling reason to believe that

measures of specific (as opposed to global) aspects of self-concept might well show more effects of college milieux and educational attainment. Thus, self-esteem or self-direction for specific roles and contexts may well be the wave of the future in improving the reliability and validity of measures.

23. This leads us to add our voices to others in suggesting that more concrete and specific assessments of self-concept should be developed.

In Pursuit of Educational Experiences

*haven't got the nerve to break out of the bellglass
four years under the ethercone breathe deep gently
now that's the way be a good boy one two three four
five six get A's in some courses but don't be a grind
be interested in literature but remain a gentleman
don't be seen with Jews or socialists
and all the pleasant contacts will be useful in
Later Life
say hello pleasantly to everybody crossing the yard
         sit out looking out into the twilight of the
pleasantest four years of your life . . .
         and I hadn't the nerve
                  to jump up and walk out of doors and tell
         them all to go take a flying*
                                         Rimbaud
                                         at the moon

                  John Dos Passos, *The 42nd Parallel*

In a perverse way, even the alienated despair of Dos Passos's barbed critique acknowledges how formidable the hallowed target of Harvard undergraduate life has become through its legitimacy. Indeed, it is an aesthetic repudiation of the capacity of the members of elite institutions to collaborate in working "symbolic violence" (Bourdieu and Passeron 1977, 1-68) to legitimize and perpetuate the class structure. Would Dos Passos's response not have been stronger almost anywhere else? Perhaps not, since his is a radical perspective on the school of an elite.

Opposed to this heretical excoriation of higher education as profoundly numbing are true believers in large numbers, the depth of whose conviction may be hypothesized to be in proportion to their educational credentials. Since, in America, "the customer is always right," it is certainly in the interests of a college or university to be well regarded by its clientele. As Alexander Astin most democratically and trenchantly puts it, "Given the considerable investment of time and energy that most students make in attending college, the student's perception of value should be given substantial weight. *Indeed, it is difficult to argue that student satisfaction can be legitimately subordinated to any other educational outcome*" (1977, 164; emphasis ours).[1] Or, as a bumper sticker on a car in the parking lot of a major state university propagandized to seduce prospects for higher learning, "I'm a college experience. Enjoy me."

Do the consumers in the main regard their own educational experiences as having been worthwhile? And what is it about the experience that promotes favorable client judgments? Questions of individual responses to milieux are the crux of this chapter. They also help us learn something of the social psychology of higher education institutions. Both will shed light on how particular kinds of educational institutions and, even more, higher education itself are legitimated, in short, how higher education provides ideological support for its hegemony. If the Meyer (1977) thesis is correct, former students should have positive reflections on their educational experiences precisely to the extent that the educational process or degree opened the door to higher status. Accordingly, we expect level of educational attainment to have effects at least as powerful as in any of the preceding chapters.

The very interest in individual satisfactions with education[2] rather than with the social and civic uses of education should not mislead us. It exhibits the entrenchment of individualism. Bellah and his associates (1985) would say that these evaluative opinions of individual preference by themselves fail to encompass social commitments and public moral engagement. From a different perspective, however, the sharing of satisfactions may be the basis for collective, solidary ritual affirmation of a particular educational institution. Conceived more broadly, satisfaction with the college experience supports higher education as an institution—hence, it even supports the society itself since education is integral to its legitimation and maintenance.

Despite their limitations, the views of individuals regarding their educational experiences constitute yet another arena in which to examine the lasting effects of higher education. Satisfactions with and reported experiences of educational institutions are our final group of outcomes that postsecondary education can effect. In previous chapters we have examined the shifts in values, goals, and activities attributable to higher education. We have sought to distinguish the extent to which alterations would have occurred anyway in the usual course of young adult development, the degree to which changes result from particular environments or student experiences in them, and the pervasiveness of a certification effect whereby the attainment of educational levels is accompanied by taking on values and activities consistent with the social status conferred. Unlike our previous analyses, however, the referent is not external to the schooling process (as were life goals or criteria for choosing a line of work), but rather consists of responses to the experience of going to college.

ASSESSING THE SUCCESS OF HIGHER EDUCATION INSTITUTIONS

There are many subjective measures used to assess the success of colleges, such as reported satisfactions or aspirations of students or graduates. Yet others include portrayals of the culture of an institution through questionnaire responses of students or faculty (Stern 1970; Pace 1979).[3] This psychological approach seems only natural in a culture in which individual dignity and freedom are held to be sacrosanct, and individual motives are seen as the causes of actions that are freely chosen. However, a vocabulary developed to describe and analyze the individual psychologically and behaviorally is simply inadequate to characterize social structures[4] by itself, although it may be inferentially useful.

Yet other measures used to appraise college programs and environments are objective, such as attrition rates, students' academic achievements, or graduates' subsequent attainments. These are attempts to circumvent some of the difficulties of subjectivity by being event-oriented. Tinto (1975, 1987), Terenzini and Pascarella (1980) and Munro (1981) have been exponents of using dropping out, or attrition, as an event that indicates the relative failure of institutions. These observers have treated leaving the institution as a sign of dissatisfaction, known among many administrators interested in retention as students "voting with their feet." Tinto (1975) pointed out that withdrawal from college could be either chosen or forced, that is, voluntary or not. Involuntary withdrawals may have many causes, principally economic, while voluntary withdrawals (and satisfactions) may be among factors that an institution has some control over (Gielow and Lee 1988) and, hence, conditioned by social structural factors. Nevertheless, since attrition may be unintentional and may stem from causes beyond the individual's control, retention or attrition rates have limitations as indicators of satisfaction (Tinto 1975, 1987; Gielow and Lee 1988).

In contrast, Gielow and Lee (1988) suggest that "satisfaction votes"[5] are freely given and, hence, more likely to be voluntary than attrition-based measures. In addition to Astin's assertion (at the start of this chapter) that it is difficult legitimately to place other outcomes ahead of student satisfaction, Gielow and Lee add their voice: "Although an affective measure, it may be argued that *student satisfaction is one of the most direct tests of postsecondary success.* . . . Given that individual students are the primary beneficiaries of the college experience, asking them how satisfied they are with those experiences is an obvious way to measure this success" (1988, 3; emphasis ours).

Sociologists are likely to couch their discussions in social structural terms instead of individual terms, such as affect or dropping out, which only imply something contextual. Durkheim's original work on social integration permeates the work of sociologists on educational satisfactions. Anderson (1981) defined and measured satisfaction as integration into college life and found that it was related to finishing college. Tinto goes one step further by drawing the useful distinction between the academic and social integration of an institution (1975, 1987). Tinto argues that students need not be equally integrated into a milieu in both senses and that variations in type of integration differentially affect decisions about continuing in an institution. One aim of this chapter is to establish a provisional general account of the structural and experiential factors accounting for integration in one or both senses.

Of course, to invoke only satisfaction measures as indicators of social structure would be naive, for this both assumes the validity of subjective opinion and oversimplifies a complex reality. In practice, such measures also suffer from being taken too literally and are often used to buttress administrative apologies in the service of strengthening a college's market position. Exaggerated and naive emphasis on hedonic satisfaction surely deflects attention from many consequential features of learning and thwarts understanding the process of education.[6]

Since people cannot reflect on what has not yet occurred, there will be no controls for earlier views.[7] This changes the essential nature of our models—which are in all other respects identical to those in previous chapters—so that, rather than isolating changes in the outcome over time, they instead estimate raw levels of satisfaction or the probabilities of reporting particular college experiences.[8]

Nevertheless, studying the relationships between educational attainment, college characteristics, and student careers, on the one hand, and educational satisfactions and reported collegiate experiences, on the other, contributes to our investigation of the certifying and socializing functions of higher education. A powerful socializing function suggests that educational milieux will elicit systematic differences in the postsecondary experiences reported, and perhaps in satisfaction with particular dimensions as well. (However, the latter is harder to gauge since satisfaction depends partly on individual needs and expectations.)

To the degree that postsecondary education is successful in conferring social statuses, we can expect general consensus regarding the value of college-going on the whole. However, subgroups (defined in terms of race, gender, or educational attainment) may vary in their valuation of specific dimensions of the collegiate experience. The compatibility of the dimensions of postsecondary schooling most salient to these groups with their differing social roles will provide further evidence of the part higher education plays in conferring social statuses.

In particular, we examine gender differences in the effects of educational attainment and all other independent variables for all outcomes.

MEASURING SATISFACTIONS AND PERCEPTIONS

We used ten different measures to assess satisfactions and perceptions.[9] The first five items dealt with educational satisfactions. First was a general factor,[10] "academic satisfaction." The items defining this factor are: "the quality of instruction," "the ability, knowledge, and personal qualities of most teachers," "the course curriculum," "my intellectual growth," and "the development of my work skills." Second were four questions, analyzed as single items, that concerned satisfaction with: "the social life," "the sports and recreational facilities," "the counseling and job placement," and "the prestige of the school."

Finally, we also used five single items about perceptions of educational experiences: difficulty of courses, courses being interesting, the student's own performance, the amount learned, and meeting people with new ideas. The items were responses to a question asking that respondents select statements describing their last year in school as "was my experience" or "was not my experience." All the items for each individual concerned the last high school or undergraduate school attended. For those not going beyond high school, the school was high school, but for all of the others it was the last postsecondary undergraduate educational setting before responding to the survey.

EDUCATIONAL LEVEL:
SATISFACTIONS AND PERCEPTIONS

At the outset, we present the relationship between level of education and the separate outcomes of satisfactions and perceptions for the most recent educational setting before 1979.[11] This will give us a snapshot of the gross differences between educational experiences at various educational levels that further analyses will seek to explain. The central concern here is on postsecondary education,[12] although we do include a comparison with responses to high school.

Academic satisfactions, as indicated by the first five rows in Table 6.1, increase quite consistently with each increment in educational level. Satisfaction with the domain of curricular instruction goes hand in hand with educational attainment. It is sensible to think of causation as reciprocal, with satisfactions with the academic realm being both cause and consequence of educational progress. Positive attitudes and perceptions of education not only can encourage the further pursuit of education,[13] but can also result in the completion of steps in the process of educational attainment itself. From these data, we cannot estimate the strength of causation in one direction or the other. There are, however, so many factors motivating the pursuit of education that we prefer to interpret the satisfactions, not as predictions of future efforts, but as our respondents' evaluations of their educational experiences that justify present and past commitments. We also assume this is warranted by the age of the cohort.

Satisfactions with extracurricular matters, unlike the curricular ones, do not vary systematically with educational attainment. The pattern of relationships for satisfaction with the social life is similar to that of sports and recreational facilities. The highest percentages are for both those who have only finished high school and those who have completed no more than a four- or five-year degree. Those with graduate degrees are next highest. Last are those in the two categories whose college experience did not result in a bachelor's degree. For the high school only and the four- or five-year degree categories the percentages may reflect greater access to a fuller round of social life and superior recreational and athletic facilities in high schools and four-year colleges than elsewhere.[14] Many, if not most, community and

Table 6.1
Educational Satisfaction and Descriptions of College Experience by Educational Attainment, Gender, and Race

	Academic Satisfaction[a]	Social Life[a]	Recreational Facilities[b]	School Prestige[b]	Counseling and Placement[b]	Courses Harder than Expected[c]	Courses Interesting[c]	Performed Well[c]	Learned a Lot[c]	Met People with New Ideas[c]
Educational Attainment										
High School Only	44	65	65	53	35	6	55	61	56	44
Less than Two Years College	54	50	37	50	31	16	77	78	72	68
Two Years or More College	59	47	43	51	33	18	85	82	83	76
Bachelor's Degree	66	62	61	66	34	12	89	90	87	85
Advanced Degree	70	56	54	70	37	11	90	97	90	90
Gender										
Men	54	57	55	57	32	13	75	76	73	70
Women	60	56	48	58	35	12	81	84	79	72
Race										
Black	60	64	57	63	33	12	78	80	76	71
White	57	56	51	57	45	23	80	81	80	73

N = 5409

[a]Percent above mean.
[b]Percent "Very Satisfied" or "Satisfied."
[c]Percent checking "Was My Experience."

two-year colleges are less well endowed in these respects than the typical high school or four-year college. Furthermore, in addition to the lack of well-developed opportunities for leisure and sociability in two-year schools, students at two-year colleges are often disadvantaged by commitments to work and family that dilute their opportunities to engage in extracurricular pursuits. This same interpretation may apply to those who have not yet finished a four-year degree by 1986. Not only are such persons likely to have many other commitments precluding social participation, but by now they are much older than the typical undergraduate and thus less likely to have similar interests. The intermediate scores of those with advanced degrees may reflect extracurricular inadequacies of the undergraduate institution less than they reflect a reduction of extracurricular involvements with an increased focus on studies as a means of mobility to graduate school.[15] Such a pattern might also constitute an instance of socialization that anticipates graduate school priorities.

Satisfaction with the prestige of the school remains around 50 percent "very satisfied" or "satisfied" among those with less than a baccalaureate degree, but jumps sharply with bachelor's degree completion and is even slightly higher for those with advanced degrees. The differences are so distinctive that they appear to reflect a certifying effect. Satisfaction with job counseling or placement does not differ significantly with educational attainment. Self-reported perceptions of the educational experience largely resemble those reported above for academic satisfactions.

Educational attainment's relationships to these perceptions parallel those for academic satisfaction perceptions that the courses were interesting, that one's performance was good, that one learned a great deal, and that one met people with new ideas. That the percentages rise with each increment of education suggest an interpretation identical to that for the academic satisfactions. However, here the largest differences are between those who only completed high school and those with less than two years of college. By a large margin our respondents perceive any amount of education beyond high school, however slight, to expose them to curricular influences that are interesting and to people with new ideas. That similar differences, though somewhat smaller, remain for performing well and for learning a great deal indicates that respondents also tend to hold virtually any college as a place for exercising their talents and for acquiring knowledge superior to high school. Finally, few at any educational level experienced course work as more difficult than expected. One can speculate either that American students are not being challenged enough or that they are simply well acquainted with what to expect from courses at each level of education. Those who have some college beyond high school, but not a four- or five-year degree, however, are the most likely groups to concur. Perhaps the data reflect a disjuncture between educational aspirations and the abilities[16] or opportunities to attain them. Alternatively, belief in the difficulty of the courses perhaps rationalizes not going further educationally. We will discover more about this in the next section, when we take individual abilities into account.

THE WHOLE SAMPLE:
EDUCATION LEVEL AND SATISFACTIONS

This section deals with how educational attainment affects satisfactions, after we remove other major possible causes of variation in satisfactions. Additionally, we will be able to address the question of how race, gender, socioeconomic status, and abilities affect college satisfactions and perceptions.

When we control on background characteristics, all levels of postsecondary education remain highly related to the academic satisfaction factor (Table 6.2). Both the bachelor's and graduate degrees yield highly elevated levels of academic satisfaction, but both groups with less than a bachelor's degree also differ significantly from those who did not go on to college. Other things being equal, women are more satisfied than men with the academic side of higher education.[17] This is in proportion to their relatively greater earnings dividend from higher education.

The other satisfactions are analyzed in terms of the effects on the odds of being higher or lower on a given item. Again, level of education emphatically influences these nonacademic satisfactions. For both of the extracurricular satisfactions the results (Table 6.3) are like those reported above. Satisfactions with the social life and recreational facilities are sharply lower among those with some college but less than a bachelor's degree than for those with no postsecondary education. However, those with bachelor's and advanced degrees do not differ significantly from high school graduates. This clearly reinforces the earlier interpretation that the social life of those attending two-year institutions may be curtailed. One of the reasons may actually be inadequate facilities in two-year institutions. Another may be, for many, lack of participation (opportunities to participate) among those who did not complete a four-year degree. Often, we

Table 6.2
Effects of Educational Attainment on Academic Satisfaction

	Academic Satisfaction
Postsecondary Educational Attainment	
Less than Two Years	.24*** (.11)
Two Years or More	.37*** (.15)
Bachelor's Degree	.53*** (.24)
Advanced Degree	.65*** (.22)
Background Factors	
Whites	-.08 (.02)
Women	.12** (.06)
Family Socio-economic Status	-.01 (-.04)
Academic Abilities	-.00 (-.03)
R^2	.05

N = 5409
* p < .05   ** p < .01   *** p < .001

NOTES: Figures in this table are unstandardized regression coefficients (standardized coefficients are in parentheses). Each category of educational attainment is compared with the reference category of those having no more than a high school education.

may have a vicious circle with decision makers opting not to develop extracurricular programs because they believe that the lifestyles of many students preclude their participation.

The other non-curricular items exhibit a different pattern. Those with bachelor's and advanced degrees have sharply higher odds of reporting satisfaction with the prestige of the school—odds that are about double those of the comparison group. The odds that advanced degree holders will report satisfaction with counseling and job placement are two-thirds higher than high school graduates. Graduate degree holders may indeed be satisfied with the prestige and counseling support because they are moral exemplars who expressed the academic ideals of their undergraduate institutions and, by doing so, drew favorable attention upon themselves on their way to graduate school. The satisfaction with prestige of the undergraduate institution of advanced degree holders is not necessarily related to their satisfaction with the counseling and placement support of the undergraduate institution. Given current patterns of graduate school enrollment, in all likelihood, advanced degree holders had gone to schools that were in fact more prestigious. Generally positive views of schools can be expected from those who choose (and are chosen) to pursue further education. Probably such students do get more than their share of counseling resources.

While race and socioeconomic status have no relationship to any of the satisfactions discussed here (Tables 6.2 and 6.3), gender and academic abilities do. As noted above, women tend to rate their academic satisfactions higher than men. Moreover, the effect on the odds that they will think the recreational and sports facilities satisfactory is only three-fourths that for men. This may reflect the past and persistent disproportionate allocation of funds by institutions to traditionally male sports and recreation. Is it that women don't care very much about such things or that women's sports facilities are not very good? In chapter 3, we learned that adult women are less likely than men to participate in sports. Sports and recreation may not be salient to many women, but, as already noted, there may be a vicious circle of inadequate facilities and inadequate opportunities. Women, in general, may be dissatisfied, given what we know about inequalities in the sports and recreation facilities available to women in educational institutions. Women who don't care much for sports and recreation may be denied an opportunity to discover an untapped potential for self-expression and participation.[18] Women are, then, more academically satisfied than men but find active recreation and sports facilities wanting.

Finally, net of educational attainment, as academic abilities rise, the odds of being satisfied with the social life and counseling and job placement fall. If the academically more gifted are not necessarily more alienated than others, they are more critical of social life and counseling opportunities.

THE WHOLE SAMPLE:
EDUCATION LEVEL AND EXPERIENCES

Controlling for background factors did not alter the apparent relationship between educational attainment and experiences. All categories of those who went beyond high school have radically higher odds than those who did not of saying they met

Table 6.3
Effects of Educational Attainment on Educational Satisfaction

	Social Life	Recreation	School Prestige	Counseling and Placement
Postsecondary Educational Attainment				
Less than Two Years	.64***	.39***	.91	1.24
Two Years or More	.59***	.47***	.97	1.27
Bachelor's Degree	1.24	1.01	1.86***	1.11
Advanced Degree	.99	.78	2.20***	1.66**
Background Factors				
Whites	.89	.70	.79	.89
Women	1.02	.75**	1.08	1.07
Family Socio-economic Status	1.03	1.03	1.00	.98
Academic Abilities	.94**	.97	.98	.93***
-2 Log Likelihood =	10184.60	9802.96	10147.11	10550.41

N = 5409
* p < .05   ** p < .01   *** p < .001

NOTES: Figures in table are the effects on the odds of being higher rather than lower on educational satisfaction.
Each category of educational attainment is compared with the reference category of those having no more than a high school education.

people with new ideas, found courses interesting, performed well, and learned a lot (see Table 6.4). Moreover, the effects are consistently greater with more education. For example, having a bachelor's degree markedly elevates the odds of agreeing to the propositions. And while the odds are consistently higher for those with advanced degrees, they are much higher than the bachelor's degree holders only for the items on academic performance and meeting people with new ideas. Thus, the odds of having positive perceptions of academic experience generally go up with each educational step upward. When we link this to the increasing magnitudes of academic and curricular satisfaction (Table 6.2), the notion that students and former students perceive that each step beyond high school adds academic value becomes nearly inescapable. (This meshes neatly with results from chapter 2.)

Complementing this finding are the markedly lower odds of perceiving the courses as more difficult than expected for all postsecondary educational categories than for those who did not go beyond high school. For both post-high school categories having less than a bachelor's degree, this effect is the strongest. Are some educational milieux, like two-year technical and community colleges, not perceived as challenging simply because they are not? Given the data, this is not provable.

To qualify the entire discussion, those who find school rewarding may self-select and be selected for higher levels of attainment. But, all else being equal, either the experiences at higher educational levels are more positive or there is a belief to that effect—both very much the same in consequence.

For the total sample, background characteristics are consequential, too. Whites are twice as likely as blacks to say that courses were more difficult than expected. Why do the milieux appear more challenging to whites than blacks, all else equal? Should this be attributed to objective differences in how challenging the milieux are? Or does the black experience somehow create different behavioral expectations, different standards for evaluating educational challenges, or a language of aloofness? Perhaps blacks may be denying the difficulty of courses as a method of distancing themselves psychologically from an oppressive educational system.

Women and men differ in how they size up their educational experiences. As noted above, women, in general, are considerably more satisfied than men with the academic aspects of their institutions. The results here underscore that theme; the odds for women to rate courses as interesting, to think they performed well, and to believe that they learned much exceed the odds for men by more than 50 percent. In chapter 3 we also saw that women are much more likely than men to grow in the belief in the importance of getting a good education. As noted above, women are also more likely than men to report the academic aspects of their education as intrinsically gratifying. Education may promise more to women than to men in personal fulfillment as an end in itself. It may represent more of an "experience undergone" for women than men in addition to the earlier- noted higher earnings dividend for women.

Family socioeconomic status has virtually no influence on educational satisfactions and experiences once education, race, and abilities are controlled. On the other hand, the higher the academic abilities, the higher the odds of reporting that one performed well. This may be related to the inverse relationship between satisfaction with the social life and academic abilities.

Table 6.4
Effects of Educational Attainment on Descriptions of Educational Experience

	Courses Harder than Expected	Courses Were Interesting	Performed Well	Learned a Lot	Met People with New Ideas
Postsecondary Educational Attainment					
Less than Two Years	.32***	2.73***	2.34***	2.14***	2.61***
Two Years or More	.29***	4.62***	2.89***	4.13***	4.15***
Bachelor's Degree	.42**	7.09***	5.14***	6.23***	7.75***
Advanced Degree	.47*	7.34***	18.86***	8.53***	12.17***
Background Factors					
Whites	2.21**	.84	.83	.80	.84
Women	1.07	1.65***	1.82***	1.56***	1.24
Family Socio-economic Status	.96	.97	.95*	.97	.97
Academic					
Abilities	1.05	1.04	1.10***	.99	.98
-2 Log Likelihood	3543.77	4603.29	4332.73	4881.89	5257.60

N = 5409
* $p < .05$ ** $p < .01$ *** $p < .001$

NOTES: Figures in table are the effects on the odds of being higher rather than lower on descriptions.
Each category of educational attainment is compared with the reference category of those having no more than high school education.

Perhaps students with high aptitudes in high school tend to remain, to some extent, "nerds" in their outlooks and in the eyes of others. Someone whose aptitudes pay off in effective scholarship may pay the price of neglecting social life or run the risk of alienating others by succeeding in academic competition.

In general, the variations in subjective responses to high school and college, of whatever stripe, are profound. Will this picture of the massive association of educational level to these responses hold true when we look at the more homogeneous sample of those with some postsecondary education? Also, what part do college characteristics and student careers play in these subjective reports?

COLLEGE CHARACTERISTICS:
SATISFACTIONS AND PERCEPTIONS

One might expect the characteristics of colleges to have a great influence on educational satisfactions and perceptions. These effects might outweigh utilitarian, expressive, and civic consequences. One may well expect certain types of colleges to be more likely to have the resources to evoke the nostalgia of "the old alum." Possibly those under private control or those that are more selective or those that are highly residential can exert a decisive positive influence. For instance, Tinto (1975), in regarding attrition as analogous to Durkheim's suicide, holds that certain schools are more cohesive and better integrate their charges into the social fabric. In addition, there are some distinctive colleges with a unique cultural climate that have strong effects reinforced by structural factors, like a large proportion of students who reside on campus or small size of college.[19] Several studies support this argument. Jacob, in *Changing Values in College* (1957), advances this interpretation for a very few colleges that have a strong collective sense of mission and identity sustainable in part because of a smaller setting. Jacob was, however, not concerned with the satisfactions of individuals. Burton Clark also picks up the theme of uniqueness and argues for the impact of such milieux in *The Distinctive College: Antioch, Reed and Swarthmore* (1970).

Feldman and Newcomb (1969) found that the effects of size were weak and inconsistent. Alexander Astin found that large institutions tend to have a variety of negative effects and a considerable number of them (1977, 230-1). He also found that the pattern of satisfactions was mixed at large institutions compared with small. At the smaller institutions students felt more satisfied with relations to faculty and with classroom instruction, whereas at large institutions they felt more satisfied with the social life, the institution's academic reputation, and curricular variety. In general, how college characteristics affect student satisfactions is becoming clearer, but they still are not explanatory touchstones.

Gielow and Lee (1988) use *High School and Beyond* data to investigate how institutional characteristics affect both academic and social satisfactions, but they did not take variations in educational attainment into account. They found substantial direct influences of several college characteristics on both academic and social satisfactions among those attending four-year colleges. They found that academic satisfaction was associated with a college's being religiously affiliated, with the geographical diversity of the student body, with college selectivity, and with the proportion of students residing on campus. The larger the student body at a four-year college, the less the academic satisfaction. On the other hand, both college size and the proportion of students living on campus had strong positive relationships to the social satisfaction of students, while a college's being religiously affiliated had a weaker relationship to social satisfaction.

By contrast, our evidence indicates weak and scattered direct effects of college characteristics on college satisfactions. In the top six rows of Tables 6.5 and 6.6 there are significant effects only on the social life and the sports and recreation facilities items. The greater the student enrollment, the greater the effect on the odds of being satisfied with recreation and sports facilities. The higher the proportion of full-time students, the higher the odds of reporting satisfaction with the social life; for each 10 percent increment in the proportion of full-time students, the odds of reporting this kind of satisfaction are 8 percent higher. For this same sample, each higher increment of full-time students also yields a 10 percent greater probability of reporting satisfaction with sports and recreational facilities.

The proportion of full-time students may be a crude measure of structural integration, of a denser and more closed interactive network. Increases in their proportion, then, may make it more likely to find others for participation in leisure activities than is the case with more open networks. One may think of "facilities" (as worded in the item) as reflecting more activities because there are more potential participants.

To the degree that a postsecondary institution is residential, the odds of satisfaction with the social life and recreational facilities rise, but not significantly so.[20] It is somewhat disappointing that "residentiality," even as assessed here in terms of proportion of freshmen living on campus, does not have significant effects on academic satisfactions and perceptions. One can readily think of superior measures of the residential nature of a college. More refined measures of the quantity and quality of interpersonal interactions accompanying different living arrangements would almost certainly yield greater insight and a closer convergence with the findings of others. However, the direction of the relationship is positive on all of the items except "satisfaction with counseling and placement" and "I met interesting people." How residence is configured and the proportions of various groups residing on a campus are structural features of postsecondary institutions that certainly may have academic and extracurricular effects. Certainly, the direction of the rela-

Table 6.5
**Effects of College Characteristics and Student Careers
on Academic Satisfaction**

	Academic Satisfaction
College Characteristics[a]	
Student Enrollment	-.02
	(-.03)
Selectivity	-.08
	(-.00)
Private Control	.06
	(.03)
Full-Time Students	-.12
	(-.03)
Vocational Emphasis	.03
	(.05)
Highly Residential	.07
	(.03)
Student Careers	
Business Major	-.16
	(-.07)
Education Major	-.06
	(-.02)
Arts & Sciences Major	-.13
	(-.06)
Ever Lived on Campus	.07
	(.04)
College Grades	.11***
	(.13)

tionships we found accords with the work of Feldman and Newcomb (1969), Chickering (1974), and Astin (1977). All of them report that residence has a wide range of beneficial effects, although they usually mean residence as an individual experience, not as a contextual characteristic.

As discussed above, the advantages and disadvantages of institutional size have been a perennial topic of debate among students of education and sociologists. The sheer size of an institution in terms of student enrollment may mean that more abundant sports and recreational facilities are available there than in smaller institutions. Each increment in the size of student enrollment elevates the odds of satisfaction with recreational and sports facilities for the total college sample. In part, we agree here with Gielow and Lee (1988), who found a relation-

Table 6.5 (continued)

	Academic Satisfaction
Postsecondary Educational Attainment	
Two Years or More	.23* (.10)
Bachelor's Degree	.36*** (.19)
Advanced Degree	.38** (.16)
Background Factors	
Whites	.03 (.01)
Women	.06 (.03)
Socioeconomic Status	-.00 (-.02)
Academic Abilities	-.00 (-.07)

R^2 = .06
N = 2702
* p < .05   ** p < .01   *** p < .001

NOTES: Figures in this table are unstandardized regression coefficients (standardardized
           coefficients are in parentheses).
           Each category of college major is compared with the reference category of all other
           majors.
           Each category of educational attainment is compared with the reference category
           of those having less than two years of postsecondary education.

[a]For persons attending more than one institution, the one attended longest; in case of ties, the
more recently attended.

ship between size and social satisfaction. Larger institutions
probably not only have more recreational facilities, but they may
have a greater variety of them. They may also contain students
with a wider variety of interests, thus making it possible for
students with similar leisure interests to pursue them together.
Gielow and Lee found a significant negative relationship between
institutional size and academic satisfactions,[21] but while the
direction of the relationship we found was the same, the magnitude of the relationship was smaller and not statistically significant. Beyond this, size causes no consistent differences for our
array of satisfaction and perception variables.

Last, the vocational emphasis of the school has a significant
effect among women. Among women this increases the odds of

Table 6.6
Effects of College Characteristics and Student Careers on Educational Satisfaction

	Social Life	Recrea-tion	School Prestige	Counseling and Placement
College Characteristics[a]				
Student Enrollment	1.01	1.02**	1.01	1.00
Selectivity	.94	.99	1.17	.99
Private Control	.89	.79	1.39	1.13
Full-Time Students	1.08*	1.10*	1.02	1.03
Vocational Emphasis	1.03	1.10	1.06	1.02
Highly Residential	1.37	1.37	1.26	.96
Student Careers				
Business Major	.97	.97	.89	.79
Education Major	1.11	1.37	.92	.73
Arts & Sciences Major	1.08	.99	.79	.64**
Ever Lived on Campus	2.24***	1.33	1.37*	1.02
College Grades	.91	.90	1.02	1.17*
Postsecondary Educational Attainment				
Two Years or More	.83	1.15	1.05	1.29
Bachelor's Degree	1.12	1.43	1.56*	1.12
Advanced Degree	.84	1.15	1.51	1.55
Background Factors				
Whites	1.26	1.08	.68	.66
Women	1.01	.75*	1.24	.98
Family Socioeconomic Status	1.03	1.02	1.01	.98
Academic Abilities	.95	.98	.96	.94*
-2 Log Likelihood =	4436.48	4419.76	4486.43	4644.36

N = 2702
* p < .05   ** p < .01   *** p < .001

NOTES: Figures are the effects on the odds of being higher rather than lower on the educational satisfaction.
Each category of college major is compared with the reference category of all other majors.
Each category of educational attainment is compared with the reference category of those having less than two years of postsecondary education.

[a]For persons attending more than one institution, the one attended longest; in case of ties, the more recently attended.

perceiving the courses to have been interesting by 46 percent, but there is no parallel effect for men.[22] More work to interpret this contextual effect is clearly in order. Hearn and Olzack (1981) found that women and other minority groups tend to select majors that are vocationally linked, but that is an individual matter, not the contextual one we have here.

STUDENT CAREERS: SATISFACTIONS AND PERCEPTIONS

How do student careers affect student satisfactions with higher education? We shall examine the effects of field of study, whether or not the individual ever resided on campus, and college grades (see Tables 6.5, 6.6, and 6.7).

While the evidence may hint that business majors may be somewhat disengaged from learning as an exciting intellectual process, our groupings into majors have no statistically significant effects at all and do not reveal any particular patterns of college satisfactions or experiences.

Having lived on a campus has two significant effects. It brings about dramatic increases of in the odds of reporting satisfaction with the social life, and it is associated with a higher likelihood of reporting satisfaction with the prestige of the school. Residing on a campus may well reflect the prestige of an institution, for superior financial endowments often purchase an institution's prestige, one dimension of which actually is the presence of residence facilities. The crude nature of the measurement probably conceals other relationships.[23] Owing to limitations of the current data we must simply reserve judgment, but our findings are consistent with those of other scholars, previously noted, who conclude that campus residence has a wide range of effects, including satisfactions of various kinds.

College grades have more significant effects than other academic career factors, and these have some consistency. It would be shocking if college grades were unrelated to academic satisfaction. Indeed, grades are powerfully associated with academic satisfaction for the college sample. The effects of grades on the odds of the experiential report items are significant across all the items. The better one's college grades, the lower the odds of finding the courses harder than expected, and the greater the odds of reporting that courses were interesting, that one performed well, that one learned a lot, and that one met interesting people. Grades are also positively related to satisfaction with counseling and placement (Table 6.6). However, grades are virtually unrelated to extracurricular satisfactions. These findings support the general conclusion that payoffs in the form of grades have an impact on one's evaluation of the academic side of college life, but probably not on other aspects. To the extent that one has been rewarded, one forms positive conclusions that buttress one's identity as a good student.[24] Of course, the causation may be the other way around, with absorption in a positive educational process resulting in good grades.

EFFECTS OF EDUCATIONAL LEVEL OF THE COLLEGE SAMPLE

Among those who went to college, educational attainment still has many sweeping and powerful effects. All three categories, those with more than two years of college, with a bachelor's degree, and with an advanced degree, are significantly more satisfied with the academic aspects of going to college than those with less than two years of postsecondary education (Table 6.5). Both the categories of bachelor's and advanced degree holders have strikingly high levels of academic satisfaction. Although those with two years or more of higher education but no bachelor's degree are also more satisfied than those who did not complete two years of college, the coefficients are lower.

The compelling effects we have just noted can be attributed to educational attainment after we remove variations in student careers and college characteristics. The persistence of the effects of educational attainment on academic satisfaction suggests again that degree attainment has the strong effect of conferring a status identity. Only one of the extracurricular items (Table 6.6) has a significant relationship to education: the elevated odds of satisfaction with the prestige of the school for bachelor's degree holders—again, most likely a matter of status conferral. Actually, more prestigious schools also typically have lower attrition rates and, hence, succeed in getting students to complete degrees.

The results shown in Table 6.7 lead one to conclude that educational level is paramount. While there are no significant effects of educational attainment on the "courses more difficult than expected" item, there are on all the others. And they are patterned like academic satisfaction. For each educational level the odds of concurring that the courses were interesting, that one performed well, and that one met people with new ideas are always higher than those for the reference category. And for all items the odds are always higher for both bachelor's and advanced degree recipients than they are for those with more than two years of college but with neither of these degrees.

While the effects of educational attainment parallel those of grades, one must remember that they are net of them and, indeed, net of all college characteristics, student careers, and background factors. And it is here that a certification interpretation is most illuminating, something quite impossible with grades alone. Finding that courses were interesting, that one met people with new ideas, that one performed well, and that one learned a great deal all imply that the bachelor's or advanced degree holder have shared similar experiences leading to newly transformed status identities. Similar experiences and status similarities are the stuff of solidarities of acquaintance and friendship. It is arguable that collegians typically feel more comfortable with each other than with non-collegians because their perspectives are similar and their identity as graduates may signal enhanced compatibility.

EFFECTS OF BACKGROUND FACTORS FOR THE COLLEGE SAMPLE

Neither race, nor gender, nor socioeconomic origins, nor measured abilities play a prominent direct part in affecting the evaluation of satisfactions and the assessment of the nature of college experiences. This does not mean that background factors are irrelevant. Our model may simply have obscured any of their indirect connections with the outcomes we are examining here (see the section headed Limitations of This Study in chapter 1).[25] Background factors have two effects (Table 6.6). First, women have only three-fourths the chance of men to find the social life satisfying. Second, the higher one's measured abilities, the lower the probability of reporting satisfaction with anything, a whisper of alienation that only attains significance on dissatisfaction with the counseling and placement opportunities.

CONCLUSION

In the main, the findings for educational satisfactions and reports of experiences parallel those of Hyman and his associates. Focusing on somewhat different outcomes, these authors found that general knowledge and the proclivities both to call on it and to use it inferentially increased with each step upward in higher education (Hyman, Wright, and Reed 1975). Hyman and

Table 6.7
Effects of College Characteristics and Student Careers on
Descriptions of Educational Experience

	Courses Harder than Expected	Courses Were Interesting		Performed Well	Learned a Lot	Met People with New Ideas
College Characteristics[a]						
Student Enrollment	1.00	1.00	1.00	1.00	.99	.99
Selectivity	1.14	.88	.88	.78	.97	1.03
Private Control	.70	1.08	1.08	1.39	.89	.74
Full-Time Students	1.01	1.03	1.03	1.00	1.02	1.09
Vocational Emphasis	.97	1.17	1.05	1.01	1.08	1.08
Highly Residential	1.02	1.51	1.51	1.45	1.07	.84
Student Careers						
Business Major	1.08	.69	.68	.81	.62	.80
Education Major	.64	.76	.77	1.06	.70	1.63
Arts & Sciences Major	.83	.82	.83	.74	.78	1.10
Ever Lived on Campus	.98	1.07	1.06	.76	.83	.94
College Grades	.61***	1.27*	1.27*	2.59***	1.41***	1.21*
Postsecondary Educational Attainment						
Two Years or More	1.12	2.30**	2.30**	1.83*	2.78***	2.23**
Bachelor's Degree	.66	3.86***	3.85***	3.42***	4.57***	3.73***
Advanced Degree	.84	3.74***	3.67***	7.36***	5.14***	5.36***

Wright also found that liberality of social and political values increased with each upward step in education (1979). Unfortunately, we do not have direct, objective evidence of knowledge acquisition for our sample, and, unfortunately, the authors just cited did not have the advantages of panel design.[26] However, to the conclusions of these authors, we can tentatively add two others for undergraduate education. First, the more education one has, the more one is satisfied with the academic aspects of the higher educational milieu. Second, there is a relatively large gap on experiential items concerning learning and intellectual growth between those with some form of postsecondary education and those with none. Secondary and postsecondary education are, as a practical matter, so qualitatively different that going to college is a distinctive educational experience contrasting sharply with high school.

Table 6.7 (continued)

	Courses Harder than Expected	Courses Were Interesting		Performed Well	Learned a Lot	Met People with New Ideas
Background Factors						
Whites	.53	.76	.74	.81	.60	1.10
Women	1.32	1.29	.31	1.21	1.26	1.07
Family Socioeconomic Status	1.02	.96	.96	.94	.98	.99
Academic Abilities	1.01	.99	.99	1.01	.96	.96
Interaction Effects						
Gender x Vocational Emphasis			1.27			
-2 Log Likelihood =	1661.48	1723.03	1720.71	1409.31	1854.28	1995.13

N = 2702

$* p < .05$ $** p < .01$ $*** p < .001$

Effects of Vocational Emphasis on Courses Were Interesting Conditional on Gender, Controlling for College Characteristics and Student Experiences	
Men	1.05
Women	1.33

NOTES: Figures in this table are the effects on the odds of being higher rather than lower on descriptions. Each category of college major is compared with the reference category of all other majors. Each category of educational attainment is compared with the reference category of those having less than two years of postsecondary education.

[a]For persons attending more than one institution, the one attended longest; in case of ties, the more recently attended.

Some of the characteristics of educational institutions appear to help determine responses to the higher educational experience. The proportion of full-time students is associated both with enhanced satisfaction with sports and recreation facilities and satisfaction with the social life, while student enrollment is associated only with the former. Their influence is greater and more consistent in this chapter than in chapters 3, 4, and 5.

Table 6.8 shows that the addition of educational attainment greatly improves upon a model using only background characteristics. And the addition of college characteristics and student career factors improves still further the model that incorporates both background factors and educational attainment.

In particular, further work on the social integration of institutions and the integration of the individual into educational milieux is promising. In the future, however, it may well be more useful to examine the interstices of educational institutions as organizations and look for niches that vary in integration. Our measures of institutional characteristics are provisionally useful, but flawed since they are so global. As the size of an institution rises, subjective measures may become less specific diagnostically. Nonetheless, the sheer size of a postsecondary educational setting seems to offer diversity in extracurricular diversions, as we found, but may, as Gielow and Lee (1988) found, be associated with lower levels of academic satisfaction.

Grades have a strong relationship to many of the responses to the academic side of the college experience. They powerfully affect not only academic satisfaction but also the perceptions of college experience. Grades, too, always predict experiencing one's higher educational lot in positive terms. It is obvious that good grades indicate that one is playing the certification-credentials game well. In *Making the Grade*, Becker, Geer, and Hughes found grades to be institutionalized as central to one's student identity (1968). Our findings certainly reinforce that interpretation.

As the individual's level of education rises, levels of academic satisfaction and interest consistently and clearly rise, too. However, the odds of being satisfied with the social and recreational aspects of college are clearly depressed among those who have completed some college short of a bachelor's degree—this in contrast to both those who did not go on to college and those who hold a bachelor's degree. Both the lesser recreational endowments of two-year schools and the time students are involved in off-campus commitments probably contribute to these effects.

The level of educational attainment has signal effects going beyond the showing of retrospective gratitude for utilitarian benefits. Levels of academic satisfaction are especially great among those who attain the baccalaureate or an advanced degree. The dramatically enhanced perceptions of experienced interest, learning, and performance complement this finding. Having attained a bachelor's degree is powerfully connected with satisfaction with social life but less so with the scholarly aspects. With those who now hold advanced degrees, this picture is reversed. Those who succeed in postgraduate studies are likely to have used their undergraduate experience as a more purely academic one than other students, whereas those who only attain the baccalaureate degree seem to have more recreational

Table 6.8
The Significance of Educational Attainment, College Characteristics, and Individual Experiences in Explaining Educational Satisfactions and Descriptions of Experiences

	Educational Attainment	College Characteristics and Individual Experiences
Academic Satisfaction	**	*
Social Satisfaction	*	**
Recreational Satisfaction	*	**
Satisfaction with School Prestige	**	*
Satisfaction with Job Placement	*	*
Courses Hard	*	**
Courses Interesting	**	*
Performed Well	**	**
Learned a Lot	**	*
Met People with New Ideas	**	*
n.s. = not significant * p < .05 ** p < .01		

NOTE: Results are based on f-tests for linear regression or analogues in the case of logistic regression (see Appendix B). Column one reflects the improvement of fit achieved by adding the dummy variables for educational attainment over a model using only background variables (there are no prior values of educational satisfactions and experiences). Column two reflects improvement of fit when the college characteristics and individual experiences are added to the model tested in column one (i.e., background and educational attainment).

fun. Nonetheless, the high level of academic satisfaction of the undergraduate degree holders should not be slighted.

The similarity of higher education experiences in combination with the degree certification can then form a basis for a quasi-elite, loose collective identity as "interesting people" who have, it can be taken for granted, undergone similar "broadening" experiences and made something of them. However, the sense of camaraderie may be nearly without substance: one should not overestimate the homogeneity of college graduates except perhaps for graduates of those distinctive institutions most clearly chartered. The alma mater, too, figures in as the place to which one is indebted for having facilitated the acquisition of the new identity, but its peculiar strength inheres in something we have no measure of here: the power of shared collective experience.

Certification, as a process of institutional authorization of aspiring individuals, goes hand in hand with the individual's reciprocal legitimation of the college or university. In the words of John W. Meyer, "Educational systems themselves are thus, in a sense, ideologies. They rationalize in modern terms and remove from sacred and primordial explanations the nature and organization of personnel and knowledge in modern society" (1977, 66).

The effects of identity bestowal linked to level of education are much greater than any effects of particular institutional characteristics, as we found in earlier chapters. This argues for the preponderant validity of the allocation-certification theory and for the theory's success in accounting for and encompassing socialization effects. This interpretation, then, probably holds for the vast majority of institutions of higher education today, but not those few elite institutions with strong charters (Meyer 1970; Kamens 1971, 1974). The latter may have relatively strong socializing effects.

In fact, based particularly on the findings in this chapter, but also in others, we can conclude that the apparent uniqueness of given institutions, although real, does not prevent these institutions from consistently acting out their part in the certifying process. The concrete scene of action can be mistaken for the essential character of the process. One is watching one hand of the magician while the tricks are really performed with the other.[27] It is mostly a case of "marginal differentiation" or "narcissism with respect to minor differences"[28] that essentially finds its origin and force elsewhere. It is displaced from the self-enhancing attainment of credentials and the conferral of new and more worthy status identities.

Nonetheless, the myth of uniqueness is crucially important to particular institutions and higher education in general. As long as the fiction is operative, it has real consequences, for it strengthens attachments and loyalties to an institution and its public images. The close correspondence between occupational career rewards for various educational levels and the satisfaction levels and positive responses to the educational experience constitute a vital linkage. The extent to which college is perceived as a satisfying experience and college experiences as positive and distinctive receives its great power from enhanced life chances. Through its gatekeeping control over the allocation process, the college keeps on renewing its legitimation and can exploit to its advantage the solidarity of its alumni and its positive public image to other constituencies.

If credentials and status are of such great importance in the United States and in setting off the educated from others, the educational *process* bears some of the responsibility. The educational system, by preparing already individualistic and competitive students in an individualistic competition—however satisfying—for later individualistic competitions in the world of work, may compound the process of estrangement from self-realization and civic purposes.

NOTES

1. Of course, the notion of students pursuing the satisfaction of their wants in the marketplace of competing colleges smacks naively of Adam Smith and the "invisible hand."

2. Young consumers obviously may be the best judges of satisfactions and may believe they know how they perceive the world. However, the blind spot here is in the omission of questions of the common good. Why should the world be better if student opinions are the principal benchmarks of institutional success? Rarely are questions asked in terms of the quality of life or the survival of a collectivity. Satisfaction means some mixture of expressive fulfillment and utilitarian advantage for the individual and does not necessarily result in societal benefits.

3. The latter technique often entails the assumption that a good fit between personality and milieu is mutually propitious for student and school. Consequently, such researchers also often include personality measures of some kind. It is worth noting that, in analyzing data from *High School and Beyond*, another nationally representative survey, Gielow and Lee (1988) found significant correlations between self-concept measures like self-esteem and self-direction, on the one hand, and educational satisfactions, on the other. There are, thus, other models that include personality variables for fuller explanation of satisfaction effects. Nonetheless, the problem of the halo effect constitutes a methodological obstacle. In other words, people who are satisfied with themselves may also be satisfied with their environments. The argument may simply be circular.

4. Pace (1979), who criticized Stern's (1970) work on measuring environments as representing a projection of personality needs upon a sociocultural system, nonetheless does not fully escape from "psychologizing" the educational milieu either.

5. Many scholars have used satisfaction measures only as intervening variables to predict student attrition or retention (Bean 1980; Howard and Maxwell 1980; Hendel 1985; Lee 1988). Both Higgerson (1985) and Johnson and Richardson (1986) also examined the positive relationship between academic satisfaction and persistence.

6. Do such measures capture what John Dewey discusses as "undergoing" educational experiences (1916, 163)? An experience undergone is one that engages the self and transforms

perspectives. A particularly glaring deficiency of empirical student satisfaction measures now in general use inheres in their global and general nature, often taking the form of "How satisfied were you with your college experience?" Many items fail to differentiate the various bases for satisfaction. This sin of omission means not only a failure to integrate the content of learnings with responses to them but also a disregard for the economic and prestige rewards of educational attainment. Similarly, most measures capture only the rudiments of satisfaction, which is a complex matter. There is satisfaction in being entertained, there is satisfaction in being extrinsically rewarded or receiving a good grade, there is satisfaction in mastery of something extrinsically useful beyond the educational process itself, and there is satisfaction in mastering whatever is intrinsically rewarding. Cutting across all of these are yet other considerations. Few researchers consider the implications of whether the measure is general and global or specific to a particular subject matter or to specific domains of skills or functions.

Although assessing student satisfactions with educational experiences may be valuable, it is a mistake to treat them as the only indicator of the education's value. Students inexperienced in a scholarly field or method may not be the best judges of what is useful or important.

7. While the topic certainly can and should be studied at two or more points in time, the NLS-72 data did not allow this.

8. The absence of controls for initial views, however, exacerbates the question of causality. Consequently, we will be able to describe the types of experiences and satisfactions corresponding to each education level, and we can do this net of the effects of important individual background characteristics and abilities. But, as we repeatedly note, other unmeasured factors that determine the amount of education individuals eventually complete may also predispose them to particular views of their college experiences. We will not be able fully to disentangle the web of causality here.

9. Asking questions retrospectively can introduce biases of unknown magnitude, for to remember what one anticipated and what the experience actually was like is cognitively complex and invites interpretive reconstructions. Still, satisfactions remembered may tell us something important about the long-term responses to a context.

10. For technical details of the factor analysis and the factor loadings, the reader should consult Appendix B under Factor Analyses and also Educational Satisfactions and Experiences.

11. In other chapters we have included cross-tabulations of 1986 data by educational attainment and race and gender. However, here we shall wait for subsequent analyses to clarify how these background factors affect satisfactions and reports of experiences.

12. We selected 1979 data on satisfactions and perceptions of experiences to restrict them to the undergraduate years and earlier (see Appendix B under The Missing Data Problem and both appendixes under Educational Satisfactions and Experiences for a fuller explanation of how we did this). Since we used the 1986 responses to supplement missing 1979 values, there is a slight chance that in some cases the items refer to graduate school experience. Also, there may be some contamination since 1979 items could refer to the graduate milieu for those few who continued studying for a graduate degree after college with no interruption to the educational career.

13. We have already noted that some analysts regard satisfactions as intervening variables that predict other outcomes.

14. There are other plausible explanations for those who completed more than two years but did not achieve a degree. Dissatisfaction with social life may be a factor in deciding not to complete the degree. It seems unlikely that unhappiness with not finishing the degree program may color the recollections of the social life, for it does not affect the academic satisfactions.

15. Perhaps those who go on to graduate studies are more critical of these opportunities than other groups, but this is unlikely since their academic satisfactions and their other reported experiences exhibit a highly positive pattern. There may be some contamination from the inclusion of some reactions to the graduate school milieu, for many graduate students sacrifice some aspects of sociability and leisure "for the duration" as part of the price of pursuing an advanced degree.

16. Clark (1960) was the first to suggest the cooling-out function of two-year colleges, a process by which the person comes to realistic terms with unrealistically inflated aspirations.

17. At each level of education, however, women do not differ significantly from men.

18. Of course, for many women the presence of abundant sports and recreational facilities may be too late to change sentiments that may have crystallized much earlier in school and family.

19. The individuality of such colleges is, of course, lost by our aggregating colleges and universities according to certain analytical characteristics.

20. Recall that the measure is simply a dichotomy based on reports of ever having lived on a campus. Clearly, we cannot ascertain the possibly magnified effects of longer periods of campus residence beyond some critical threshold. Also, the measure is somewhat flawed in that it does not pertain unambiguously to the particular postsecondary institution addressed by the subjective reports.

21. Gielow and Lee (1988) found more institutional effects than we did. There are several methodological reasons for this, among them the greater homogeneity of their sample and the shorter time span between college experience and the survey questions. First, Gielow and Lee studied only those who went to four-year colleges. These institutions may have greater effects for several reasons, especially their homogeneity, the homogeneity of the college-going population, and their gatekeeping and certifying role. Second, the time between the retrospective satisfaction responses and the college experience was much shorter than ours, and it is possible that subjective effects attenuate with long periods of time. Contributing to this may be the contamination of the judgment of the past from events and situations contemporary with the taking of the questionnaire. Third, Gielow and Lee's sample of 3,492 is somewhat larger than our 2,702, which makes it easier for them to obtain statistically significant results than for us, but this must be scarcely appreciable. Fourth, it is not clear that Gielow and Lee applied weights and corrected for design effects. At any rate, our correction for design effects alone militates strongly against finding results significant, as discussed in Appendix B. Finally, while they include grade point average, they incorporate neither level of educational attainment nor degree completion in their models, and both of the latter play a central role in our work. We discuss the importance of grades in the next section.

22. The interaction effect between vocational emphasis of a program and gender on perceiving the courses as interesting is only significant at the .10 level. Therefore, we did not include it in the table.

23. The measure is simply a dichotomy based on the report of ever having lived on a campus. Clearly, we cannot ascertain the possible effects of longer periods of campus residence. Also, the measure does not pertain unambiguously to the particular postsecondary institution addressed by the subjective reports.

24. This does not necessarily mean that colleges should give everyone A's to elicit approval, for the differential symbolic rewards of the grading system would thereby be eliminated. Hence, differential judgments of the academic side of institutions

by students would not be predicated on grades, but on some other, more elusive basis deriving perhaps from considerations such as morality and loyalty.

25. There are almost certainly indirect effects as Gielow and Lee (1988) found.

26. That both studies included those who did not go to high school increases the overall variability and hence differences attributable to educational level.

27. Bourdieu and Passeron (1977, 14) point out the difficulty the members of a society may have in perceiving the bases for pedagogical legitimacy objectively, especially with the concealment practices of legitimate authority.

28. Riesman uses these memorable images. He borrowed the former from economics, and the latter, from Sigmund Freud.

7

Conclusions: The Triumph of Credentialism?

If education is a myth in modern society it is a powerful one. The effects of myths inhere, not in the fact that individuals believe them, but in the fact that they "know" everyone else does, and thus that "for all practical purposes" the myths are true. We may all gossip privately about the uselessness of education, but in hiring and promoting, in consulting the various magi of our time, and in ordering our lives around contemporary rationality, we carry out our parts in a drama in which education is authority.

John W. Meyer, *The Effects of Education as an Institution*

The justification for a university is that it preserves the connection between knowledge and the zest of life, by uniting the young and the old in the imaginative consideration of learning. . . . A university which fails in this respect has no reason for existence.

Alfred North Whitehead, *The Aims of Education*

"Uniting the young and the old in the imaginative consideration of learning" is a lofty ideal for higher education. Cultivation of the intellect is only one of the high expectations Americans have for colleges. Others are the personal development of students, preparation for citizenship and for positions in the workforce, and enjoying collegiate life. To reiterate the questions at the outset of this book, is higher education fulfilling all these high expectations that are largely contradictory? What, in fact, does higher education do for young adults?

We have framed three major issues. First, what are the long-term effects of higher education on life goals, social activities, self-concept and, educational satisfaction? Second, are these effects the result of differences in college environments and student careers or status transformation? Finally, how are these influences related to basic American values—utilitarian and expressive individualism and civic commitment?

Colleges make many claims about what they do for students. The following, published in a major college guide (Peterson's Guides 1990b), deal with college characteristics and student experiences we have analyzed:

> Because . . . is a residential college, *campus life is an important part of its students' learning experience.*
>
> The College encourages students to take full advantage of the wide range of intercollegiate teams, student-sponsored activities, clubs, community activities, services, professional organizations, and recreational events, believing that *extracurricular activities contribute to a full college experience.*
>
> *Career development is an integral aspect of the College's mission,* and graduates are in great demand by the high-technology community.
>
> The College is dedicated to the belief that a *liberal arts education is the best preparation for life as well as for careers.*
>
> To the courses that *prepare students for careers* in business, industry, and the professions, the University adds a solid base of liberal studies to ensure the formation of a fully educated and *responsible* person.
>
> Each year, about one third of . . . students go on to graduate and professional school, and virtually all of those who seek immediate employment *find jobs* within six months after graduation.
>
> . . . committed to the task of liberally educating its students for the *well-being of the individual* and the *welfare of society* (emphasis ours).

On the basis of our analysis, we must be skeptical of such claims for higher education as a whole or these college characteristics in general. Instead, our results confirm Meyer's (1977) argument that the most powerful effect of education on students is to confer new social identities upon them. Insofar as this changes students' attitudes and behavior, it is a result of or in anticipation of their transformed status. If Meyer is correct, first, differences in college environments and students' careers should have less impact than differences in educational attainment;

and, second, changes that do occur should be consistent with the new status. The analysis of the material rewards of income and job prestige, life goals, social participation, self-concept, and satisfaction with education shows that, in general, educational level and credentials do have the most powerful impact. College characteristics and varying aspects of student experience are not especially influential in determining lasting outcomes of higher education. Some variations in the effects of educational attainment, on the one hand, and college characteristics and student experiences, on the other, will be discussed below. Overwhelmingly, however, our findings support Meyer's contention that the primary impact of education is to define people's legitimate identities and to allocate them to positions in society.

In modern industrial societies, educational institutions have the authority to establish categories and levels of social status and to certify individuals to occupy these positions. One's educational credentials take on "overwhelming ceremonial significance" (Meyer 1977, 75). Education, as Merton (1957) and many others have argued, is the major legitimized institutionalized ladder to individual success in America. The findings in chapter 2 underscore this and show the well-developed articulation between education and the economy from the standpoint of individual occupational careers.

Clarifying the lasting consequences of higher education for students is our aim. In this final chapter we will review our findings about how education transforms the status of individuals, reflecting and reinforcing American core values. Could colleges do more than they do for students? What are the implications of our work for curriculum policy? We offer some advice to those who advise prospective students. Finally, we place the experiences of the High School Class of 1972 in historical context and briefly summarize the contributions of our study.

STATUS TRANSFORMATION AND AMERICAN VALUES

How, then, does this status transformation that higher education performs affect the basic values of young adults? Educational level is especially important for those behaviors and attitudes related to work and less so for expressive and leisure activities and goals. Far from undermining or providing an alternative to American society's emphasis on utilitarian individualism, higher education reinforces and supports it. Chapter 2 develops the impact of postsecondary education on the development of success goals and the acquisition of material rewards related to work. As expected, more years of education and higher degrees attained enhance prospects of higher earnings and greater occupational prestige. College strengthens commitment to the dominant American values of work, success, and achievement through competition. In contrast, among college characteristics and individual educational experiences, only college major and grades have a significant impact on material rewards. No other aspects of the college milieu or experience affect success goals. Differences between college environments do not appear to have lasting consequences. The transformation of status through certification has the paramount influence on utilitarian individualism.

Attaining educational credentials enhances some aspects of expressive individualism but not others, as we showed in chapter 3. The importance of a good education and participation in cultural groups are the goals most influenced by increases in educational status. Changes in educational status do not alter goals having to do with marriage, family, friendship, and leisure. These goals are central to seniors in high school, and they are still highly valued when these graduates reach their early thirties. In contrast, postsecondary schooling intensifies the desire for a good education, apparently as a stairway to intrinsically rewarding occupations. It is completing more education, not differences in college environments or student experiences, that reinforces this work-related expressive goal.

In chapter 4, achieving higher levels of educational status once again has an impact; this time, on civic engagement. Only a small minority of the public participate in civic activities other than voting. Most choose to exercise their "precious American right to not think about politics" (Updike 1971, 44). But bachelor's and advanced degree holders, above all, were more likely than high school graduates to engage in political and community activity. Thomas Jefferson's contention that the best hope for sustained democratic government rests in educating the people was almost prescient. While commitment to community leadership and social justice as life goals declined for everyone as these high school graduates reached early adulthood, the decline was smaller for those achieving higher educational levels. The only college characteristic to affect civic and community participation was the proportion of full-time students at the institution, which had a small positive effect on non-worship church activities.

Compared to high school graduates with no further formal education, persons achieving higher degrees tend to gain in self-esteem and self-direction (see chapter 5). This is not surprising in a society where higher education creates and legitimates occupational statuses and is the major gatekeeper for access to these positions. To graduate from college is, in itself, an accomplishment highly valued in the culture. Increased self-esteem and self-direction may often be associated with experiences of material success. They may also be a necessary, if not sufficient, condition for civic participation. This may be one means by which attaining educational credentials persists in eliciting greater participation in the pursuit of the common good.[1]

The patterns of satisfaction with higher educational experience described in chapter 6 further reveal the ways higher education integrates the individual into society. Postsecondary education provides a distinctive educational experience contrasting sharply with high school. The more education people have, the more they are satisfied with the academic aspects of their schools and the more they report intellectually challenging, interesting, and successful learning experiences during their college years. Obtaining good grades especially strengthens the sense of having valuable college experiences. Campus residence and attending schools with higher proportions of full-time students also have positive effects on the perceptions of alumni. Having successfully climbed several rungs of the legitimate mobility ladder, former students attribute to the rungs provided by their own institution a peculiar and legitimate value.

Often these satisfactions are expressed through loyalty to one's institution. Much more than as a stepping stone to later careers, the alma mater is a continuing affective focus for many Americans. Many alumni and their families manifest intense loyalty and the conviction that their school or college is superior. Alumni who regard the alma mater as an inextricable part of their personae are both legendary and legion. The alma mater provides many middle-class Americans a sense of attachment and solidarity in a society in which the strength of the local community, the church, and family are diminished. The alma mater, then, can help provide the individual with a social identity in an increasingly privatized society.

The overwhelming significance of higher education for material rewards and utilitarian goals and activities, in contrast to expressive and civic ones, can be shown in yet another complementary way. Chapters 2 through 6 give ample details on the effects of levels of education, college characteristics, and student experience for each outcome. Now we gain an overview, contrasting all the findings in the separate domains, by comparing figures in these chapters (see Tables 2.7, 3.4, 4.6, and 6.8).[2] The first column of these figures shows those goals and activities for which educational attainment adds significantly to background factors and previous goals and activities in explaining differences in the various goals and activities. The extent to which college characteristics and individual experiences work their impact is shown in column two. With regard to utilitarian rewards, goals, and activities, college characteristics and student careers, as well as educational attainment, make a significant difference. Both groups of factors also have a strong impact on educational satisfactions. On the other hand, for civic goals and activities, while educational attainment has some effects, college characteristics and student careers count for almost nothing in explaining these outcomes. For expressive goals and activities, it is only the goal related to education—desire for a good education—that is affected, and that only by educational attainment. Variations in most expressive goals and activities, as well as self-concept, are not significantly accounted for by differences in higher education. These figures show, then, how strongly higher education reinforces utilitarian concerns, in contrast to expressive and civic ones. Satisfactions with education, like utilitarian outcomes, are related to both educational attainment and differences in campus milieux and student experiences. Once again, we see how alumni give legitimacy to the system that has conferred identity upon them. Our empirical findings are not inconsistent with the perspective of critical theorists such as Jackman and Muha:

> On one level, we might agree that the well educated are indeed more democratic. Bourgeois democratic systems, with their apparent emphasis on political equality and responsiveness, have not produced tangible commitments to the elimination of inequalities between groups. Instead, the democracies have developed individualism and symbolic responsiveness as a means of diverting and muting the demands of subordinated groups. We suggest that the training and the experience of the well educated make them the natural leaders in the development of such a defense of dominant interests. (1984, 765)

The system of higher education, then, in myriad ways supports, encourages, and legitimates the dominant individualism of the middle and upper middle class and the social structures of the economy. For our cohort of 1972 high school graduates, postsecondary education is an integral part of social mobility and labor market processes. Most alumni are satisfied—the system perpetuates itself in a self-justifying cycle of attainment and satisfaction. Our conclusions, however, prompt us to ask whether higher education might do more for future cohorts of high school graduates.

COULD HIGHER EDUCATION DO MORE
FOR STUDENTS?

Societies, in Peter Berger's image, are prisons comprised of social structures and cultural beliefs and values (1963). We internalize these values and devote ourselves to rebuilding the walls of our prison. This study shows the long-term stability of life goals developed by the senior year in high school and subsequent activities soon afterwards. These early patterns are strong determinants of goals and activities of thirty-two year olds, regardless of experiences in higher education. This kind of analysis, Berger acknowledges, may leave one with a feeling of "sociological claustrophobia" (1963, 122). Is there no way out of this cycle of structures, institutions, and values? Is everything determined by the families we are born into and the abilities we develop in childhood? Do even the schools, our greatest hope to equalize and broaden American youth, serve only to reinforce or legitimate preexisting differences? Berger suggests that there are, in fact, ways in which human societies are more like a stage drama than a prison. Actors in society—individuals and groups—sometimes deviate from the traditional patterns, creating new or changed configurations. Could higher education have more personal impact on students? Could it create conditions for encouraging self-esteem and social concern for graduates? Based on the evidence, our skepticism runs deep. Yet there may be grounds for guarded optimism.

We are skeptical because education is so deeply intertwined with utilitarian individualism. Students go to college for degrees to help them get jobs. If it were not for the constraints of the existing labor market, many would not pay the cost—in earnings foregone, in time, or in subjecting themselves to sometimes boring and frustrating experiences. Since they "have to" be in school, the rational thing for students to do is to pass their courses as quickly and efficiently and with as little interference with their other interests as possible (Becker, Geer, and Hughes 1968). The system encourages cutting corners and cheating, as well as ritualism. Professors respond to this narrow focus by adding courses and requirements and assignments. Thus the war between students and professors escalates.[3] Colleges lost their educational innocence by getting so fully into the certification business. To discuss reforms in teaching or curriculum idealistically seems to ignore the social reality that "the reasons for going to school are extraneous to whatever goes on in the classroom" (Collins 1979, 192). Collins would prefer to solve the problem by "credential abolitionism," whereby obtaining jobs could no longer be based on school credentials. He recognizes, however, that this is not a practical suggestion and that the present policy of "credential Keynesianism" (or constant expansion of education) is likely to continue. Credential requirements for jobs continue to inflate, and both high school and college degrees continue to decline in value. This is, in fact, what has been happening and has been documented recently by the Commission on Skills of the Work Force (National Center on Education and the Economy 1990).

Needing postsecondary educational credentials to attain good pay and prestige means that more and more students will attend higher education institutions for utilitarian motives. The utilitarian motivations of the students generate demand for the institutions to provide practical curricular offerings. These career-oriented programs at once allow the institution to compete successfully for students and shape the requirements for the occupational structure (as Meyer argues). Thus, the relationship is circular, but constantly escalating: a spiral, if you will. Notice how much the whole cycle depends on utilitarian motives.

A number of studies have linked increased rates of postsecondary educational attainment with a mismatch between the skills of the workforce and the skills required in the economy (though whether changes in the occupational structure are in the direction of "up-skilling" or "de-skilling" continues to be debated). Sidestepping this debate, let us simply note that the number of college-educated people continues to exceed the number of jobs requiring a college education.[4] Higher education and occupational structures have become intertwined as many fields have come to rely on specific educational requirements. However, whether they are merely screening devices or sources of training necessary for job performance probably varies.

What good is coming out of the attainment of increasing levels of education by succeeding generations of Americans? This process has not served to equalize the affluence or attainments of the wealthy and the disadvantaged. It has, instead, perpetuated them (Kingston 1981; Useem and Karabel 1986). Moreover, deferring productive roles until the mid- or even late twenties seems an unnecessary waste of productive capacity. One mitigator of credential inflation is the development of systems whereby individuals can develop or prove they have the skills and attributes necessary for viability as a worker and as a contributing member of society. Another possibility is now receiving much public attention. This is a comprehensive national apprenticeship system (e.g., Hamilton 1990). Yet another possibility is the development of reliable indicators of work performance (as advocated in Bishop 1989).

Despite this, there are grounds for believing that higher education could do more for students, even within the constraints of the certification system. Social inertia is powerful, but differences in values and social participation and self-concept offer hope. For some of the outcomes, educational attainment has stronger effects for women: earnings, instrumental individualism, occupational groups, and self-esteem. Only for occupational prestige does educational attainment have stronger effects for men. One college characteristic, the proportion of vocational programs, has a more positive effect on women's perception that courses were interesting than on men's. In addition, the effects of specific college characteristics and student careers taken together do make a difference in most of the utilitarian goals and activities. (These effects could not be attributed to isolated college characteristics and student experiences.) College environments and experiences probably can be manipulated to achieve more desirable effects. Further research might search for mechanisms to produce these different effects.

Specifically, but to a small degree, educational attainment does encourage civic responsibility and participation. Opportunities for women and blacks have been opened in higher education, and these are just the groups predisposed to be a vanguard for renewed civic concern. Women value strong friendships, work with friendly people, good education, and working for social justice more than men do. Women are more involved in cultural groups, church activities, and community volunteer and youth work. Similarly, with all else equal, blacks are more likely than whites to value good education, working for social justice, and community leadership. Blacks, bolstered by enhanced self-esteem and an ideology of oppression, are more often involved than whites in political discussion, community and volunteer work, and church activities. Higher education helps to boost intellectual interests to a slight degree if participation in cultural groups is the indicator. Higher education could, then, contribute more to other forms of individual expression as well as to social vision and civic involvement. If college helps develop among students healthy self-esteem (not to be confused with self-absorption), this could encourage a spirit of mutuality with concern for both self and others. Personal growth and social vision beyond the goals of individual competition and success can be fostered.

INTEGRATING LIBERAL ARTS AND
PROFESSIONAL EDUCATION

The debate between advocates of liberal arts and advocates of professional education has a long history. Among the earliest societies having writing and reading—Egypt, Mesopotamia, and Syria, for example—education had both utilitarian and expressive goals. Education was the gateway to privileged positions for a tiny elite of civil servants and administrators as well as a source of developing character, wisdom, and morality (Marrou 1956). The medieval European universities, too, offered professional education: law, medicine, and theology. Early in the seventeenth century, Sir Francis Bacon questioned this emphasis: "I find it strange that they are all dedicated to the professions, and none left free to arts and science at large" (Meyerson 1974). Meyerson tells of an English clergyman who, when asked why his nephew should study classical languages, answered, "In order to read Scripture in the original, have proper contempt for those who cannot, and eventually rise to a position of emolument in the Church" (Meyerson 1974, 174). Education has been conferring status, then, for a long time. What distinguishes colleges and universities today, especially in the United States, is that they affect the lives of the staggering proportion of the population who attend, whether they graduate or drop out along the way.

The ongoing debate about curriculum has reflected one of the major contradictions in American higher education (Carnoy and Levin 1985). American higher education has become increasingly stratified into prestigious research universities and liberal arts colleges versus lower-status state universities and colleges and community colleges stressing practical skills and training. Enrollment patterns, too, reflect this difference. In the last twenty years, there has been a hemorrhage of students moving out of liberal arts into business and other practical fields (Astin 1985; Boyer 1987). While one of ten bachelors' degrees in 1970 were in business, one of four are today. Arts and sciences degrees declined in the same period from one in four to one in ten (Bowen and Sosa 1989). Over one-third of students at public universities and slightly fewer at private colleges would leave school if they did not believe college would help them in the job market (Boyer 1987). Many students put up with liberal arts requirements, but prefer to move on to specialized training for careers. Still, students are ambivalent; they also want to develop themselves as whole people (Boyer 1987). Professors are ambivalent, too. In a national survey, 56 percent say undergraduate education would be improved if there were less specialized training and more broad liberal education (Carnegie Foundation 1989). This varies by discipline, with humanities and social science professors strongly preferring more liberal education, engineering professors strongly preferring more specialized education, and business professors evenly split on the question.

Supporters of liberal arts point out that most work skills are in fact learned not in school but on the job, and that this is true even for those with professional degrees and certificates (Berg 1971; Collins 1979). With rapidly changing technology, students need to learn critical thinking skills that can be applied to changing situations and multiple occupations. Yet, advocates of professional education argue that the liberal arts are a luxury for the elite but impractical for the majority of students. Most students can afford college only to get degrees for jobs. Their economic future depends on learning marketable skills. Findings in chapters 2 and 6 suggest that if one wants to make a lot of money, one should not major in arts and sciences or in education, and if one wants to learn a lot, one should not major in business. If these were the only options, it would be a discouraging dilemma. There is another way, suggested as early as 1917 by Alfred North Whitehead in an address to the Mathematical Association of England: "There can be no adequate technical education which is not liberal, and no liberal education which is not technical: that is, no education which does not impart both technique and intellectual vision. In simpler language, education should turn out the pupil with something he knows well and something he can do well" (1929, 56).

Whitehead argues what many students would say today: course content that seems relevant to their lives motivates students to be interested. We have seen in chapter 6 that women found their courses more interesting in schools that had higher proportions of vocational programs. A bachelor's degree in liberal arts, followed by graduate or professional school, may be excellent for those who can afford it. But for students with only four years or less of college, some combination of liberal arts and professional education would be more appropriate. Double majors and minors make it possible to get adequate training in both a professional field and the liberal arts. For example, the training of elementary and secondary school teachers is a prominent current concern. Some advocate a four-year liberal arts degree, followed by one or two years of professional training. Others claim this would keep low income and minority persons out of the teaching profession. But most agree that both liberal arts content and practical education courses are needed (Goodlad 1984).

Many higher education critics favor integration of liberal arts and professional education (Cheit 1975; Meyerson 1974; Boyer 1987). A "pure" liberal arts education is a utopian ideal that has been realized only in very limited circumstances. The values of liberal education, however, can be combined with the pursuit of specialized training. Gamson's "liberating" education (Gamson et al. 1984) provides a promising liberal arts component. It does not imply a static common curriculum for all students or one set of ideas or books. Courses could be offered for prospective lawyers in the philosophy of law, for medical students in the social and psychological setting of medicine, and for engineers in the aesthetics of engineering (Meyerson 1974). Engineers should certainly take courses transcending their narrowly technical training—courses dealing holistically with environmental issues. Boyer (1987) proposes "enriched majors," in which the undergraduate specialization includes courses that put the specialty in perspective, studying the history and tradition of the field, its social and economic implications, and characteristic ethical and moral issues involved. Grant and Riesman (1978) suggest recruiting mature scholars, who have already achieved a reputation in their fields, to organize and teach such courses.

How higher education affects self-concepts, life goals, and social participation has been our primary topic. Where educational attainment influences these outcomes, advanced degrees usually have a stronger effect than bachelor's degrees. This is for a wide range of goals and activities: utilitarian, expressive, and civic. These personal changes are precisely those claimed for liberal arts education. Practical training (in the form of professional degrees or specialization in an academic field) does not necessarily dilute the effects of liberal studies at all, but in fact can be fruitfully combined with them. It is because of the status conferred and the identity received that education affects individuals' goals, values, and activities. Most obviously, the specialized curriculum of advanced degrees provides entrée into better-paying, more prestigious, or more meaningful careers. But it is not just utilitarian goals and activities that are enhanced by achieving graduate or professional degrees. People with advanced degrees are also more likely to want interesting work, to be involved in cultural and leisure groups, to participate in a wide range of civic activities, and to be more concerned about social justice. This implies the possibility of integrating liberal arts and more practical studies at the undergraduate level as well. Further study could explore just how different curricular emphases affect the skills and attitudes of graduates. Meanwhile, on the basis of our analyses, what advice would we give to prospective students?

ADVICE FOR PERSONS ADVISING PROSPECTIVE COLLEGE STUDENTS

Credentials are crucial in the social context in which students make choices. Whether justified or not, most firms and occupations use education credentials as screening devices. Thus, obtaining degrees and certificates is one way to maintain or open up more choices. Not all degrees or certificates open specific occupational doors, however. Students should begin learning about occupations and work environments they find interesting early in their education careers, to ascertain which type and levels of formal education are desirable or necessary in those fields.

If one's aim is to make more money, our results confirm the conventional wisdom—opportunities for higher paying jobs come to those with more education. If the aim is a job with high prestige, almost by definition, the higher the education level, the more prestigious the job. While it is important to get a degree, our research implies that it is much less important where one obtains the degree. Yet, one study has shown that senior managers in major corporations are more likely to have undergraduate or professional degrees from an elite group of the most prestigious universities (Useem and Karabel 1986). In contrast, for the broader population of all high school graduates, our research shows that neither income nor occupational prestige depends significantly on attending more selective or larger or private schools. Finally, among 1972 high school graduates, liberal arts and education majors tend to have lower annual incomes than business and other majors fourteen years after high school. It is possible that liberal arts majors may catch up in the future. Moreover, recent increases in teachers' salaries, an oversupply of business graduates, and various other job market factors make long-term predictions precarious.

If meaningful, interesting work and freedom to make decisions are nonetheless important, obtaining the necessary educational credentials becomes critical. For these kinds of jobs are more likely to be available to persons with postsecondary certificates and degrees.

Some prospective students will also ask about differences in the quality of academic or social experience between colleges. Only one difference in college characteristics affected students' academic experience in this study. Women found courses more interesting at schools with a higher proportion of vocational programs. Most of all, however, academic satisfaction is associated with getting good grades and achieving higher levels of education. Yet, if a satisfying college social life is one's goal, residential schools with high proportions of full-time students may have some advantages. The larger the school and the higher the proportion of full-time students and those who live on campus, the more likely students are to be satisfied with the social life and sports and recreation facilities.

LEARNING FROM ONE COHORT

The class of 1972 left high school for their respective postsecondary pursuits—college, work, family—at a unique point in history. On campus and elsewhere they were immersed in the disillusionment and uncertainty of the winding down of the Vietnam conflict and the turmoil surrounding the Watergate scandal. These historic circumstances must have affected the values, goals, and activities examined in this study. Consequently, we must appraise the extent to which we can generalize about the impact of higher education from the experience of a particular high school class in a singular historic period.

Viewing the circumstances and attitudes of many generations of college students provides a much-needed perspective to this appraisal. Mapping levels of political activism and the strength of student political organizations over the past century, Altbach (1974) demonstrates that political involvement among college students varies cyclically. Indeed, Levine (1980) argues that the patterned variation in both the level of student activism and the content of student concerns vary systematically around periods of war. Levine likens these societal oscillations and corresponding student orientations to an individual person's periods of frenzied wakeful activity followed by exhausted rest. The societal pattern of "community ascendancy" in the years preceding and during World Wars I and II and the Vietnam conflict parallels heightened student activism, while the "individual ascendancy" prevailing in postwar years entails student expressive and utilitarian concerns. As Levine argues:

> The relationship between the individual and the community is continually changing. At times when society is perceived to be moving toward the community ideal, individual ties with the community are strengthened and community is the dominant theme. In times when the society appears to be moving in the

opposite direction, individual ties with the community are attenuated and the individual is dominant. An emphasis on "me" is what differentiates periods of individual ascendancy from periods of community ascendancy. The orientation of individual ascendancy is hedonistic, emphasizing the primacy of duty to one's self, while that of community ascendancy is ascetic, stressing the primacy of duty to others. Individual ascendancy is concerned principally with rights, community ascendancy with responsibilities (1980, 25).

Altbach's and Levine's interpretations help specify Karl Mannheim's understanding of the "stratified consciousness" of different generations into sharply divergent perspectives by showing how it comes about (Bush and Simmons 1981, 142). But for two observations, this fluidity might appear to contradict what Bellah et al. (1985) portrayed as a unidirectional trend toward greater individuation. One is that both the American cultural vocabulary of motives and political and economic structures persist throughout this century-long period in assuming an individualistic motivation and goal system. Even in periods of community ascendancy, both Altbach (1974) and Levine (1980) note that only a fraction of the young people on campuses actively pursue this orientation.

Second, the cycles described here derive from limited data. A longer time perspective on more inclusive indicators of civic values and goals might show a pattern of decline in the intensity or extent of the periods of community ascendancy. Further, the observation that elevated levels of civic concern center around extraordinary cataclysmic events is not a particularly sanguine argument for American society's ability to sustain a commitment to the common good.

Attending college in the post-Vietnam years, the late adolescence and early adulthood of the high school class of 1972 falls in an age of individual ascendancy. Most apropos to the concerns of this study, Levine concludes: "During periods of individual ascendancy, students are more committed to the material aspects of the American dream and believe more strongly in their likelihood of achieving them" (Levine 1980, 124). Thus, the powerfully utilitarian and indifferently civic-minded perspectives of the class of 1972 can be depicted as a natural occurrence in the larger historical context of our times that will not necessarily be replicated in future generations. Although these cyclical patterns help us understand this cohort's absolute levels of subscription to civic and individualistic goals and values, they leave unanswered the question of the role of higher education in the development of different perspectives in succeeding cohorts.

To say that postsecondary education elicits changes in individual students' values differently in various historical eras is to suggest that the experience of attending college serves as a mechanism through which the historical circumstances promote particular values among young people. In fact, Levine suggests that schools, as well as other institutions, do play this role: "The level of altruism among (1970s) undergraduates is low. It has been replaced by an ethic of 'looking out for number one' and an almost singleminded concern with material success. In part, this is a reflection of the mood of the times, but it is also encouraged, often unwittingly, by actions of the family, the schools, the media, and the government" (Levine 1980, xvii).

For these students of the 1970s, attaining higher education reinforced already high levels of instrumental goals and intrinsic work values while contributing only a little to initially low civic commitments and activity levels. This is consistent with the tenet that higher education—perhaps inadvertently—encourages views already largely formed by other social actors (particularly, Levine would argue, the media).

It is impossible to reach firm conclusions regarding the impact of higher education for earlier or future groups of students based on the experience of a single high school class, just as it is difficult to guess where a line is drawn given only one point. Nevertheless, placing our findings in the context of the cycles observed by Levine yields a working hypothesis: The nature and extent of higher education's effects on individuals' goals and values depend on whether the particular outcomes of interest are consistent with the prevailing societal orientation. This dovetails neatly with Meyer's assertion of a legitimating function of higher education; only in this case, rather than certifying individuals or making credible specific bodies of knowledge, colleges validate the focus and values of the larger society with regard to individualism and community involvement.

If higher education currently simply reinforces the prevailing societal orientation, can conscious efforts to cultivate orientations that are not ascendant be fruitful? Because this has not been attempted on a massive scale, this question cannot be addressed with national-level aggregate data such as those used here. Rather, this question can best be answered through well-designed intensive small-scale studies and field demonstrations in social engineering. One interesting aspect of any attempt consciously to cultivate particular goals and values is that to do so requires making these aims explicit. Given the multiple and often conflicting expectations held by students, parents, professors, and business leaders, individually and as groups, agreeing on desirable outcomes may be even more challenging than attempting to effect any particular set of changes.

CONTRIBUTIONS OF THIS STUDY

Finally, how does this book contribute to understanding the lasting effects of higher education? We have taken a close, careful look at the goals and activities of a cohort of American high school graduates. To clarify what higher education is really doing and not doing in their lives was the aim. The benefits of the approach derive both from its empirical and its conceptual bases.

A rich base of data combined from several sources provides an advantage over many earlier studies. The nationally representative sample permits generalizing about the whole population of high school graduates. Having information for the same persons when they were high school seniors and fourteen years later allows us to take account of the impact of previous goals and activities and to assess the impact of postsecondary education in the intervening years. The comparison group of people with no more than a high school education makes it possible to isolate what higher education is and is not doing for its clientele.

The dominant American values described by Bellah and his associates and Meyer's theory of education's place in modern societies have formed the conceptual framework. In spite of limitations of the data discussed in chapter 1, many of the survey questions provided useful measures of utilitarian and expressive individualism and of civic commitment. We have been able to observe the development of a broad range of core values and activities among adults in their first fourteen years after high school.

The theoretical framework helps us illuminate reasons for the strength and persistence of utilitarian individualism in American society. For success goals are sustained by schools—the very organizations that define knowledge and occupational positions and train and certify persons for these positions. Utilitarian individualism has strong cultural and historical roots, and the contemporary institutions that reinforce this individualism are pervasive and powerful. To understand the depth and breadth of their power is essential for clarifying the effects of higher education on students.

What higher education does is to confer status upon its alumni, and in the process, at least for this cohort, to strengthen utilitarian values. Moreover, higher education undergirds the legitimacy of the social and economic system. People want a good education so they can get better-paying and more meaningful work. They get the results they expect, and they are pleased with what they receive. The myths and norms of society are upheld. Finally, to a small degree, education enhances civic concerns and commitment.

Where higher education fails is in affecting seriously the expressive side of the lives of these alumni, their leisure activities and goals, their view of self, and to a lesser degree, their civic participation. There is precious little evidence that higher education really contributes to the personal development of its students beyond certifying them. Colleges are not fulfilling the high hopes many Americans have placed in them in this one regard.

We have also argued, however, that what existed for the high school class of 1972 does not necessarily determine what shall always be in the future. For there are hints in our results that colleges could do far more for the personal growth and civic commitment of students. It would be a shame if the inertia of "business as usual" and "more of the same" stifled critical scrutiny and prevented real change.

NOTES

1. College grades, on the other hand, enhance neither self-esteem and sense of efficacy nor commitment to political activity and social change. Grades in college are positively related to occupational status and to participation in church-related activities. Beyond this, grades have no discernable effects on the activities and goals of young adults. Grades, like certificates and degrees, are indicators of academic status. The status conferred by grades is useful primarily for schools, where good grades serve as administrative sorting criteria and gatekeepers for further higher education. But undergraduate grades are seldom important in the process of obtaining employment. Moreover, academic learning has little relation to job performance (Collins 1979). As one of Walker Percy's (1980) characters puts it, "I got all A's in college, but I failed life." College grades reflect dutiful conformity to the conventional norms of school, and by extension, family, church, and occupation.

2. Recall that in chapter 5 neither level of education nor college characteristics nor experiences improved predictive power of a model beyond background characteristics and initial values of self-concept.

3. Conflict between the culture of students and the culture of teachers is endemic in education (Waller 1961). Its extent in high schools has been recently documented by Goodlad (1984) and Sizer (1984).

4. Definitions of the education needed for adequate performance in a job tend to be rather loose, often relying on the average level of educational attainment of incumbents and rarely actually comparing job tasks to skills transmitted in the educational process.

Appendix A

Variables in Models of Outcomes

EDUCATIONAL ATTAINMENT (1986)[1]

Only High School Scored 1 if no college attended, 24.6%; 0 otherwise.[2]

Less than Two Years of College Scored 1 if some higher education but less than two years, 21.7%; 0 otherwise.

Two Years or More of College Scored 1 if two years or more of college but less than bachelor's degree, 24.9%; 0 otherwise.

Bachelor's Degree Scored 1 if four- or five-year degree, 18.0%; 0 otherwise.

Advanced Degree Scored 1 if M.A., Ph.D., M.D., or other advanced professional degree, 10.8%; 0 otherwise.

COLLEGE CHARACTERISTICS

Student Enrollment Total student enrollment of an institution for 1972 (Tenison 1976). Mean = 11,894; standard deviation = 11,947. Smallest postsecondary institution had 117 students and the largest had 55,858. Median = 4599. (Natural log used in linear regression; the enrollment was divided by 1,000 for logistic regression.)

Selectivity The median Scholastic Aptitude Test (SAT) score for an institution's 1973 freshman class. American College Test (ACT) scores converted to SAT scores (Higher Education Research Institute 1985) supplemented by data on missing institutions (Tenison 1976). Mean = 956.7; standard deviation = 116.3. Lowest median SAT was 580; highest was 1400. (Divided by 100 for ordinary and logistic regression.)

Private Control Scored 0 if publicly controlled institution; 1
    if private (Tenison 1976). Of the college students, 75.4 %
    attended public institutions.
Full-Time Students Percent full-time students enrolled
    (Tenison 1976). Mean = .648; standard deviation = .209.
    The minimum was .02; maximum, 1.00. (Multiplied by 10
    for logistic regression.)
Vocational Emphasis The proportion of educational pro-
    grams that are vocational (Carroll 1979). Mean = 60.1;
    standard deviation = 13.8 with a minimum of .00 and a
    maximum of 100. (Divided by 10 for ordinary and logistic
    regression).
Highly Residential The proportion of freshmen residing on
    campus (Carroll 1979). Coded 1 for greater than 75%; 0
    for other.

INDIVIDUAL HIGHER EDUCATIONAL CAREERS

Business Major Last reported undergraduate major in busi-
    ness (coded 1 for business; 0 for other). 19.7% of the total.
Education Major Last reported undergraduate major in edu-
    cation (coded 1 for education; 0 for other). 14.1% of the
    total.
Arts & Sciences Major Last reported undergraduate major in
    arts and sciences (coded 1 for arts and science; 0 for other).
    Arts and sciences majors were 23.5% of the total.
Ever Lived on Campus Self-report of ever having lived on a
    campus (coded 1 if any report; 0 if none). Of the respon-
    dents, 42.7% had lived on campus.
College Grades The mean of all self-reported undergraduate
    grade point averages. "Mostly A" = 7; "About half A and half
    B" = 6; "Mostly B" = 5; "About half B and half C" = 4; "Mostly
    C" = 3; "About half C and half D" = 2; "Mostly D or below"
    = 1. For ordinary regression, recoded: 1 through 2.67 = 3;
    mean = 5.103; standard deviation = 1.057; 17 categories
    from 3 to 7. For logistic regression: lowest = 1; highest =
    7; mean = 5.087; standard deviation = 1.097; 23 categories
    from 1 to 7.

BACKGROUND FACTORS

Academic Abilities A composite score resulting from adding
    standardized scores of tests on vocabulary, reading,

mathematics, and letter groups (a test of inductive reasoning) administered during the senior year in high school (Riccobono et al. 1981, Vol. 2, Appendix K, p. 2). Deciles used in logistic regression.

Family Socioeconomic Status   An equally weighted linear composite based on mother's and father's education, father's occupational status, parents' income, and amount and type of material possessions in the home (Riccobono et al. 1981, Vol. 2, Appendix K, pp. 4-11). Deciles used in logistic regression.

Women   Scored 0 if male (49.6%); scored 1 if female (50.4%).

White   Scored 0 if black (6.6%); scored 1 if white (93.4%).

IN PURSUIT OF SUCCESS   (Chapter 2)

1986 Earnings   Annual salary and wages for 1986.   Mean = $22,447; standard deviation = 14,262.2 and a minimum of $70 and a maximum of $99,995; median = $20,000. Natural log used in linear regression.

Occupational Status   Socioeconomic index of most recent job from Stevens and Featherman (1981; see Appendix B) revision of Duncan Socioeconomic Index.   Mean = 44.22; standard deviation = 19.06 with a minimum of 11.13 and a maximum of 88.65; median = 46.0.

Job Security (1972 & 1986)   A composite score computed by adding responses to items dealing with the importance of the following in "determining the kind of work you plan to be doing for the rest of your life": "openings available"; "good starting income now or in a few years"; and "job security and permanence."   Scores ranged from 1 to 9. Recoded for logistic regression: 1,2,3 = 0; 4,5,6 = 1; 7,8,9 = 2.   For 1972, 0 = 7.1%; 1 = 43.5%; 3 = 49.3%. For 1986, 0 = 1.2%; 1 = 20.3%; 2 = 78.4%.

Occupational Groups (1974 and 1986)   Participation in union, trade, or farm association.   Scored 2 if "active participant"; 1 if "member only"; 0 if "not at all."   For 1974, 2 = 4.5%; 1 = 11.3%; 0 = 84.1%.   For 1986, 2 = 11.4%; 1 = 20.3%; 0 = 68.3%.

Opportunities for Children (1974 & 1986)   The importance of the life goal, "being able to give my children better opportunities than I've had."   Scored 2 for "very important"; 1 for "somewhat important"; and 0 for "not important."   For 1972, 2 = 62.9%; 1 = 30.3%; 0 = 6.8%.   For 1986, 2 = 56.2%; 1 = 34.9%; 0 = 8.9.

Intrinsic Work Value (1972 & 1986) A composite score from sum of responses to items about importance in life of: "freedom to make my own decisions"; and "work that seems important and interesting to me." Scores ranged from 1 to 6. Recoded: 1,2 = 0; 3,4 = 1; 5,6 = 2. For 1972, 0 = .9%; 1 + 21.2%; 2 = 77.9%. For 1986, 0 = .6%; 1 = 12.0%; 2 = 87.4%.

Success Goal (1972 & 1986) (The importance in life of: "Being successful in my line of work." Scored same as foregoing item. For 1972, 2 = 83.5%; 1 = 15.4%; 0 = 1.1%. For 1986, 2 = 67.9%; 1 = 30.3%; 0 = 67.9%.

Money Goal (1972 & 1986) The importance in life of "having lots of money." Scored same as Opportunities for Children (above). For 1972, 2 = 14.9%; 1 = 60.0%; 0 = 25.1%. For 1986, 2 = 15.3%; 1 = 67.9%; 0 = 16.8%.

Opportunities for Promotion and Advancement (1972 & 1986) The importance of "opportunity for and promotion and advancement in the long run" in "determining the kind of work you plan to be doing for most of your life." Scored same as Opportunities for Children (above). For 1972, 2 = 41.4%; 1 = 41.6%; 0 = 17.0%. For 1986, 2 = 60.7%; 1 = 33.3%; 0 = 6.1%.

IN PURSUIT OF SELF-EXPRESSION (Chapter 3)

Strong Friendships (1972 & 1986) The importance in life of "having strong friendships." Scored 2 for "very important"; 1 for "somewhat important"; and 0 for "not important." For 1972, 2 = 80.6%; 1 = 17.8%; 0 = 1.6%. For 1986, 2 = 70.5%; 1 = 27.7%; 0 = 1.8%.

Marriage and Family (1974 & 1986) The importance in life of "finding the right person to marry and having a happy family life." Scored 2 for "very important"; 1 for "somewhat important"; and 0 for "not important." For 1972, 2 = 82.5%; 1 = 13.2%; 0 = 4.3%. For 1986, 2 = 86.0%; 1 = 10.8%; 0 = 3.2%.

Working with Friendly People (1972 & 1986) The importance in life of "meeting and working with friendly, sociable people." Scored 2 for "very important"; 1 for "somewhat important"; and 0 for "not important." For 1972, 2 = 56.5%; 1 = 35.7%; 0 = 7.8%. For 1986, 2 = 54.8%; 1 = 40.2%; 0 = 5.0%.

Leisure (1974 & 1986) The importance in life of "having leisure to enjoy my own interests." Scored 2 for "very important"; 1 for "somewhat important"; and 0 for "not important." For 1972, 2 = 57.3%; 1 = 40.7%; 0 = 2.0%. For 1986, 2 = 60.6%; 1 = 38.1%; 0 = 1.2%.

Good Education (1974 & 1986) The importance in life of "having a good education." Scored 2 for "very important"; 1 for "somewhat important"; and 0 for "not important." For 1972, 2 = 56.8%; 1 = 39.7%; 0 = 3.6%. For 1986, 2 = 58.3%; 1 = 38.9%; 0 = 2.8%.

Cultural Groups (1974 & 1986) Participation in a "literary, art, discussion, music or study group." Scored 2 if "active participant"; 1 if "member only"; 0 if "not at all." For 1972, 2 = 9.2%; 1 = 2.9%; 0 = 87.9%. For 1986, 2 = 6.0%; 1 = 3.1%; 0 = 90.9%.

Social Groups (1974 & 1986) Participation in a "social, hobby, garden, or card playing group." Scored 2 if "active participant"; 1 if "member only"; 0 if "not at all." For 1972, 2 = 18.2%; 1 = 3.9%; 0 = 77.9%. For 1986, 2 = 17.4%; 1 = 6.1%; 0 = 76.4%.

Sports Clubs (1974 & 1986) Participation in "sports teams or sports clubs." Scored 2 if "active participant"; 1 if "member only"; 0 if "not at all." In 1974, 2 = 25.7%; 1 = 4.3%; 0 = 70.0%. In 1986, 2 = 26.0%; 1 = 5.8%; 0 = 68.2%.

IN PURSUIT OF THE COMMON GOOD (Chapter 4)

Voting (1974 & 1986) In 1986: Has respondent voted in last presidential or any subsequent election? "Yes" = 75.9%. In 1974: Prior to 1974, has respondent ever voted in a local, state or national election? "Yes" = 66.5%. Scored 0 if "no" and 1 if "yes."

Political Activities (1974 & 1986) A composite score computed by adding responses to items regarding activities in the prior two years: talking about public problems with officials; canvassing voters; monetary political contributions; attending political meetings; working for a candidate; participation in political organizations. Scored 2 for "frequently"; 1 for "sometimes"; and 0 for "never." 1974 mean = 7.72; standard deviation = 2.09; ranging from 5 to 18. 1986 mean = 7.50; standard deviation = 2.08; with a range from 6 to 18.

Political Discussion (1974 & 1986) A composite score computed by adding responses to items regarding activities in the prior two years: talking about political problems with family; with friends; and with work associates. Scored 2 for "frequently"; 1 for "sometimes"; and 0 for "never." Scores ranged from 1 to 9. Recoded for logistic regression: 1,2,3 = 0; 4,5,6 = 1; 7,8,9 = 2. For 1974, 2 = 48.2%; 1 = 49.3%; 0 = 2.5%. For 1986, 2 = 42.8%; 1 = 55.2%; 0 = 1.9%.

Social Justice (1972 & 1986) The importance in life of "working to correct social and economic inequalities." Scored 2 if "very important"; 1 if "somewhat important"; and 0 if "not important." In 1972, 2 = 25.7%; 1 = 53.0%; 0 = 21.3%. In 1986, 2 = 8.2%; 1 = 55.3%; 0 = 36.5%.

Community Leadership (1972 & 1986) The importance in life of "being a leader in the community." In 1972, 2 = 10.2%; 1 = 44.6%; 0 = 45.2%. In 1986, 2 = 3.1%; 1 = 31.0%; 0 = 65.9%.

Non-Worship Church Activities (1974 & 1986) "Church or church-related activities (not counting worship services)." Coded 2 for "active participant"; 1 for "member only"; 0 for "not at all." In 1974, 2 = 16.1%; 1 = 16.7%; 0 = 67.2%. In 1986, 2 = 24.5%; 1 = 19.6%; 0 = 55.9%.

Community Groups (1974 & 1986) "Community centers, neighborhood improvement, or social-action associations or groups." Coded 2 for "active participant"; 1 for "member only"; 0 for "not at all." In 1974, 2 = 4.5%; 1 = 3.6%; 0 = 91.8%. In 1986, 2 = 5.9%; 1 = 7.5%; 0 = 86.6%.

Volunteer Work (1974 & 1986) "Organized volunteer work- such as in a hospital." Coded 2 for "active participant"; 1 for "member only"; 0 for "not at all." For 1974, 2 = 4.7%; 1 = 1.4%; 2 = 93.9%. For 1986, 2 = 5.6%; 1 = 2.1%; 0 = 92.3%.

Youth Organizations (1974 & 1986) "Youth organizations— such as Little-League Coach, scouting, etc." Coded 2 for "active participant"; 1 for "member only"; 0 for "not at all." For 1974 2 = 6.8%; 1 = 2.1%; 0 = 91.1%. For 1986, 2 = 13.8%; 1 = 5.0%; 0 = 81.3%.

IN PURSUIT OF SELF (Chapter 5)

Self-Direction (1972 & 1986) A weighted factor score from factor analysis of items: planning only makes one un- happy—plans hardly ever work out; something or someone stops one from getting ahead; happiest when one accepts condition in life; and good luck is more important than hard work for success. High scores show perception of self-di- rection while low scores indicate perception of direction by outside forces or others. 1972 mean = .059; standard deviation = .755, with a minimum of -3.09 and a maximum of 1.24. 1986 mean = .076; standard deviation = .767, with a minimum of -3.73 and a maximum of 1.19.

Self-Esteem (1972 & 1986) A weighted factor score from factor analysis of items: positive attitude toward self; person of worth on equal plane with others; able to do things as well as others; and satisfied with self. High scores show high self-esteem. 1972 mean = -.006; standard deviation = .827, with a minimum of -3.90 and a maximum of 1.31. 1986 mean = .014; standard deviation = .870 with a minimum of -5.354 and a maximum of 1.103.

IN PURSUIT OF EDUCATIONAL EXPERIENCES (Chapter 6)

For 1979 items, the referent is the most recent educational institution attended, including high school (1986 items were used only to supplement missing 1979 responses). 1986 items refer only to the most recent postsecondary school attended.

Academic Satisfaction A weighted factor score from factor analysis (Harman 1967) of the most recent school or college attended. Highest loading items: satisfaction with "quality of instruction"; "quality of teaching"; "quality of teachers"; "course curriculum"; "my intellectual growth"; and "development of my work skills." Mean = -.003; standard deviation = .932, with a minimum of -3.54 and a maximum of 1.58. The satisfaction items with their factor loadings after varimax rotation (Kaiser 1958) on the academic factor follow:

Quality of instruction	(.81)
Quality of teachers	(.73)
Courses and curriculum	(.68)
My intellectual growth	(.66)
Development of work skills	(.60)
The social life	(.19)
Sports and recreational facilities	(.07)

Social Life Satisfaction with "the social life." Recoded for logistic regression: Scored 2 if "very satisfied"; 1 if "somewhat satisfied"; 0 if "neutral", "somewhat dissatisfied", or "very dissatisfied." 2 = 21.9%; 1 = 34.6%; 0 = 43.4%.

Recreational Facilities Satisfaction with "sports and recreational facilities." Recoded for logistic regression: Scored 2
if "very satisfied"; 1 if "somewhat satisfied"; 0 if "neutral",
"somewhat dissatisfied", or "very dissatisfied." 2 = 19.9%;
1 = 31.8%; 0 = 48.3%.

School Prestige Satisfaction with "the prestige of the school."
Recoded for logistic regression: 2 if "very satisfied" or
"somewhat satisfied"; 1 if "neutral"; 0 if "somewhat dissatisfied" or "very dissatisfied." 2 = 56.9%; 1 = 35.3%; 0 =
43.0%.

Counseling-Job Placement Satisfaction with "counseling and
job placement." Recoded for logistic regression: 2 if "very
satisfied" or "somewhat satisfied"; 1 if "neutral"; 0 if "somewhat dissatisfied" or "very dissatisfied." 2 = 33.8%; 1 =
37.1 %; 0 = 29.2%.

Difficulty of Courses "Courses harder than expected." Coded
1 for "was my experience"; 2 for "was not my experience."
1 = 12%.

Interesting Courses "Courses were interesting." Coded 1 for
"was my experience"; 2 for "was not my experience." 1 =
78%.

Academic Performance "I performed well academically."
Coded 1 for "was my experience"; 2 for "was not my
experience." 1 = 80%.

Learned a Lot "I learned a lot." Coded 1 for "was my experience"; 2 for "was not my experience." 1 = 76%.

Met People with New Ideas "I met people with new ideas."
Coded 1 for "was my experience"; 2 for "was not my
experience. 1 = 71%.

NOTES

1. Source is the *National Longitudinal Study of the High School
Class of 1972* (Tourangeau 1987) and subsequent waves unless
otherwise noted. See Appendix B for the statistical reliabilities
of all composite measures constructed of two or more variables.
2. Throughout this appendix the percentages that are given
represent the proportion, after weighting, of all cases in the
particular category.

Appendix B

Research Design and Methods

INTRODUCTION

This appendix reports the essential technical details of how we did this study. We excluded most technical material from the body of the book because we wanted our sociological interpretations to be straightforward, intelligible, and provocative. Thickets of technical detail might easily bore or distract the reader, thereby defeating our purpose.

The process of data analysis spanned several years. During that time, we made countless choices, which we describe here. We have tried to make this appendix accessible to the general reader. Even so, longitudinal analyses with many variables are intrinsically complex. Where we could not simplify further without extending the book to absurd lengths, some knowledge of quantitative research methods may help the reader.

STRENGTHS OF RESEARCH DESIGN AND METHOD

Smart, Ethington, and McLaughlin (1985, 5-6) noted that methodological deficiencies in the design of many previous studies (see Corey 1936; Wise 1958; Feldman and Newcomb 1969; Bowen 1977) resulted in their inconclusiveness. This study does much to overcome these flaws.[1]

We shall discuss here in some detail each of our seven correctives to these prior studies' methodological deficiencies that we discussed briefly in chapter 1. To recapitulate, these are: longitudinal design; a control group of those not going beyond high school; the time span of fourteen years; the nationally representative sample; the wide array of outcomes; the inclusion of the characteristics of educational institutions; and the inclusion of the educational careers of the individual students in educational settings after high school.

Longitudinal Design

The National Longitudinal Study of the High School Class of 1972 (NLS-72) (Eckland and Alexander 1980; Riccobono et al. 1981; Tourangeau et al. 1987) included many personal and social characteristics of a sample of American high school seniors in 1972 or 1974 and again in 1986. With longitudinal designs one can determine the ordering of events and see how behavior and beliefs change over time. One can distinguish causal factors and specify their relative weights in the causal process. Panel designs, in contrast to cross-sectional or correlational ones with data gathered at one point in time, then, afford a greater opportunity to make causal inferences.

We present the measures used in our analyses above in Appendix A. We discuss how we handled particular variables and missing data below. The initial 1972 variables include gender, race, family socioeconomic status, and a measure of academic abilities. These particular items were measured only at the outset. Other measures were, however, repeated. For example, 1972 measures of values and attitudes, self-esteem, and self-direction and 1974 measures of social and political activities provided baselines. Assessing the changes in these attitudes and behaviors was possible since these questions were asked again in 1986.

The Control Group

Crucial to this study is the inclusion of those with no postsecondary education or training. The lack of a control group is a serious deficiency in almost all early studies of higher education. This flaw still characterizes most studies. How can one tell that the changes supposedly taking place in college wouldn't have taken place anyway? Sociocultural events peculiar to the historical moment could have affected the entire cohort in similar ways. Developmental or maturational events that are "normal" for persons between 18 and 32 might have done so, too. Those not going on to college comprise, then, a useful control group for us. We can see what is "value added" by educational context and attainment and we can also isolate the direct effects of higher education. We removed the effects of the many other initial dissimilarities of the groups statistically. We did this by using multivariate analyses, as reported below.

Fourteen-Year Time Span

The time span of fourteen years can give us a grasp of the duration of the effects of higher education. Too often, otherwise exemplary studies stop short of college graduation (Gruber 1979) or at graduation (Astin 1977). Or, they follow up only a short time after graduation (Smart, Ethington, and McLaughlin 1985). Or, they examine young people after graduation without assessing their preexisting characteristics (Hyman, Wright, and Reed 1975; Hyman and Wright 1979). By 1986 most of our sample was thirty-two years old. The respondents have, for the most part, concluded their formal educational experience. And they have begun to solidify a life pattern that may incorporate earlier educational experiences.

Nationally Representative Sample

The NLS-72 sample is from the fifty United States and the District of Columbia (Riccobono et al. 1981, 8; Tourangeau et al. 1987). The design represents various geographical regions, the degree of urbanization, community income levels, high school size, public and private control, proportion of minority group enrollment, and geographic proximity to institutions of higher education. Schools were sampled first, then the students within them, in a sampling design referred to as a stratified, two-stage probability sample. There are data from 16,683 students in 1,061 schools in the base year, 1972. The first (1973-74) follow-up sample survey retention rate was an exceptionally high 93.7 percent. The 1973-1974 sample added 4,450 more students from 257 additional schools. For the four later waves (1974--1975, 1976-1977, 1979-1980, and 1986-1987), response rates continued high, over 90 percent for each wave after 1973-1974. In 1986, of the 14,489 respondents contacted, 12,841 returned questionnaires. The sample chosen for 1986 was smaller than previous years, but the retention rate was 88.6 percent. This proportion compares favorably with the high proportions responding in earlier years. Since seven years had elapsed since the previous wave, it is also remarkably high. Attrition from wave to wave has, then, been extraordinarily low.

We weighted all analyses to correct for attrition and for the deliberate overrepresentation of certain types of students in the original design. This helps assure representativeness. This process adjusts the frequency distributions of critical background variables: gender, race, high school curriculum, high school grades, and postsecondary education. It makes them proportional to those of high school seniors in the United States in 1972 (for a complete explanation, see Riccobono et al. 1981, 11; Tourangeau et al. 1987). We have, then, a high level of confidence that our findings successfully represent the high school class of 1972. Since, however, we can say nothing about those who dropped out of high school before the spring of the senior year, interpreting the effects of high school completion per se will have to be left to others. Because high school dropouts have not been included, generalizing our results to the entire age cohort is unwarranted.

Wide Array of Outcomes

The NLS-72 data are an omnibus of items that interest researchers of higher education. Appendix A shows the great richness of the items we were interested in, grouped in order. First are the causal factors: educational attainment,[2] characteristics of higher education institutions, and students' college careers. Second are groups of outcomes corresponding to chapters 2-6 of the text: utilitarian individualism, expressive individualism, civic commitments, self-concept, and educational satisfactions and reports of how educational contexts were experienced. For reported activities, goals, self-direction and self-esteem, we are able to control on the previous level of a measure for an outcome. (See below for further discussion of this under Before and After Measures of Outcomes.)

Characteristics of Educational Institutions

We include information on 1,509 postsecondary educational settings that our respondents attended. These institutions represent a full spectrum of the formal educational possibilities beyond high school. We present figures on the predominant or last undergraduate postsecondary school students attended. Six hundred fifty-nine attended research universities; 237 went to doctoral granting universities; 941 attended comprehensive universities; 278 went to liberal arts colleges; and 578 attended a variety of two-year colleges.[3] This richness yields a twofold chance to show how institutional features affect outcomes. First, we can compare the effects of an educational characteristic to the effects of educational attainment itself. Second, we can compare the effects of institutional features with one another.

We used institutional data on postsecondary institutions from three sources. The first was the Basic Institutional Source File of the NLS-72—Institutional Data Base (Tenison 1976). This institutional data-set of the College Entrance Examination Board (CEEB) complemented the NLS-72 set of items for individuals. We used 1973 data from this source.[4] The final analysis used the proportion of full-time students, the total enrollment of the institution, and whether control was public or private.

The second source of institutional data was the Higher Education Research Institute's *HERI S.A.T. File with Added Institutional Characteristics* (Higher Education Research Institute 1985). HERI converted median ACT (American College Testing Program Assessment) scores of 1973 freshmen at an institution to equivalent Scholastic Aptitude Test (SAT) scores. HERI also provided estimates of median SAT scores for many institutions without CEEB selectivity data. The Higher Education Research Institute imputed median SAT scores to such institutions by using known median SAT scores from closely comparable types of colleges. This is more satisfactory than the previous method of attributing the 1973 national median of 850 of all incoming freshmen to all postsecondary schools for which the actual median scores were unavailable.

The third source was *Characteristics of Postsecondary Education Institutions* (Carroll 1979). Based on institutional self-reports, this source yielded the proportion of freshmen living on campus, the proportion of vocational versus academic programs, and the proportion of students in such vocational programs.

As is usually the case in secondary analyses with data from several different sources, particularly administrative data, there were some discrepancies. For example, the data-set from the CEEB occasionally differed sharply from the HERI data-set, such as type of control and whether the school was two-year or four-year. We resolved these by hand-checking the institution in CEEB's *The College Handbook* (1983-84) and *Barron's Profiles of American Colleges* (College Division of Barron's Educational Series 1983).

Individual Educational Careers after High School

Our models encompass three kinds of information from NLS-72 about education beyond high school. First, we incorporate grades attained after high school. Second, we use a crude measure of student involvement in campus life, reported residence on campus. Third, we include the last reported major, infrequent in studies of the effects of higher education. We discuss these under the Measures and Measurement section below.

THE LOGIC OF THE DESIGN

Isolating Causes

How did we isolate the direct effects of education beyond high school from the normal development of those who have not gone beyond high school? Explicitly comparing outcomes for individuals at each level of educational attainment with those for their peers completing only high school enables us to differentiate the direct effects of educational attainment from the changes young people would undergo regardless of whether they continued their schooling. This allows us to avoid the common error of attributing all changes among those going to college to higher education.

We can compare the relative causal weight of each institutional characteristic, each individual career factor, and each educational level by using regression or logistic regression. Thus, we look for the effect of each of these factors in turn by controlling for the effect of all the others. It is also essential that we hold constant the other factors such as family social class, abilities, race, and gender. All these controls assure us that neither selection effects nor maturation effects account for observed differences in outcomes and that institutional characteristics or educational level do.

In addition, we used the initial value—measured during high school or soon after—of the dependent variable as an additional, extremely important, control when possible. Holding these initial values constant is crucial to verify that observed changes cannot be attributed to inertia of initial differences that were not taken into account.

We distinguish the socialization effects of both institutional dimensions and individual careers after high school from the effects of level of education attained. We also contrast a degree's certification effects to those due to differences in characteristics of higher educational institutions and from student career factors there.

Except for some parts of chapter 2 and all of chapter 6, our study uses a panel or longitudinal design (i.e., with measurements at different times on the same sample of individuals.) It is recursive.[5] The construction of complete causal models is not our aim. There are no doubt many indirect effects of the independent variables that, in view of our purpose, we have chosen not to model.

Before and After Measures of Outcomes

It is crucial to remember that, whenever possible, we have controlled for early values of the goals, reported activities, self-direction, and self-esteem. Thus, through educational and background variables, we explain differences between early and 1986 values on these goals, activities, and perceptions of self. Indeed, since Heise's discussion (1970, 3-27), it is common to assume regression allows one to assess change when one has differing before-after measures of the same variable. The notion that one is assessing change, we believe, can also be extended to the case of logistic regression when one has before-after measures that differ.

In addition, one can also see throughout this book the powerful consistency of activities, goals, self-direction, and self-esteem between the first measure and the later measure. This is especially true of the extremes on single item measures; those most active or holding a value or goal "very important." This is of some substantive interest, for many observers have noted continuity or stability among postadolescents, particularly in values (Mortimer and Lorence 1979, 1980; Lindsay and Knox 1984). It is, then, the strength of the initial value that contributes particularly to this persistence. In some instances the single item measures have only a limited number of values, often three or five categories. Thus, there may be a ceiling or floor effect. This means we may be less likely to detect change because the measure does not have enough categories to allow for further movement toward the extremes.

Selection Effects

"Selection effects" are always possible alternative explanations of educational effects. That is, preexisting differences between individuals taking different educational paths may actually explain that which educational factors only seem to account for. For example, the Wisconsin Studies (Sewell and Hauser 1976) reached the conclusion that those who continue schooling past high school have fundamentally different characteristics than those who do not continue schooling. We are able to account for the effects of the most important original differences between people: data obtained in 1972, when these people were high school seniors, include race, sex, rank in class, an academic abilities score, and the socioeconomic class of parents. There are also 1972 measures of personality characteristics, attitudes and values. All of these provide critical ways of separating selection effects from the educational effects and for establishing their relative contributions. Thus, we discuss the different outcomes of educational careers as distinct from differences between these young people as they finished high school.

Interaction Effects

We examined gender differences in the effects of educational attainment and all other independent variables for all outcomes in this study. For every dependent variable, we analyzed male and female subsamples of the whole sample and the college-going sample separately. Whenever the effect of an independent variable was statistically significant for either the total sample or for men or women, we tested the statistical significance of the difference between men's and women's coefficients.

We did this by using the t-test for random variables with unequal variances: $t = (b_m - b_w)/(\text{st. err}_m^2 + \text{st. err}_w^2)^{1/2}$ (Gottfredson 1981). As in all our significance testing, we multiplied standard errors by the design effect, 1.61, in advance.

While there were many small differences between men and women, only a few were statistically significant. In each of the latter cases, we reanalyzed the equation for the given dependent variable in the combined samples of men and women by including interaction terms constructed by multiplying the value for gender by the appropriate predictor (Gottfredson 1981). Some, but not all, of the effects of the interaction terms were significant. When at least one interaction effect was significant, the coefficients are reported in the tables. In boxes at the bottom of the tables we include the conditional effects when they are significant. When none of the interaction effects are significant, we have presented the original analyses without interaction effects. These analyses of male-female differences show that, in many of the processes we have examined, the differences between men and women are not large enough to be of substantive or theoretical importance.

The Analysis Samples

The analyses in this book are limited to the white and black respondents of the 1986 survey. Unfortunately, there were too few Hispanic, Asian-Pacific, and Native American respondents for statistically reliable results. Of the original sample of 12,841, they constituted 4.5 percent, 0.5 percent, and 0.6 percent, respectively. To have included them in the black sample and labeled the whole category "non-white" would have obscured critical differences in the educational experiences of minorities in contemporary American society. Further research should address the educational issues specifically for each of these groups.

We checked the four background characteristics (gender, academic abilities, socioeconomic status, and race) as well as educational attainment of our sample of 5,409 against the total black and white sample of 11,572. After weighting each analysis (as explained above under Nationally Representative Sample), there was a close correspondence on two of the five measures: educational attainment and gender. Educational attainment is slightly higher for our sample. The proportion of respondents with only a high school diploma was 22.9 percent in the total sample and, in our sample, 21.1 percent. Corresponding percentages of those who had completed high school and had less than two years of college were 29.7 and 25.5 percent; two years of college or more with no degree, 17.0 and 18.0 percent; four- or five-year college degree, 21.6 and 24.6 percent; advanced degree, 8.8 and 10.8 percent. The proportion of males in the total sample was 48.7 percent, and in our sample, 49.6 percent.

There was a reasonable correspondence, yet not quite so close, on two others: academic abilities and socioeconomic status. Abilities scores were somewhat higher in our sample, with a mean of 211 rather than 205 (the standard deviation of our sample is 31). Socioeconomic status scores also were greater: from a mean of 122 to one of 1,009 (the standard deviation of our sample was 6,850). The groups were less comparable in the case of race. The proportion of blacks in the total sample was 10.5 percent, while in our sample it was 6.6 percent.

Any findings concerning race must be tempered owing to the high attrition rate of blacks in our study. However, since the sample is so representative in other respects, one can place considerable confidence in findings for the other background factors.

Most important, where samples vary in composition, one cannot confidently compare the magnitude of the effects between one analysis and another. Thus, it was essential to have two entirely consistent samples for all of the analyses: one consisting of those with as well as those without postsecondary educational experience; the other, of those with some education beyond high school.

Treatment of Missing Data

Missing data endemically plague survey research with the threat of loss of information. The most acceptable and rather frequent approach is simply to drop the case from the analysis if there is a missing response on even one item, a step that often results in unacceptably few cases and a consequent inability to generalize results.

Many researchers, like us, prefer to make an attempt to save cases for analysis. As an alternative to dropping a case when data were missing, for a number of variables we imputed meaningful estimates for missing data from other data. This is a commonly accepted technique for supplying estimates for missing data. One device was to use responses to identically worded questions from the year nearest the one for which the data were missing. For example, we substituted 1974 data for 1972, or 1985 data for 1986. The other major technique was to estimate the missing values from regression analyses of highly correlated items. An account of what we did follows.

First, in some cases the abilities score (measured in the high school senior year) was missing, but rank in high school class was available. The correlation between abilities and rank is quite high (Pearsonian R = +.59). We regressed abilities on rank when the values of both were known. We then used the resulting slope to predict unknown values of abilities and substituted the predicted values for cases where an abilities score was missing.

Second, in the rare event that the respondent reported no 1986 educational level, we imputed one from the 1979 data. Obviously, it is highly likely that respondents had attained at least the level of education reported in 1979.

Third, data on subjective states, such as life goals, values, and self measures, were missing for some individuals in 1972 but not in 1974. We directly substituted 1974 values when 1972 values were missing. The correlations between identical items from years so close together are substantial, with Gammas generally in the range of .40 to .70 (Davis 1971).

Fourth, when 1986 income figures were missing, we used 1985 or 1984 figures when available, provided the respondent was employed in 1986 at a job of roughly comparable level. We discuss other steps we took with income below, under Measuring Status Outcomes.

Fifth, we used the 1979 responses for satisfactions with the educational milieu and careers there, but in a few cases we supplemented them with 1986 data when there were missing 1979 responses. Thus, we can address with some confidence any observed relationships between high school or pre-graduate school college characteristics and respondents' evaluations. There may be a trifling degree of error owing to the method of imputation for missing values, for using data from the later date may have—in a small number of cases—resulted in responses to a graduate school environment being substituted for responses to the undergraduate experience.

Sixth, because of the large number of institutions with missing values for the proportion of students in vocational programs, we dropped it. The proportion of programs that were vocational is highly correlated with it (R = +.67), and that is what we used. Then, for cases with missing values for the proportion of vocational programs, we used regression to estimate and impute the proportion of vocational programs in an institution from the proportion of students in vocational programs.

After we cleaned all the data, we eliminated every case with any missing data on any one of the variables to be analyzed. A total sample of 5,409 persons survived. We based much of our analysis of the effects of educational attainment on this sample, which includes both those who attended postsecondary institutions and those who did not. Some variations are accounted for not only by educational attainment but also by postsecondary institutional characteristics and individual careers. For these, we used a subsample of 2,702 who had attended postsecondary institutions and for whom all institutional and experiential data were present.

MEASURES AND MEASUREMENT

Institutional Measures

The six institutional measures are: the size of student enrollment, the proportion of full-time students, emphasis on vocational curriculum versus academic, selectivity of admissions, private versus public control, and the proportion of freshmen who reside on campus. We dropped several institutional variables as either theoretically unpromising or as confounded with other variables in the study. Highly correlated items in a model create uninterpretable statistical anomalies. The principal example is the relative wealth of the student body as measured by reports of family income. We eliminated the income of the families of student bodies from the analysis because of its high correlation (Pearsonian R = +.60) with the selectivity of the institution.

Individual Higher Educational Careers

For each calendar year throughout the survey respondents reported what school they had attended. Throughout the fourteen years many students attended more than one college. In much of the literature the first school attended is used. But we do not believe that the first school attended could be of as great importance as the school attended for the longest time. The first school attended need not reflect the socializing impact of prolonged exposure to a milieu. We gave priority to the college each individual most frequently reported cumulatively over all the years of the survey up to a four- or five-year degree. When there were ties in the number of years two colleges were attended, we used the most recently attended of the tied schools. In so doing, we hoped to capture the impression of a school upon people as they emerged from the student role into later roles. The impact of the environment in which graduate studies were undertaken was also thus ruled out.

We also examine three self-reported components of the individual's college career: the mean of undergraduate grades reported, student residence on campus, and student major. In contrast to the common usage of many other studies, we used the last reported major, not the first. Our reasoning resembles that for choosing the higher education institution most frequently reported or last mentioned. We believe that the first major (or other major earlier than last) simply does not mirror the possible socializing impact of prolonged immersion in a field of study. Furthermore, the last major is more likely than prior ones to play a part in individual identity and status allocation, for example through the hiring decisions of employers.

Educational Satisfactions and Perceptions as Outcomes

NLS-72 included data on educational satisfactions and perceptions of educational experiences in both 1979 and 1986. In 1979 the instructions preceding the items dealing with satisfactions with the educational milieu and perceptions of educational experience refer to the "last year you were in school." The self-reports of students or former students used here refer to the last educational institution attended before the 1979 survey wave. We used the 1986 data only to supplement missing 1979 data. By doing this, we gain reasonable assurance that, for those with some postsecondary education, the last undergraduate institution attended, and not graduate school, is the referent. The 1979 responses were in terms of the last educational institution attended. For those who went on to postsecondary education, this usually means some kind of college or university. For those who did not go on to higher education after high school, the point of reference is the high school.

That respondents often reconstruct recollections of experiences and place them in a more favorable light is minimized by thus shortening the retrospective time span. Nevertheless, if respondents do put on "rose-colored glasses," they are engaged in a self-presentation tactic that reveals something meaningful and normative about their experience in context. Given our research problem, that may be even more important to know than respondents' perceptions during their education.

In the analyses that include those who did not go on to college we compare the responses of collegiates to their last college and the responses of the non-collegiates to the senior year of high school. We are not comparing apples and oranges, for the unit of analysis is responses to milieux, not literally the milieux themselves.

FACTOR ANALYSES

Factor analysis is a technique that identifies clusters of interrelated items and allows the analyst to construct a composite measure or measures. Each empirical cluster defines and isolates a factor (or component or dimension) distinct from other factors. One advantage is that a large set of items can be reduced to a few clear dimensions. Another is enhanced measurement reliability. All the factor analyses in this study employed principal axis factoring with deletion of a case when response was missing for any item. For a basic discussion of the statistical reasoning underlying the factor analytic techniques we used, see Harman (1967).

Self-Esteem and Self-Direction

The social psychology and educational literature amply documents self-esteem and self-direction, and many researchers have used the particular items in this study. Unlike exploratory factor analyses, we analyzed the set of self-esteem items separately from those of self-direction. We did this for 1972 and 1986. Thus, we were using exploratory factor analytic techniques to confirm the presence of a dimension (self-esteem or self-direction) and to isolate it. For missing 1972 factor scores we substituted the closely comparable factor scores from 1974 responses. We used only the original four items comprising each set that appeared in the first wave (Research Triangle Institute 1972). Items added to NLS-72 in subsequent waves not only did not improve the reliability of the measures appreciably but also rendered the factors more difficult to interpret.

Incorporated in the base year and in each wave of the NLS-72 is a short selection of Rosenberg's (1979) self-esteem scale items. Feeling oneself to be a person of worth, taking a positive attitude toward oneself, feeling oneself to be as capable as others, and feeling satisfied with oneself comprised strong factors in both 1972 and 1986. Positive responses and high factor scores all represent high levels of self-esteem. The factor loadings for each item are all acceptably high. For 1972 they are, respectively, .67, .61, .59, and .44. The 1986 loadings for the same items are .80, .72, .67, and .57. Loadings of .40 or higher help give some assurance of reliability to the resulting scales. In contrast, a loading close to zero means that the particular item varies at random with the factor and does not appreciably improve the scale. The eigenvalue is, however, critical for establishing reliability. It is related to the total common variance that the items comprising a factor explain, and virtually all authorities (Harman 1967) judge a value of 1.00 or higher to be acceptable. For 1972 and 1986, the eigenvalues were, respectively, 1.34 and 1.92.

A four-item measure of perceived self-direction appears in the first year and in each wave of the study. Three of these items appeared originally in Coleman et al.'s *Equality of Educational Opportunity* (1966). Rejection of all the following items and high factor scores all indicated a perception of self-direction: "Planning only makes one unhappy," "Something or someone stops me from getting ahead," "One is happier if one accepts one's condition in life," and "Good luck is more important than hard work in bringing success." Agreement with these statements means a perception that one does not control events. Most of the factor loadings lag slightly behind those for self-esteem. Respectively, for 1972 they are .68, .55, .40, and .37, while for 1986 they are .74, .63, .45, and .38. The eigenvalues are acceptable, but not as high as those for self-esteem: 1.07 for 1972 and 1.29 for 1986.

Educational Satisfactions and
Perceptions of Experiences

One strong factor emerged from our factor analysis of college satisfaction items.[6] We discussed factor analysis and these particular types of analysis earlier in this section. Since the items loading highly on this factor all have to do with satisfaction with the strengths of the academic programs of the school, we called it "academic satisfaction." The eigenvalue indicating the explanation of much common variance was 2.74 and Cronbach's Alpha was .74. The satisfaction items with their factor loadings after rotation[7] on the academic factor follow:

Quality of instruction	+.81
Quality of teachers	+.73
Courses and curriculum	+.68
My intellectual growth	+.66
Development of work skills	+.60
The social life	+.19
Sports and recreational facilities	+.07

The last two items did not have high loadings on this factor[8] and in fact they defined an independent factor. Since the eigenvalue of this factor was, however, less than 1, there was not much common explained variance. While we dropped it as unacceptably weak, we used these items singly in our linear and logistic regression analyses since they each appeared to reveal something important and different about the extracurricular aspects of the milieu. Satisfaction with counseling and placement and the prestige of the school were excluded from our eventual factor analysis because they did not contribute clearly to one factor. Also, they both appeared to address something conceptually distinct that we wanted to examine separately.

BASE YEAR COMPOSITE MEASURES

Academic Abilities

Riccobono et al. (1981) constructed this composite score of academic abilities. This score resulted from adding standardized scores of the tests on vocabulary, reading, mathematics, and letter groups (a test of inductive reasoning) administered during the senior year in high school (Riccobono et al 1981, Appendix K:2). That a factor analysis of these four items had a latent root greater than 1 for the resultant factor, which explained 56 percent of the total variance, indicates adequate reliability. We did not use the weighted factor scores in our analyses. As noted above, when data were missing, we inferred a score from class rank in that year.

Family Socioeconomic Status (SES)

Riccobono et al. (1981, 4-11) also deal extensively with the score of family socioeconomic status. It is an equally weighted linear composite based on the education of both parents, father's occupational status, parents' income, and amount and kind of material possessions in the home. It was derived from a principal components factor analysis that indicated about equal weights of the items and that yielded an acceptable factor solution of a single factor (thus, reasonably high reliability). See Appendix A for how we recoded these items.

Other Composite Measures

Often two or more items were conceptually homogeneous, with reasonably high correlations between them. To simplify matters we added the item values to create a composite score. We also checked the reliability of these measures.

Cronbach's Alpha is an estimate of the reliability, or internal consistency, of items in a composite measure (Cronbach 1951; Cronbach 1984, 169-171; Nunnally 1978, 225-55). This statistic assesses the extent of intercorrelation among a set of items. A value of .70 or higher indicates a high degree of reliability, but in preliminary work values of .50 or .60 are adequate. Scores of .30 or lower indicate the items do not overlap sufficiently to be combined. High scores result from both high intercorrelations among items and the number of items. Since all of our scores stem from what are to the psychometrician a small number of items, our results justify the construction of these composites as first approximations.

The composite score for 1974 and 1986 and Cronbach's Alphas for each year respectively are: political activism (.76, .82); talking about politics (.72, .80); job security (.73, .63); and intrinsic work value (.42, .54).

MEASURING EXTRINSIC REWARDS

Income

We performed several transformations on 1986 income other than those already reported above for missing values. Respondents had the option of reporting a current salary in hourly, weekly, biweekly, monthly, or yearly terms. We converted all reported wages for 1984, 1985, and 1986 to weekly units. Labor economists typically use weekly wages, and this common unit helped us with our checking on a case by case basis. We examined all cases in which the reported income was greater than $30 per hour. This enabled us to catch apparent misreports. The National Opinion Research Center (NORC) had declared cases with very high or very low incomes to be missing. In some cases there were obviously misplaced decimals, resulting in absurdly high or low income. We had available not only the reported income from other years but also the reported number of hours worked per month and the census category of the reported occupation. The NORC had flagged and declared missing forty-five cases with high wages in excess of $99,995 per year. In thirty-one of these cases we decided to accept the self-report. Typically, the high reported 1986 wages made sense when we looked at the status of the reported occupation, such as doctor, lawyer, or accountant, together with the report of number of hours worked per week. We also checked against the figures for 1985 and even 1984. In fourteen cases we accepted the NORC assignment of "missing" as reasonable.

From among the 206 cases with very low reported wages we judged forty-nine to be accurate. These were usually people who had part-time jobs resulting in low weekly wages.

When we finished the entire process of saving cases, we converted the weekly figures to annual ones. Some inaccuracy may have resulted in those cases when the respondent did not work all year. We assume that any inaccuracy, virtually impossible to check, would affect such a small proportion of the cases that overall statistical relationships would not be distorted. In addition, since very high values distort computations of means or averages, we converted values of $100,000 or more to $99,900.

Occupational Status

Social scientists have been comparing the prestige or social standing of occupations for decades. Early waves of the NLS used the census occupational category to arrive at the Duncan status ranking for each occupation, but we did not. The Duncan Socioeconomic Index (SEI), originally constructed in the 1950s, has been one of the most popular. Duncan used the prestige rankings of experimental subjects to calculate the relationship between the occupational prestige ranking and the education and income characteristics of workers in a few occupations. The calculations allowed him to estimate proxy prestige scores for the remaining large number of specific occupations and array them on a 100 point scale (Duncan 1961).

Since Duncan published his socioeconomic scores in 1961, researchers have tackled a variety of issues in trying to refine or update this "prestige" index.[9] In view of the many critical reservations of the original index,[10] Stevens and Featherman developed several alternatives that improved on it and updated it (1981, 364-395). Following their recommendation, we adopted their TSEI2 scores, which are based on the proportion of the total work force with one or more years of college and incomes of $10,000 or over for an inclusive set of occupations, as a metric of occupational standing. Scores range from college law teachers and dentists at 90.45 and 89.57 to clothing ironers and pressers, sewers and stitchers, shoemaking and machine operatives, textile operatives, bootblacks, and private maids, all scoring between 14 and 15 (Stevens and Featherman 1981).

We used these scores for the occupational status of the first reported and the 1986 full-time jobs.[11] That gave us some indication of change in occupational standing for each respondent.[12]

STATISTICAL PROCEDURES

We set out to make our results plain to the largest possible audience. Both linear and logistic regression are statistical tools relatively transparent to large numbers of people with relatively little training in multivariate analysis.

Choosing Linear or Logistic Regression

Regression analysis (ordinary least-squares) allows multivariate causal modeling of outcomes (Achen 1982). Each antecedent factor's effect on a dependent variable can be isolated from the effects of all the others. When possible, we use regression. Sometimes, however, we do not meet the assumptions for ordinary regression: relationships are non-linear; error variances are heteroscedastic (not constant); variables are not normally distributed; or the dependent variable is categorical. When the dependent variable is categorical, we use logistic regression, a useful option for rank-ordered or categorical outcomes (Winship and Mare 1984; Aldrich and Nelson 1984). The regression models include initially the four background factors and, first, the increases in the proportion of variance explained, by including level of education, and second, the increase in variance explained by adding to that model educational characteristics and individual career observations. This is straightforward with ordinary regression. Although ordered logit models do not estimate the proportion of variance explained as precisely analogous to R-squared, the method produces a ratio statistic that is approximately like a chi-square distribution. As a result, the difference between -2 logged likelihood of nested models serves as an analog to the f-test (Alridge and Nelson 1984). This allows the presentation of results in terms of the effects on the odds of an outcome, that is, the likelihood that each given increase in the causal factor will be accompanied by a different outcome (e.g., voting or not). Thus, for each change in the category of an ordered antecedent factor, the odds of falling into a given category of an outcome become higher or lower. And logistic regression, like its linear cousin, allows one to hold the effects of other antecedent conditions constant. We transformed dependent variables into categorical form when other assumptions were violated as well. Dependent variables can have two, three, or more categories, but we allowed ourselves no more than three for simplicity of interpretation. Since skewness of the distribution is not problematic with logistic regression, when we recoded dependent variables we tried to retain a representation of the range of responses in the categories chosen.

Interpreting Linear and Logistic Regression

Although the logic of logistic regression parallels that of the more familiar analysis of linear regression, the interpretation does not. It is, at once, both more and less difficult. For linear regression estimates, the standardized Betas bear a crude resemblance to Pearsonian correlation coefficients with all else in the model constant. Therefore, one can directly compare the magnitude of coefficients for the same sample in the same analysis. The unstandardized regression coefficient (b) conveys how many units of raw change in a dependent variable result from one unit of change in the independent variable, all else constant. Logistic regression precludes these kinds of comparisons. Furthermore, unlike regression, one cannot estimate exactly the proportion of variance explained, although -2 times the log-likelihood is an analogue to R^2 (the proportion of explained variance in linear regression). However, logistic regression adds a sense of concreteness to how each increment affects each outcome. For each specified change in the independent variable, one can state precisely and comparatively the effects on the odds of the outcome, all else being equal.

Treating categorical variables as dependent variables precludes the use of linear regression models, which assume continuous, interval-level dependent variables. Rather, the effects of a combination of categorical and continuous explanatory variables on ordered categorical dependent variables are best estimated with an ordered logit model. (For a thorough discussion, see Winship and Mare 1984.) In essence, for a three-category dependent variable, this logistic regression technique simultaneously estimates the effects of the explanatory variables on the log odds of having values in the top two categories rather than the bottom category *and* of having values in the single top category rather than in the bottom two categories. Thus, two intercepts are estimated, but a single set of coefficients is constrained to fit both sets of comparisons (the probability of being in categories 2 and 3 versus 1, and the probability of placement in category 3 versus 1 and 2). These coefficients are presented in terms of their effects on the odds of having higher values on the dependent variable. Consequently, coefficients resulting in odds less than one detract from horizontal fit, while odds greater than one increase it. These are multiplicative effects that can be interpreted as "*b* times the odds of having higher rather than lower fit."

We had two different sets of regression models and two different sets of logistic regression models according to the sample under investigation and the nature of the dependent variable. This was necessary to compare those who went to college with those who did not and to search separately for the differential effects of college characteristics and individual careers. In the first set of linear and logistic regression models we used the whole sample of 5,409 to examine the effects of differing levels of higher education and background characteristics on outcomes. In the second set, we included in analyses only the subsample of 2,702 who attended some type of postsecondary institution and for whom all institutional and educational career data were present.

Levels of Statistical Significance

We chose three conventional levels of significance: $p < .05$; $p < .01$; $p < .001$. These mean, respectively, that the probabilities that an observed relationship could have occurred by chance alone are, respectively, less than: 5 in 100, 1 in 100, and 1 in 1000. In a few instances, we relaxed the confidence level to $p < .10$, a 1 in 10 probability. To test for significance in linear regression models we used a one-tailed t-test. For the logistic regression analyses, we used the chi-square test. In both cases we corrected for the design effect. By making this conservative correction, we take an extra step to bolster confidence in the statistical significance of observed relationships between variables; thus, we have enhanced the assurance that observed relationships are unlikely to have occurred by chance alone. The complex nature of NLS-72 sampling—involving sample stratification, disproportionate oversampling of certain groups, and multistage sampling—necessitated this adjustment for design effects due to the consequent greater sampling variability of statistical estimates. To adjust for this, we used the method recommended by the National Opinion Research Center (Tourangeau et al. 1987). We had produced coefficients expressing the strength of relationships by using SAS and SPSS-X statistical programs (see below under Statistical Software). Before testing for statistical significance, we multiplied the standard error of each coefficient by 1.61, the average square root of the design effect (DEFT). In essence, this raised by nearly two-thirds the level required for statistical significance. This conservative approach means that fewer of our coefficients attain acceptable levels of statistical significance, but it does give us more assurance that those that do so are valid population estimates.

Statistical Software

With one exception, for all of the statistical analyses and data transformations we used SPSS-X, Release 3.0 for VAX-VMS (SPSS 1986). For the logistic regression analyses, however, we used the Experimental Release of LOGIST PROCEDURE for the VAX/SAS System (SAS Institute 1988).

CONCLUSION

We hope this appendix answers most of the methodological questions readers may raise. The reader who has borne with us this far may now appreciate why we placed this material in an appendix and not in the main text.

NOTES

1. Pascarella and Terenzini (1991) flatteringly reference our unpublished 1988 American Educational Research Association (AERA) draft paper (Knox, Lindsay, and Kolb 1988) in several chapters of their update of Feldman and Newcomb's classic and exhaustive review of empirical findings of the individual effects of higher education (1968). There are, however, three major methodological and substantive differences between that paper and the analyses for this book. Accordingly, Pascarella and Terenzini graciously included a caveat concerning the tentative nature of our paper and referred the reader to this book for these more comprehensive and precise analyses.

First, we added more variables having to do with the individual student careers in educational milieux. Second, we performed all of the analyses again on identical samples to afford comparability. We amplify on this need for identical samples in this appendix in the section entitled Interpreting Linear and Logistic Regression. Third, we made a major, and conservative, correction for design effects. The last change resulted in a loss of the statistical significance of some relationships. The first two also modified the findings somewhat. Some particular findings reported in the AERA paper do not hold true under these more stringent requirements.

Since the AERA paper we have also added an analysis of satisfactions with educational settings and of self-reports of educational experience there. Also, we dropped the Carnegie Classification as a baseline for analysis. Neither the additional analyses of responses to educational settings nor the deletion of the Carnegie Code affects the other findings.

2. It is somewhat disconcerting that there is a tendency to misreport the attainment of bachelor's and advanced degrees (Adelman 1990). The extent of misreporting is probably not great enough to vitiate the evidence advanced here for the allocation-certifying hypothesis. It is probable also that the effects on outcomes of incorrect reports of degree attainment are self-canceling.

3. The figures total 2,693 because they are unweighted.

4. We also secured the Carnegie Classification Code of Higher Education Institutions from this source. However, after extensive preliminary analyses we did not use the Carnegie Code, which is an amalgam and is essentially a rank ordering, with some confounding across categories. The categories, although concrete and administratively useful, are unwieldy in regression models and contributed nothing to explaining outcomes of interest. The analytical attributes we selected or constructed captured theoretically meaningful notions less redundantly and more cleanly.

5. According to Heise, "A relation between two variables is called recursive if it is linear, if the two variables are not in a loop, and if the source variable is uncoordinated with the disturbances of the dependent variable. If all the causal relations in a system are recursive, the entire system is said to be recursive" (1975, 153).

6. Using the *High School and Beyond* data with items identical to those from NLS-72, Gielow and Lee (1988) isolated two factors. These were an academic factor and a social factor, with items like "social life" and "sports and recreational facilities" forming a second, weaker factor. It is probably largely the longer time period involved with NLS-72 and our less homogeneous sample that explain why we isolated only one factor and they isolated two. Gielow and Lee did not provide eigenvalues in their paper, but their Cronbach's Alpha for social satisfaction is +0.55, indicating considerably lower reliability than for their academic satisfaction factor, for which Alpha = +0.78.

7. Rotation was, strictly speaking, not necessary since there was only one clear factor (Kaiser 1958).

8. We did leave them in for the computation of the factor scores.

9. "Prestige" is in quotes here, because although prestige ratings form the original core of the ranking system, the prestige of most occupations is only inferred from observed socioeconomic relationships; hence, the Duncan SEI is not strictly a prestige scale. For a comparison of prestige and socioeconomic scales see Featherman and Hauser (1976), and for a wide range of estimation procedures see Stevens and Featherman (1981).

10. These reservations include: the occupational attributes of 1950 and 1949 income levels were outdated; the occupational classification scheme used by the census changed somewhat during the years; and estimates originally based on male workers may no longer be valid for the occupational hierarchy of a

workforce with increasing numbers of women (Powers and Holmberg 1978).

Furthermore, Powell and Jacobs (1984) found that respondents do not accord men and women in the same occupation the same prestige. Consequently, the relationships between income, schooling, and social standing are essentially different for men and women. This implies the necessity for two different scales, one for men and the other for women. Christine Bose addressed this in creating indices that were based on occupational prestige, but modified by the gender of the job incumbent (1985). Unfortunately, the lack of a common metric between the separate Bose indices for both genders precludes its use in comparing the status attainment of men and women.

11. For the last occupation, we gave to census occupational category 280, "Salesmen and Sales Clerks, n.e.c.," nonexistent in Stevens and Featherman, a weighted mean (40.54) of the categories 281-285 (specific sales occupations) in proportion to the category's frequency of occurrence in our sample.

12. There are often elaborate prestige differences within a particular occupation that the measures of occupational standing do not entirely capture. Thus, the measures are rather crude but not so crude as to be unreliable for our purposes.

REFERENCES

Achen, Christopher H. 1982. *Interpreting and Using Regression*. Beverly Hills, Calif.: Sage Publications.

Clifford Adelman. 1990. The Data Game: Success Depends on How—and about Whom—You Ask the Question. *Change: The Magazine of Higher Learning* 22:44-45.

Albert, Elizabeth M. 1988. In the Interest of the Public Good? New Questions for Feminism. In *Community in America: The Challenge of Habits of the Heart*, edited by Ralph Norman and Charles Reynolds. Berkeley: University of California Press.

Aldrich, John H., and Forrest D. Nelson. 1984. *Linear Probability, Logit, and Probit Models*. Beverly Hills, Calif.: Sage Publications.

Alexander, Karl L., Martha Cook, and Edward L. McDill. 1978. Curriculum Tracking and Educational Stratification: Some Further Evidence. *American Sociological Review* 43:47-66.

Alexander, Karl L., and Bruce K. Eckland. 1973. *Effects of Education on the Social Mobility of High School Sophomores Fifteen Years Later (1955-1970)*. Chapel Hill: Institute for Research in Social Science, University of North Carolina.

Alexander, Karl L., and Edward L. McDill. 1976. Selection and Allocation within Schools: Some Causes and Consequences of Curriculum Placement. *American Sociological Review* 41:963-80.

Almond, Gabriel A., and Sidney Verba. 1963. *The Civic Culture*. Princeton, N.J.: Princeton University Press.

Altbach, Philip G. 1974. *Student Politics in America: A Historical Analysis*. New York: McGraw-Hill.

American Council on Education. 1986. *American Universities and Colleges*. 12th ed. New York: Walter de Gruyter.

Anderson, Kristine L. 1981. Post-High School Experiences and College Attrition. *Sociology of Education* 54:1-15.

———. 1984a. *Institutional Differences in College Effects: Final Report*. National Institute of Education, Washington, D.C.: ERIC Document # ED 256 204.

————. 1984b. *The Effects of College Type and Characteristics on Educational Attainment*. National Institute of Education, Washington, D.C.: ERIC Document # ED 256 206.

————. 1985. College Characteristics and Change in Students' Occupational Values: Socialization in American Colleges. *Work and Occupations* 12:307–28.

Angle, John, and David A. Wissman. 1981. Gender, College Major, and Earnings. *Sociology of Education* 54:25–33.

Aronowitz, Stanley. 1983. *Working Class Hero: A New Strategy for Labor*. New York: The Pilgrim Press.

Arrow, Kenneth J. 1973. Higher Education as a Filter. *Journal of Public Economics* 2:193–216.

Astin, Alexander W. 1965. *Who Goes Where to College?* Chicago: Science Research Associates.

————. 1977. *Four Critical Years: Effects of College on Beliefs, Attitudes, and Knowledge*. San Francisco: Jossey-Bass.

————. 1985. *Achieving Educational Excellence*. San Francisco: Jossey-Bass.

Astin, Alexander W. and Calvin B.T. Lee. 1972. *The Invisible Colleges: A Profile of Small, Independent Colleges*. New York: McGraw Hill.

Astin, Alexander W., Kenneth C. Green, Williams S. Korn, and Ellyne Berz. 1988. *The American Freshman: National Norms for Fall, 1988*. Los Angeles: Higher Education Research Institute, Graduate School of Education, University of California, Los Angeles.

Astin, Helen S., and Louise Kent. 1983. Gender Roles in Transition. *Journal of Higher Education* 54:309–324.

Bachman, Jerald G., and Patrick M. O'Malley. 1977. Self-Esteem in Young Men: A Longitudinal Analysis of the Impact of Educational and Occupational Attainment. *Journal of Personality and Social Psychology* 35:365–380.

Baker, Therese L., and Judith A. Bootcheck. 1985. The Relationship of Marital Status and Career Preparation to Changing Work Orientations of Young Women: A Longitudinal Study. *Research in Sociology of Education and Socialization* 5:327–49.

Baum, L. Frank. 1984 (1900). *The Wonderful Wizard of Oz*. New York: New American Library.

Bean, John P. 1980. Dropouts and Turnover: The Synthesis and Test of a Causal Model of Student Attrition. *Research in Higher Education* 12:155–187.

Becker, Gary. 1975. *Human Capital: A Theoretical and Empirical Analysis, with Special Reference to Education*. New York: Columbia University Press.

Becker, Howard S., Blanche Geer, and Everett C. Hughes. 1968. *Making the Grade: The Academic Side of College Life*. New York: Wiley.

Behuniak, P., Jr., and Robert K. Gable. 1979. A Longitudinal Study of Self-Concept and Locus of Control for Persisters in Six College Majors. Paper presented at the Northeastern Educational Research Association. Ellenville, N.Y., October.

Bellah, Robert N., Richard Madsen, William M. Sullivan, Ann Swidler, and Steven M. Tipton. 1985. *Habits of the Heart*. New York: Harper and Row.

Berg, Ivar E., with the assistance of Sherry Gorelick. 1971. *Education and Jobs: The Great Training Robbery*. New York: Praeger.

Berger, Peter. 1963. *Invitation to Sociology: A Humanistic Perspective*. Garden City, N.Y.: Anchor Books.

Bills, David B. 1988a. Educational Credentials and Hiring Decisions: What Employers Look for in Entry Level Employees. *Research in Social Stratification and Mobility* 7:71–97.

———. 1988b. Educational Credentials and Promotions: Does Schooling Do More than Get You in the Door? *Sociology of Education* 61:52–60.

Bishop, John. 1989. Incentives for Learning: Why American High School Students Compare So Poorly to Their Counterparts Overseas. In *Investing in People: A Strategy to Address America's Workforce Crisis, Background Papers* Vol. 1. Commission on Workforce Quality and Labor Market Efficiency. Washington, D.C.: U.S. Department of Labor.

Blau, Peter M., and Otis Dudley Duncan. 1967. *The American Occupational Structure*. New York: Wiley.

Bloom, Allan David. 1987. *The Closing of the American Mind: How Higher Education Has Failed Democracy and Impoverished the Souls of Today's Students*. New York: Simon and Schuster.

Bose, Christine E. 1985. *Jobs and Gender: A Study of Occupational Prestige*. New York: Praeger.

Bourdieu, Pierre. 1977. Cultural Reproduction and Social Reproduction in *Power and Ideology in Education*, edited by Jerome Karabel and A. H. Halsey. New York: Oxford University Press.

Bourdieu, Pierre, and Jean-Claude Passeron. 1977. *Reproduction in Education Society and Culture*. Translated by Richard Nice. London: Sage Publications.

———. 1979. *The Inheritors: French Students and Their Relation to Culture*. Translated by Richard Nice. Chicago: University of Chicago Press.

Bowen, Howard R. 1977. *Investment in Learning: The Individual and Social Value of American Higher Education*. San Francisco: Jossey-Bass.

Bowen, William G., and Julie Ann Sosa. 1989. *Prospects for Faculty in the Arts and Sciences: A Study of Factors Affecting Demand and Supply, 1987 to 2012*. Princeton, N.J.: Princeton University Press.

Bowles, Samuel, and Herbert Gintis. 1976. *Schooling in Capitalist America: Educational Reform and the Contradictions of Economic Life*. New York: Basic Books.

Boyer, Ernest L. 1987. *College: The Undergraduate Experience in America*. New York: Harper and Row.

Brint, Steven, and Jerome Karabel. 1989. *The Diverted Dream: Community Colleges and the Promise of Educational Opportunity in America*. New York: Oxford University Press.

Buchmann, Marlis. 1989. *The Script of Life in Modern Society: Entry into Adulthood in a Changing World*. Chicago: University of Chicago Press.

Bush, Diane M., and Roberta G. Simmons. 1981. Socialization Processes Over the Life Course. In *Social Psychology: Socialization Perspectives*, edited by Morris Rosenberg and Ralph H. Turner. New York: Basic Books.

Carlson, R. 1965. Stability and Change in the Adolescent's Self-Image. *Child Psychology* 36:659–666.

Carnegie Commission on Higher Education. 1973. *A Classification of Institutions of Higher Education: A Technical Report*. Carnegie Commission on Higher Education.

Carnegie Foundation for the Advancement of Teaching. 1989. *The Condition of the Professoriate*. Princeton, N.J.

Carnoy, Martin, and Henry Levin. 1985. *Schooling and Work in the Democratic State*. Stanford, Calif.: Stanford University Press.

Carroll, C. Dennis. 1979. *Characteristics of Postsecondary Education Institutions: Computer File Version 7907* (Machine Readable Data File) Washington, D.C.: Office of Evaluation and Dissemination, U.S. Office of Education.

Cheek, Neil H., Jr., and William R. Burch, Jr. 1976. *The Social Organization of Leisure in Human Society*. New York: Harper and Row.

Cheit, Earl F. 1975. *The Useful Arts and the Liberal Tradition*. New York: McGraw Hill.

Chickering, Arthur W. 1974. *Commuting versus Resident Students*. San Francisco: Jossey-Bass.

Clark, Burton R. 1960. The Cooling Out Function in Higher Education. *American Journal of Sociology* 65:569-576.

————. 1970. *The Distinctive College: Antioch, Reed and Swarthmore*. Chicago, Aldine.

Coleman, James S. 1971. *The Adolescent Society*. New York: Free Press.

Coleman, James S., Ernest Q. Campbell, Carol J. Hobson, James McPartland, Alexander M. Mood, Frederic D. Weenfeld, and Robert L. York. 1966. *Equality of Educational Opportunity*. Washington, D.C.: U.S. Government Printing Office.

College Division of Barron's Educational Series. 1983. *Barron's Profiles of American Colleges*. 13th ed. Woodbury, N.Y.: Barron's Educational Series, Inc.

————. 1990a. *Barron's Profiles of American Colleges*. 17th ed. New York: Barron's Educational Series, Inc.

————. 1990b. *Barron's 300 Best Buys in College Education*. New York: Barron's Educational Series, Inc.

College Entrance Examination Board. *The College Handbook: 1983-84*. 22nd ed. New York: CEEB.

Collins, Randall. 1971. Functional and Conflict Theories of Higher Education. *American Sociological Review* 36:1002-19.

————. 1979. *The Credential Society: An Historical Sociology of Education and Stratification*. New York: Academic Press.

Commission on the Humanities. 1980. *The Humanities in American Life*. Berkeley, Calif.: University of California Press.

Corey, Stephen M. 1936. Attitude Differences between Different Classes: A Summary and Criticism. *Journal of Educational Psychology* 27:321-30.

Cronbach, Lee J. 1951. Coefficient Alpha and the Internal Structure of Tests. *Psychometrika* 16:297-334.

————. 1984. *Essentials of Psychological Testing*. 4th ed. New York: Harper and Row.

Davis, James A. 1971. *Elementary School Analysis*. Englewood Cliffs, N.J.: Prentice-Hall.

Dewey, John. 1916. *Democracy and Education*. New York: The MacMillan.

DiMaggio, Paul. 1982. Cultural Capital and School Success: The Impact of Status Culture Participation on the Grades of U.S. High School Students. *American Sociological Review* 47:189-201.

DiMaggio, Paul, and John Mohr. 1985. Cultural Capital, Educational Attainment, and Marital Selection. *American Journal of Sociology* 90:1231-61.

DiMaggio, Paul, and Michael Useem. 1978a. Social Class and Arts Consumption: The Origins and Consequences of Class Differences in Exposure to the Arts in America. *Theory and Society* 5:141-61.

———. 1978b. Cultural Democracy in a Period of Cultural Expansion: The Social Composition of Arts Audiences in the United States. *Social Problems* 52:179-97.

Dore, Robert P. 1976. Human Capital Theory, The Diversity of Societies and the Problem of Quality in Education. *Higher Education* 5:79-102.

Dos Passos, John. 1930. *The 42nd Parallel*, Part 1 of *U.S.A.* New York: The Modern Library.

Duncan, Otis Dudley. 1961. A Socioeconomic Index for All Occupations. In *Occupations and Social Status*, edited by A. J. Reiss, Jr. New York: Free Press.

Durkheim, Emile. 1956. *Education and Sociology*. Translated by Sherwood D. Fox. New York: Free Press.

Eagle, Eva, Robert A. Fitzgerald, Antoinette Gifford, John Tuma, and C. Dennis Carroll. 1988. *A Descriptive Summary of 1972 High School Seniors: Fourteen Years Later, National Longitudinal Study 1972*. Contractor Report, National Center for Education Statistics, Washington, D.C.

Eckland, Bruce K., and Karl L. Alexander. 1980. The National Longitudinal Study of the High School Senior Class of 1972. In *Research in Sociology of Education and Socialization: Longitudinal Perspectives on Educational Attainment*, edited by Alan C. Kerckhoff. Greenwich, Conn.: JAI Press.

Ellison, Christopher G., and Bruce London. 1992. The Social and Political Participation of Black Americans: Compensatory and Ethnic Community Perspectives Revisited. *Social Forces* 70:681-701.

Engel, Mary. 1959. The Stability of the Self-Concept in Adolescence. *Journal of Abnormal and Social Psychology* 58:211-15.

England, Paula, George Farkas, Barbara Stanek Kilbourne, and Thomas Dou. 1988. Explaining Occupational Sex Segregation and Wages: Findings from a Model with Fixed Effects. *American Sociological Review* 53:544-58.

Featherman, David L., and Robert M. Hauser. 1976. Prestige or Socioeconomic Scales in the Study of Occupational Attainment? *Sociological Methods and Research* 4:402-22.

———. 1978. *Opportunity and Change*. New York: Academic Press.

Feldman, Kenneth A. 1972. Some Theoretical Approaches to the Study of Change and Stability of College Students. *The Review of Educational Research* 42:1-26.

Feldman, Kenneth A., and Theodore M. Newcomb. 1969. *The Impact of College on Students*. Vols. 1 and 2. San Francisco: Jossey-Bass.

Freedman, Mervin B. 1962. Studies of College Alumni. In *The American College*, edited by Nevitt Sanford. 847-93.

Freeman, Richard B. 1976. *The Over-Educated American*. New York: Academic Press.

Freeman, Richard B., and James L. Medoff. 1984. *What Do Unions Do?* New York: Basic Books.

Gamson, Zelda F., Nancy B. Black, Jamie Beth Catlin, Patrick J. Hill, Michael R. Mills, John Nichols, and Terry Heitz Rogers. 1984. *Liberating Education.* San Francisco: Jossey-Bass.

Gardner, Howard. 1983. *Frames of Mind: The Theory of Multiple Intelligences.* New York: Basic Books.

Gecas, Victor. 1982. The Self-Concept. *Annual Review of Sociology* 8:1–33.

Gielow, C. Robert, and Valerie E. Lee. 1988. The Effect of Institutional Characteristics on Student Satisfaction with College. Paper presented at the American Educational Research Association Annual Meeting. New Orleans, April.

Goldthorpe, John H., David Lockwood, Frank Bechhofer, and Jennifer Platt. 1968. *The Affluent Worker: Industrial Attitudes and Behavior.* London: Cambridge University Press.

————. 1969. *The Affluent Worker in the Class Structure.* London: Cambridge University Press.

Goodlad, John I. 1984. *A Place Called School: Prospects for the Future.* New York: McGraw Hill.

Goodman, Jerry D. 1979. The Economic Returns of Education: An Assessment of Alternative Models. *Social Science Quarterly* 84:269–83.

Gottfredson, Denise C. 1981. Black-White Differences in Education Attainment Processes: What Have We Learned? *American Sociological Review* 46:542–57.

Gottfredson, Linda S. 1985. Education as a Valid but Fallible Signal of Worker Quality. In *Research in Sociology of Education and Socialization,* edited by Alan C. Kerckhoff. Greenwich, Conn.: JAI Press.

Grant, Gerald, and David Riesman. 1978. *The Perpetual Dream: Reform and Experiment in the American College.* Chicago: University of Chicago Press.

Griffin, Larry J., and Karl L. Alexander. 1978. Schooling and Socioeconomic Attainments: High School and College Influences. *American Journal of Sociology* 84:319–47.

Gruber, James E. 1979. *Self in Transition: Change and Continuity in Self-Esteem after High School.* Palo Alto: R & E Research Associates.

Gujarati, Damodar. 1988. *Basic Econometrics.* 2nd ed. New York: McGraw Hill.

Gustafson, James M. 1982. Professions as "Callings." *Social Service Review* 3:501–15.

Halvorsen, Robert, and Raymond Palmquist. 1980. The Interpretation of Dummy Variables in Semilogarithmic Equations. *American Economic Review* 70(3):474–5.

Hamilton, Stephen F. 1990. *Apprenticeship for Adulthood: Preparing Youth for the Future.* New York: Free Press.

Harding, Vincent. 1988. Toward a Darkly Radiant Vision of America's Truth: A Letter of Concern, An Invitation to Re-Creation. In *Community in America: The Challenge of Habits of the Heart,* edited by Ralph Norman and Charles Reynolds. Berkeley: University of California Press.

Harman, Harry H. 1967. *Modern Factor Analysis.* 2nd. ed. Chicago: University of Chicago Press.

Hearn, James C. 1984. The Relative Roles of Academic, Ascribed, and Socioeconomic Characteristics in College Destinations. *Sociology of Education* 57:22–30.

Hearn, James C., and Susan Olzack. 1981. The Role of College Major Departments in the Reproduction of Sexual Inequality. *Sociology of Education* 54(July):195–205.

Heise, David R. 1969. Problems in Path Analysis and Causal Inference. In *Sociological Methodology*, edited by Edgar F. Borgatta and George W. Bohrnstedt. San Francisco: Jossey-Bass.

————. 1970. Causal Inference from Panel Data. In *Sociological Methodology*, edited by Edgar F. Borgatta and George W. Bohrnstedt. San Francisco: Jossey-Bass.

————. 1975. *Causal Analysis.* New York: John Wiley & Sons.

Hendel, Darwin D. 1985. Effects of Individualized and Structured College Curricula on Students' Performance and Satisfaction. *American Educational Research Journal* 22:117–22.

Herzog, A. Regula. 1982. High School Seniors' Occupational Plans and Values: Trends in Sex Differences 1976 through 1980. *Sociology of Education* 55:1–13.

Higgerson, Mary Lou. 1985. Understanding Why Students Voluntarily Withdraw From College. *NASPA Journal* 22:15–21.

Higher Education Research Institute. 1985. *HERI S.A.T. File with Added Institutional Characteristics.* (Machine Readable Data File) Los Angeles: Graduate School of Education, UCLA.

Hochschild, Arlie. 1989. *The Second Shift: Working Parents and the Revolution at Home.* New York: Viking.

Holland, Dorothy C., and Margaret A. Eisenhart. 1990. *Educated in Romance: Women, Achievement, and College.* Chicago: University of Chicago Press.

Howard, George S., and Scott E. Maxwell. 1980. Correlation between Student Satisfaction and Grades: A Case of Mistaken Causation? *Journal of Educational Psychology* 72:810–20.

Hudis, Paula M. 1976. Commitment to Work and Family: Marital-Status Differences in Women's Earnings. *Journal of Marriage and the Family* 38:267–78.

Hyman, Herbert H., and Charles R. Wright. 1971. Trends in Voluntary Association Memberships of American Adults: Replication Based on Secondary Analysis of National Data Samples. *American Sociological Review* 36:191–206.

————. 1979. *Education's Lasting Influence on Values.* Chicago: University of Chicago Press.

Hyman, Herbert H., Charles R. Wright, and John S. Reed. 1975. *The Enduring Effects Of Education.* Chicago: University of Chicago Press.

Independent Sector. 1988. *Giving and Volunteering in the United States.* Washington, D.C.: Author.

Jackman, Mary R., and Michael J. Muha. 1984. Education and Intergroup Attitudes: Moral Enlightenment, Superficial Democratic Commitment, or Ideological Refinement? *American Sociological Review* 49:751–69.

Jacob, Philip E. 1957. *Changing Values in College.* New York: Harper and Brothers.

Jacobs, Jerry A. 1989. *Revolving Doors: Sex Segregation and Women's Careers.* Stanford, Calif.: Stanford University Press.

James, Estelle, Nabeel Alsalam, Joseph C. Conaty, and Duc-Le To. 1989. College Quality and Future Earnings: Where Should You Send Your Child to College? *American Economic Review* 79:247–52.

Janowitz, Morris B. 1983. *The Reconstruction of Patriotism: Education for Civic Consciousness*. Chicago: University of Chicago Press.

Jencks, Christopher, Susan Bartlett, Mary Corcoran, James Crouse, David Eaglefield, Gregory Jackson, Kent McClelland, Peter Mueser, Michael Olzeck, Joseph Schwartz, Sherry Ward, and Jill Williams. 1979. *Who Gets Ahead? The Determinants of Economic Success in America*. New York: Basic Books.

Johnson, Naomi T., and Richard C. Richardson, Jr. 1986. *A Causal Model of Academic Factors Affecting Student Persistence*. ERIC Document # 271-075.

Kaiser, Henry F. 1958. The Varimax Criterion for Analytic Rotation in Factor Analysis. *Psychometrika* 23:187-200.

Kamens, David H. 1971. The College "Charter" and College Size: Effects on Occupational Choice and College Attrition. *Sociology of Education* 44:270-96.

———. 1974. Colleges and Elite Formation: The Case of Prestigious American Colleges. *Sociology of Education* 47:354-78.

———. 1977. Legitimating Myths and Educational Organization: The Relationship between Organizational Ideology and Formal Structure. *American Sociological Review* 41:208-19.

———. 1979. Student Status Aspirations: A Research Note on the Effects of Colleges. *Youth and Society* 11:83-91.

Kanouse, David E., Gus W. Haggstrom, Thomas J. Blaschke, James P. Kahan, William Lesowski, and Peter A. Morrison. 1980. *Effects of Postsecondary Experiences on Aspirations, Attitudes, and Self-Conceptions*. Santa Monica, Calif.: Rand.

Kaplan, Howard B. 1975. The Self-Esteem Motive and Change in Self-Attitudes. *Journal of Nervous and Mental Diseases* 161:265-75.

Katchadourian, Herant A., and John Boli. 1985. *Careerism and Intellectualism among College Students*. San Francisco: Jossey-Bass.

Kemper, Theodore G. 1980. Altruism and Voluntary Action. In *Participation in Social and Political Activities*, edited by David Horton Smith and Jacqueline Macauley. San Francisco: Jossey-Bass.

Kerckhoff, Alan C. 1976. The Status Attainment Process: Socialization or Allocation? *Social Forces* 55:368-81.

Kerckhoff, Alan C., Richard T. Campbell, and Jerry M. Trott. 1982. Dimensions of Educational and Occupational Attainment in Great Britain. *American Sociological Review* 47:347-64.

Kerckhoff, Alan C., and Robert A. Jackson. 1982. Types of Education and the Occupational Attainments of Young Men. *Social Forces* 61:24-45.

Kingston, Paul W. 1981. The Credential Elite and the Credential Route to Success. *Teacher's College Record* 82(Summer):589-600.

Kingston, Paul W., and Lionel S. Lewis. 1990. *The High-Status Track: Studies of Elite Schools and Stratification*. Albany: State University of New York Press.

Knox, William E., Paul Lindsay, and Mary N. Kolb. 1988. Higher Education Institutions and Young Adult Development. Unpublished paper presented at the American Educational Research Association Annual Meeting, New Orleans, April.

———. 1992. Higher Education, College Characteristics and Student Experiences: Long Term Effects on Educational Satisfactions and Perceptions. *Journal Of Higher Education* 63:303-28.

Kohn, Melvin L. 1969. *Class and Conformity: A Study in Values.* Homewood, Ill.: Dorsey Press.

Kohn, Melvin L., and Carmi Schooler. 1983. Stratification, Occupation, and Orientation. In *Work and Personality: An Inquiry into the Impact of Social Stratification,* edited by Melvin Kohn and Carmi Schooler. Norwood, N.J.: Ablex.

Kolb, Mary N. 1990. *Linking Education and Work: A Study of the Fit between College Majors and Careers.* Unpublished Ph.D. dissertation, University of North Carolina, Chapel Hill.

Langley, Noel, Florence Ryerson, and Edgar Allen Woolf. 1989. *The Wizard of Oz: The Screenplay.* New York: Dell.

Lasch, Christopher. 1978. *The Culture of Narcissism: American Life in an Age of Diminishing Expectations.* New York: Norton.

Lee, Valerie E. 1988. *Racial/Ethnic Differences in Prediction Pattern for Persistence to College Graduation.* Unpublished manuscript.

Lefcourt, Herbert M. 1981. *Research with the Locus of Control Construct: Assessment Methods.* Vol. 1. New York: Academic Press.

———. 1983. *Research with the Locus of Control Construct: Developments and Social Problems.* Vol. 2. New York: Academic Press.

———. 1984. *Research with the Locus of Control Construct: Extensions and Limitations.* Vol. 3. New York: Academic Press.

Leslie, Larry L. 1985. Quality of Education and Economic Growth. *Economics of Education Review* 4:273-90.

Leslie, Larry L., and Paul T. Brinkman. 1988. *The Economic Value of Higher Education.* New York: Collier Macmillan.

Levine, Arthur. 1980. *When Dreams and Heroes Died: A Portrait of Today's College Student.* San Francisco: Jossey-Bass.

Lewis, Sinclair. 1929. *Dodsworth.* New York: Harcourt, Brace.

Lindsay, Paul, and William E. Knox. 1984. Continuity and Change in Work Values among Young Adults: A Longitudinal Study. *American Journal of Sociology* 89:918-31.

Lindsay, Paul, William E. Knox, and Mary N. Kolb. 1988. Gender, Race, Schooling, and Job Status: Some New Evidence. Unpublished paper.

Lindsay, Paul, and Caroline H. Lindsay. 1987. Teachers in Pre-Schools and Child Care Centers: Overlooked and Undervalued. *Child and Youth Care Quarterly* 16:91-105.

Little, Angela. 1984. Education, Earnings and Productivity—the Eternal Triangle. In *Education versus Qualifications?,* edited by John Oxenham. London: George Allen and Unwin.

London, Howard B. 1978. *The Culture of a Community College.* New York: Praeger.

Marrou, H. I. 1956. *A History of Education in Antiquity.* Translated by George Lamb. New York: Sheed and Ward.

Merton, Robert K. 1957. *Social Theory and Social Structure.* rev. and enl. ed. Glencoe, Ill.: Free Press.

Meyer, John W. 1970. The Charter: Conditions of Diffuse Socialization in Schools. In *Social Processes and Social Structures,* edited by W. R. Scott. New York: Holt, Rinehart and Winston.

———. 1977. The Effects of Education as an Institution. *American Journal of Sociology* 83:55-77.

Meyerson, Martin. 1974. Civilizing Education: Uniting Liberal and Professional Learning. *Daedalus* 103:173-79.

Miller, Arthur. 1947. *All My Sons*. New York: Reynal and Hitchcock.

Moen, Phyllis, and Ken R. Smith. 1986. Women at Work: Commitment and Behavior over the Life Course. *Sociological Forum* 1(3):450–75.

Moll, Richard. 1985. *The Public Ivys: A Guide to America's Best Public Undergraduate Colleges and Universities*. New York: Viking.

Mortimer, Jeylan T., and Jon Lorence. 1979. Work Experience and Occupational Value Socialization: A Longitudinal Study. *American Journal of Sociology* 84:1361–85.

———. 1980. Self-Concept Stability and Change from Late Adolescence to Early Adulthood. In *Research in Community and Mental Health*, Vol. 2, edited by Roberta G. Simmons. Greenwich, Conn.: JAI Press.

Mueller, Ralph O. 1988. The Impact of College Selectivity on Income for Men and Women. *Research in Higher Education* 29(2):175–91.

Munro, B. H. 1981. Dropouts from Higher Education: Path Analysis of a National Sample. *American Educational Research Journal* 55(6):133–41.

Nam, Charles, and Mary G. Powers. 1983. *The Socioeconomic Approach to Status Measurement: With a Guide to Occupational and Socioeconomic Status Scores*. Houston: Cap and Gown Press.

National Center for Education Statistics. 1980. *A Longitudinal Survey of Students in the United States*. (Machine readable data file) Washington, D.C.: Center for Education Statistics.

———. 1989. *Digest of Education Statistics, 1989*. 25th ed. Washington, D.C.: U.S. Department of Education, Office of Educational Research and Improvement.

———. 1990. *The Condition of Education 1990*. Vol. 2: *Postsecondary Education*. Washington, D.C.: U.S. Department of Education, Office of Educational Research and Improvement.

National Center on Education and the Economy. 1990. *America's Choice: High Skills or Low Wages!* The Report of the Commission on the Skills of the American Workforce. Rochester, N.Y.: National Center on Education and the Economy.

Newcomb, Theodore M. 1943. *Personality and Social Change*. New York: Dryden Press.

Newcomb, Theodore M., Kathryn E. Koenig, Richard Flacks, and Donald P. Warwick. 1967. *Persistence and Change: Bennington College and Its Students after Twenty-five Years*. New York: John Wiley.

Nunnally, Jum C. 1978. *Psychometric Theory*. 2nd ed. New York: McGraw-Hill.

Oakes, Jeannie. 1985. *Keeping Track: How Schools Structure Inequality*. New Haven: Yale University Press.

Pace, C. Robert. 1979. *Measuring Outcomes of College: Fifty Years of Findings and Recommendations for the Future*. San Francisco: Jossey-Bass.

Padover, Saul K., ed. 1939. *Thomas Jefferson on Democracy*. New York: New American Library.

Parsons, Talcott. 1947. Weber's Economic Sociology. In *Max Weber: The Theory of Social and Economic Organization*, translated by A. M. Henderson and Talcott Parsons. New York: Free Press of Glencoe.

Pascarella, Ernest T. 1984. College Environmental Influences on Student's Educational Aspirations. *Journal of Higher Education* 55:751–77.

Pascarella, Ernest T., and Patrick T. Terenzini. 1991. *How College Affects Students: Insights from Twenty Years of Research.* San Francisco: Jossey-Bass.

Percy, Walker. 1980. *The Second Coming.* New York: Farrar, Straus, Giroux.

Persell, Caroline H. 1977. *Education and Inequality.* New York: Free Press.

Peterson's Guides. 1990a. *Peterson's Competitive Colleges 1990-91.* Princeton: Peterson's Guides.

————. 1990b. *Peterson's Guide to Four-Year Colleges.* Princeton: Peterson's Guides.

Powell, Brian, and Jerry A. Jacobs. 1984. The Prestige Gap: Differential Evaluations of Male and Female Workers. *Work and Occupations* 11:283-308.

Powers, Mary G., and Joan J. Holmberg. 1978. Occupational Status Scores: Changes Introduced by the Inclusion of Women. *Demography* 15:183-204.

Quayle, Dan P. 1989. *Morning Edition. PBS Radio.* January 19.

Quinn, Robert P., and Martha S. Baldi de Mandilovitch. 1977. *Education and Job Satisfaction: A Questionable Payoff.* NIE Papers in Education and Work, No. 5. U.S. Department of Health, Education and Welfare. Washington, D.C.: U.S. Government Printing Office.

Rasell, M. Edith, and Lawrence Mishel. 1989. *Shortchanging Education: How U.S. Spending on Grades K-12 Lags behind Other Industrial Nations.* Washington, D.C.: Economic Policy Institute.

Research Triangle Institute. 1972. *The Design of a Longitudinal Survey of Secondary School Seniors.* A report prepared for the National Center for Education Statistics. Research Triangle Park, N.C.: Research Triangle Institute.

Riccobono, John, Louise B. Henderson, Graham J. Burkheimer, Carol Place, and Jay R. Levinson. 1981. *National Longitudinal Study: Base Year (1972) through Fourth Follow-Up (1979) Data File Users Manual.* Washington, D.C: National Center for Educational Statistics.

Richards, James M., Jr. 1983. Validity of Locus of Control and Self-Esteem Measures in a National Longitudinal Study. *Educational and Psychological Measurement* 43:897-905.

Riesman, David. 1958. *Constraint and Variety in American Education.* New York: Doubleday.

Riesman, David, Nathan Glazer, and Reuel Denny, eds. 1955. *The Lonely Crowd: A Study of the Changing American Character.* New York: Doubleday.

Riesman, David, and Christopher Jencks. 1962. The Viability of the American College. In *The American College,* edited by Nevitt Sanford. New York: John Wiley.

Ritzer, George, and David Walczak. 1986. *Working: Conflict and Change.* 3rd ed. Englewood Cliffs, N.J.: Prentice-Hall.

Rosenbaum, James E. 1976. *Making Inequality: The Hidden Curriculum of High School Tracking.* New York: Wiley.

Rosenberg, Morris. 1979. *Conceiving the Self.* New York: Basic Books.

————. 1981. The Self-Concept: Social Product and Social Force. In *Social Psychology: Sociological Perspectives,* edited by Morris Rosenberg and Ralph H. Turner. New York: Basic Books.

Rotter, Julian B. 1966. Generalized Expectancies of Internal versus External Control of Reinforcement. *Psychological Monographs* 80:1, Whole No. 609.

———. 1975. Some Problems and Misconceptions related to the Construct of Internal versus External Control of Reinforcement. *Journal of Consulting and Clinical Psychology* 43:56-67.

Rubin, Lillian B. 1976. *Worlds of Pain: Life in the Working-Class Family.* New York: Basic Books.

SAS Institute. 1988. *Experimental Release of LOGIST PROCEDURE for the VAX/SAS System.* Cary, N.C.: The SAS Institute.

Sanford, Nevitt, ed. 1962. *The American College.* New York: John Wiley.

Schulberg, Budd. 1980. *On the Waterfront: A Screenplay.* Carbondale and Edwardsville, Ill.: Southern Illinois University Press.

Sennett, Richard, and Jonathan Cobb. 1972. *The Hidden Injuries of Class.* New York: Vintage Books.

Sewell, William H., and Robert M. Hauser. 1975. *Education, Occupation, and Earnings: Achievement in the Early Career.* New York: Academic Press.

———. 1976. Causes and Consequences of Higher Education: Models of the Status Attainment Process. In *Schooling and Achievement in American Society,* edited by William H. Sewell, Robert M. Hauser, and David L. Featherman. New York: Academic Press.

———. 1980. The Wisconsin Longitudinal Study of Social and Psychological Factors in Aspirations and Achievements. In *Research in Sociology of Education and Socialization.* Vol. 1, edited by Alan C. Kerckhoff. Greenwich, Conn.: JAI Press.

Sewell, William H., Robert M. Hauser, and Wendy C. Wolf. 1980. Sex, Schooling, and Occupational Status. *American Journal of Sociology* 86:551-83.

Shank, Susan E. 1988. Women and the Labor Market: The Link Grows Stronger. *Monthly Labor Review* 111:3-8.

Singer, Eleanor. 1981. Reference Groups and Social Evaluations. In *Social Psychology: Sociological Perspectives,* edited by Morris Rosenberg and Ralph H. Turner. New York: Basic Books.

Sizer, Theodore R. 1984. *Horace's Compromise: The Dilemma of the American High School.* Boston: Houghton-Mifflin.

Smart, John C. 1986. College Effects on Occupational Status Attainment. *Research in Higher Education* 24:73-95.

———. 1988. College Influences on Graduates' Income Levels. *Research in Higher Education* 29:41-59.

Smart, John C., C. A. Ethington, and G. W. McLaughlin. 1985. Self-Concept and Career Orientation Developmental Patterns during the College Years. Paper presented at the Annual Meeting of the American Educational Research Association, Chicago, March 31-April 4.

Smart, John C., and G. W. McLaughlin. 1985. Baccalaureate Recipients: Variations in Academic Ability, Personal Values, and Early Career Satisfaction. Paper presented at the 25th Annual Forum of the Association for Institutional Research. Portland, Oregon, April 28-May 1.

Smart, John C. and Ernest T. Pascarella. 1986. Self-Concept Development and Educational Degree Attainment. *Higher Education* 15:3-15.

Smith, David H. 1975. Voluntary Action and Voluntary Groups. In *Annual Review of Sociology*, Vol. 1, edited by Alex Inkeles, James Coleman, and Neil Smelser.

Smith, Herbert L. 1986. Overeducation and Underemployment: An Agnostic Review. *Sociology of Education* 59:85–99.

Snyder, Thomas D. 1987. *Digest of Education Statistics 1987*. Washington, D.C.: Center for Education Statistics.

Solmon, Lewis C. 1975. The Definition of College Quality and Its Impact on Earnings. *Explorations in Economic Research* 20:537–87.

———. 1985. Quality of Education and Economic Growth. *Economics of Education Review* 4:273–90.

Spence, A. Michael. 1974. *Market Signaling: Informational Transfer in Hiring and Related Screening Processes*. Cambridge, Mass.: Harvard University Press.

SPSS. 1986. *SPSS-X, Release 3.0 for VAX-VMS*. Chicago: SPSS, Inc.

Stern, George G. 1970. *People in Context: Measuring Person-Environment Congruence in Education and Industry*. New York: Wiley.

Stevens, Gillian, and David L. Featherman. 1981. A Revised Socioeconomic Index of Occupational Status. *Social Science Research* 10:364–95.

Swartz, David. 1977. Pierre Bourdieu: The Cultural Transmission of Social Inequality. *Harvard Educational Review* 47:545–55.

———. 1990. Pierre Bourdieu: Culture, Education, and Social Inequality. In *Education and Society*, edited by Kevin J. Dougherty and Floyd M. Hammack. San Diego: Harcourt, Brace, Jovanovich.

Tenison, Laurence J. 1976. *Description and Specifications for the NLS-Institutional Data Base*. (Machine Readable Data File) Washington D.C.: College Entrance Examination Board.

Thurow, Lester. 1975. *Generating Inequality*. New York: Basic Books.

Tinto, Vincent. 1975. Dropout from Higher Education: A Theoretical Synthesis of Recent Research. *Review of Educational Research* 45:89–125.

———. 1977. Does Schooling Matter? A Retrospective Assessment. In *Review of Research in Education*, Vol. 5, edited by L. S. Shulman. Itasca, Ill.: F. E. Peacock Publishers.

———. 1987. *Leaving College: Rethinking the Causes and Cures of Student Attrition*. Chicago: University of Chicago Press.

Tomala, G., and P. Behuniak, Jr. 1981. A Longitudinal Study of Locus of Control for Male and Female Persisters and Drop-Outs in Four Year Colleges. Paper presented at the Annual Meeting of the American Educational Research Association. Los Angeles: April 13–17.

Tourangeau, Roger, Penny Sebring, Barbara Campbell, Martin Glusberg, Bruce Spencer, and Melody Singleton. 1987. *The National Longitudinal Study of the High School Class of 1972 (NLS-72): Fifth Follow-Up (1986)*. (Machine Readable Data File) Washington, D.C.: Center for Education Statistics, U.S. Department of Education.

Treas, Judith, and Andrea Tyree. 1979. Prestige Versus Socioeconomic Status in the Attainment Process of American Men and Women. *Social Science Research* 8:201–21.

Updike, John. 1971. *Rabbit Redux*. New York: Alfred A. Knopf.

U.S. Bureau of the Census. 1987. Male-Female Differences in Work Experience, Occupation, and Earnings: 1984. *Current Population Reports*. P-70, no. 10. Washington, D.C.: U.S. Government Printing Office.

U.S. Bureau of the Census. 1989. *Statistical Abstract of the United States: 1989.* 109th ed. Washington, D.C.: U.S. Government Printing Office.

U.S. Bureau of the Census. 1992. *Statistical Abstract of the United States: 1990.* 112th ed. Washington, D.C.: U.S. Government Printing Office.

U.S. Department of Labor. 1983. *1983 Handbook on Women Workers.* Washington D.C.: U.S. Government Printing Office.

U.S. News and World Report. 1990. *1991 College Guide: America's Best Colleges.* Washington, D.C.: U.S. News and World Report, Inc.

Useem, Michael. 1989. *Liberal Education and the Corporation: The Hiring and Advancement of College Graduates.* New York: A. de Gruyter.

Useem, Michael, and Jerome Karabel. 1986. Pathways to Top Corporate Management. *American Sociological Review* 51:184-200.

Verba, Sidney, and Norman H. Nie. 1972. *Participation in America: Political Democracy and Social Equality.* New York: Harper and Row.

Verba, Sidney, Norman H. Nie, and Jae-on Kim. 1978. *Participation and Political Equality: A Seven-Nation Comparison.* Cambridge: Cambridge University Press.

Wagenaar, Theodore. 1984. *Occupational Aspirations and Intended Field of Study in College.* Washington D.C.: National Center for Education Statistics.

Waite, Linda J. 1981. U.S. Women at Work. *Population Bulletin* 36(2):1-43.

Waite, Linda J., Gus Haggstrom, and David E. Kanouse. 1986. The Effects of Parenthood on the Career Orientation and Job Characteristics of Young Adults. *Social Forces* 65:43-73.

Waller, Willard. 1961 (1932). *The Sociology of Teaching.* New York: Russell and Russell.

Weber, Max. 1947. Sociological Categories of Economic Action. In *Max Weber: The Theory of Social and Economic Organization,* translated by A. M. Henderson and Talcott Parsons. New York: Free Press of Glencoe.

Webster, Harold, Mervin B. Freedman, and Paul Heist. Personality Changes in College Students. In *The American College,* edited by Nevitt Sanford. 811-46.

Weil, Frederick D. 1985. The Variable Effects of Education on Liberal Attitudes: A Comparative-Historical Analysis of Anti-Semitism Using Public Opinion Survey Data. *American Sociological Review* 50:458-74.

Weis, Lois. 1988. *Class, Race, and Gender in American Education.* Albany: State University of New York Press.

Whitehead, Alfred North. 1929. *The Aims of Education.* New York: Mentor Books.

Wigdor, Alexandra K., and Wendell R. Garner, eds. 1982. *Ability Testing: Uses, Consequences, and Controversies.* Vols. 1 and 2. Washington, D.C.: National Academy Press.

Wilensky, Harold L. 1964. Mass Society and Mass Culture. *American Sociological Review,* 24:173-97.

Williams, Robin M., Jr. 1963. *American Society: A Sociological Interpretation.* 2nd rev. ed. New York: Alfred A. Knopf.

Wilson, Robert N. 1981. The Courage to Be Leisured. *Social Forces* 60:282-303.

Winship, Christopher, and Robert D. Mare. 1984. Regression Models with Ordinal Variables. *American Sociological Review* 49:512-25.

Wise, William M. 1958. Residence Halls and Higher Learning. *Personnel and Guidance Journal* 36:398-401.

Wolfinger, Raymond E., and Steven J. Rosenstone. 1980. *Who Votes?* New Haven: Yale University Press.

Wylie, Ruth. 1974. *The Self-Concept.* Vol. 1: *A Review of Methodological Considerations and Measuring Instruments.* Rev. ed. Lincoln: University of Nebraska Press.

———. 1979. *The Self-Concept.* Vol. 2: *Theory and Research on Selected Topics.* Rev. ed. Lincoln: University of Nebraska Press.

INDEX

Abilities. *See* Academic abilities;
Job skills
Academic abilities, 36-37, 40, 45,
69-70; absence as control,
134 n.12; and characteristics
of college attended, 12-18, 47;
among the college sample, 80;
dissatisfaction with counseling and placement opportunities, among the college
sample, 160; and educational
attainment, 12-18, 54 n.2; effect on educational satisfactions and perceptions, 147;
effect on satisfaction with
counseling and job place-
ment, 149; effect on satisfaction with the social life, 149;
effect on self-direction, 129,
134 n.8, 135 n.15; effect on
valuing job security, 40, 59
n.31; effect on valuing working with friendly people, 76;
lack of self-expressive findings and placement in occupations, 51, 54 n.2;
measurement of, 213-214;
and school success, 12-18;
self-concept effects, 120, 125,
128, 133 n.5; and student experiences, 12-18. *See also*
Background characteristics
Academic achievement, of stu-

dents as indicators of institutional success, 141. *See also*
Grades
Academic career. *See* Student careers
Academic emphasis of college curriculum. *See* Curricular emphasis of college
Academic major. *See* Student
major
Academic satisfaction, measurement of, 213
Achen, Christopher H., 216
ACT. *See* American College Testing Program Assessment
Activity tracks (post-secondary)
in NLS-72: 133 n.7; differences in, 134 n.8
Adelman, Clifford, 220 n.2
Advanced degree, effect on: academic satisfaction among college-goers, 159, 163;
academic satisfaction factor,
147; church-related activities,
104-105; commitment to being a community leader, 106;
commitment to social justice,
105; instrumental outcomes,
33, 35, 37-38, 41-42, 46, 48,
53; outcomes stronger than
bachelor's degree, 182; participation in community groups,
102; perceptions of educa-

About the Authors

WILLIAM E. KNOX is Associate Professor in the Department of Sociology at the University of North Carolina at Greensboro. His research interests include social psychology and the sociology of education.

PAUL LINDSAY is Associate Professor in the Department of Sociology at the University of North Carolina at Greensboro. His research interests include the sociology of education and educational policy.

MARY N. KOLB is Executive Director of the Maryland Institute for Employment and Training Professionals in Columbia, Maryland. Her research interests include the sociology of education and education and the economy.